Sites of the Ascetic Self

Sites
of the
Ascetic Self

JOHN CASSIAN AND CHRISTIAN

ETHICAL FORMATION

NIKI KASUMI CLEMENTS

University of Notre Dame Press
Notre Dame, Indiana

The author thanks Peeters Publishers for the rights to adapt for chapter 5 of
Niki Kasumi Clements, "Emotions and Ascetic Formation in John Cassian's
Collationes," *Studia Patristica.* Edited by Markus Vinzent and Ioannis
Papadogiannakis. Special Vol. 83, no. 9 (2017): 241–70.

Library of Congress Control Number: 2020007576

ISBN: 978-0-268-10785-7 (Hardback)
ISBN: 978-0-268-10788-8 (WebPDF)
ISBN: 978-0-268-10787-1 (Epub)

For John Connor Mulligan

CONTENTS

ACKNOWLEDGMENTS

To acknowledge the sources of this book is to recognize sources over decades. From California to the Northeast to Houston, I have been supported, challenged, and motivated by individuals who have modeled how to live and think differently. I could ask for no better colleagues than those at Rice University, where this book took root in conversation with April DeConick, Jeff Kripal, Anthony Pinn, Bill Parsons, Elias Bongmba, Anne Klein, Marcia Brennan, Matthias Henze, Claire Fanger, David Cook, John Stroup, and Brian Ogren. Working across disciplines has its challenges and would not have been possible without the critical and charitable engagement of interlocutors in my department at Rice, in the Humanities Research Center, and across the School of Humanities.

From my time at Brown University, I am very grateful to the following: Thomas Lewis, Susan Ashbrook Harvey, Stephen Bush, Harold Roth, Mark Cladis, Stanley Stowers, and Ross Kraemer for sharing their intellectual force and institutional acumen. The Religion and Critical Thought vertical cohort also saw this work from its time as a seedling, notably Megan McBride, Anna Bialek, Caroline Kory, David Lê, Jonathan Sozek, Douglas Finn, Alexis Glenn, Alissa Mac-Millan, and Matt Duperon. I also thank, as a bit of Brown in Houston, Bob and Nancy Carney for their years of friendship and wisdom.

To find mentors in one's academic exemplars is a singular wonder, and I thank Elizabeth Clark from Duke University for enabling this book and the next, as well as Douglas Christie, from Loyola Marymount University, for his timely encouragement. From Harvard Divinity School, past and present, I am grateful for the critical formation of Amy Hollywood, Mark Jordan, Khaled Anatolios, John Behr, Jonathan Schofer, and Sarah Coakley. Elfie Raymond, Wendy Lipp, David Bernstein, Phillis Levin, Ali Nematollahy, and Cristle Collins

Judd remind me of the best of Sarah Lawrence College and enabled my pursuit of the academic life. Cultivating the ethos of word and deed as a professor and writer has become an imperative through the examples of Biko Mandela Gray at Syracuse University and Gregory Perron at Rice University. For their exceptional generosity navigating the archives of Michel Foucault at the Bibliothèque nationale de France in 2019, Laurence Le Bras, Philippe Chevallier, and the Foucault estate have my thanks, with my regrets that most of this research could be featured only in the next book. I am also grateful to my editor, Stephen Little, that our paths crossed and for his stalwart support alongside the excellent team at the University of Notre Dame Press.

This book has been shared, shaped, and rethought in enlivening intellectual communities, including the Boston University Symposium on the Future of the Philosophy of Religion, the Center for Advanced Study in the Behavioral Sciences at Stanford University, the Elizabeth A. Clark Center for Late Ancient Studies at Duke University, the International Symposium for Contemplative Studies with the Mind & Life Institute, the Kosmoi-Leuven Centre for the Study of Religion and Worldview, the University of Chicago Divinity School, Villanova University's "Affect Camp," and the Rice Workshop in Humanistic Ethics. Special thanks to Ryan Coyne, Bob Davis, David Eckel, Sarah Hammerschlag, Anne Harrington, Jennifer Knust, Stephen Kosslyn, Laura Lieber, Margaret Mitchell, Matthew Peterson, Joseph Verheyden, and Vida Yao.

For various forms of support and solidarity through the years, I also thank Maria Aguilar, Melissa Bailar, Stephen Bradshaw, Lynn Brilhante, Kathleen Canning, Isaac Carroo, Nikki Carson, Silvia Cernea, Adam Clark, Davina Davidson, George Demacopoulos, Laura Dingeldein, Linda Dunleavy, Benjamin Dunning, Farès el-Dahdah, Elaine Howard Ecklund, Rebecca Falcasantos, Brett Grainger, Richard Harley, Diana Heard, George Hegarty, Sonam Kachru, Eva Kauppila, Jones College, Justin Kelley, David Liao, Sylvia Louie, Matthew Lyddon, Benjamin Marcus, Libby Matthews, Lynne McCabe, Zack Mezera, Jadrian Miles, Brenna Moore, the Mosles, the Mulligans, Marcie Newton, Aristotle Papanikolaou, Anya Parker, Amelia Perkins, Al Peters, Janet Peters, Daniel Picus, Aysha Pollnitz, Bilal

Rehman, Ruth Robbins, Judith Roof, Malone Sams, Paula Sanders, Claudia Solis, the Solises, Robyn Schroeder, Kerry Sonia, Zoe Tao, Diane Terrill, Andrew Tobolowsky, Nicolas Shumway, Thaya Utha-yophas, Matthew Wettergreen, Lisa Wahlander, Michelle White, Mara Willard, and Chloe Wilson.

The Clements family—TC, Michi, Sumi, Sachi, Suki, Kay, Fran-ces, and Caleb—deserves my sincerest appreciation for their love, support, and hilarity through four decades. My dearest friends— Gwendolyn Bradford, Amanda Cadogan, Becca Cain, Holly Holmes, Tamsin Jones, Kristin LeMay, Rachel Smith, and Andi Winnette—all inspired and sustained me in this work. The existential and political urgency of committing to The Work came from Ryan Gosa and Paul Otremba, whose untimely passings motivated this book from begin-ning to end. This book—and indeed my self—would not exist at all were it not for the brilliance and unfailing support of John Connor Mulligan, who has enabled me to live in this best of fractured worlds with love, whimsy, Rabbit, and Domino.

Introduction

Around 380 CE, a well-educated young man of some means leaves his lushly wooded native land of Scythia Minor near the Black Sea for the Mediterranean coast of Palestine.[1] Submitting himself at the entrance to a monastic community in Bethlehem, he gains entry and learns the rudiments of communal living along with a traveling companion and dear friend.[2] In texts he would pen forty years later along the southern coast of Gaul, this man calls himself "Iohannes" and his companion "Germanus."[3] Once established in their routine and living quarters in Bethlehem, John and Germanus receive a third inhabitant for their domicile. This old man seems to be the least amongst them — an ignoble entrant to the monastery occasioned by bodily infirmity and age as opposed to a true commitment to the monastic life.

But then come his stories. Pinufius, as the man calls himself, describes the wondrous workings of ascetics in the Egyptian desert, stressing their virtues of humility and obedience. There was Abba John, whose exemplary obedience led him to perform the most absurd of tasks: smashing a precious oil vessel, sweating while failing to move an impossibly large boulder, and watering a lifeless stick for a year simply because his elder commanded him to do so.[4] Yet more questionable was Abba Patermutus, whose obedience to his elder led him to throw his own son into the river at the elder's command to prove he had divested himself of such worldly attachments; the elder fortunately stationed fishers for the boy downstream.[5] Then there was the brother who gave up his considerable wealth to join the community. In a test of his humility and endurance in his new social station, his shoulders were loaded up with ten baskets of wares to sell in the market as a common laborer, which he did with aplomb.[6]

The most spectacular revelation of humility, however, is that of Pinufius himself. It turns out that this old man despised in Bethlehem is Abba Pinufius, the acclaimed elder of a community in Panephysis in the Egyptian desert.[7] Too esteemed and deferentially treated in his home community, Pinufius first sought the anonymity required for his exercise of humility by stealing away to a community at a great distance from his own in the Thebaid and obediently supplicating himself. His brothers, missing their shepherd, scoured the Egyptian desert, eventually finding Pinufius in a cenobium in Tabenna and dragged him back home.[8] Changing scale if not strategy, Pinufius soon departed the desert altogether, made the difficult journey by sea to the distant Bethlehem, and humbled himself as a novice at the entrance to the monastery near the Cave of the Nativity. Certain he would not be found in this world away from Egypt, Pinufius settled into life in John and Germanus's community only to be spotted by chance by brothers from his home monastery making a pilgrimage to the sacred sites in Palestine, who carried him home once again.[9]

Their imaginations captured by such stories, both told to them by Pinufius and enacted before their eyes through his example, John and Germanus receive blessings from their own superiors to set out for the desert cells of Egypt.[10] The *Conlationes XXIIII*, known in English translation as the *Conferences*, claims to chronicle conversations between the young friends and fifteen of the most esteemed elders in the desert during their travels.[11] The conversations revivified through the writings of John, known to history as John Cassian (*Iohannes Cassianus*) (c. 360–c. 435), twenty years removed from the desert and in the Gallic seaport of Massilia, detail the themes, practices, and concerns of the ascetic life.

As John and Germanus physically sat at the feet of the *abbas* in 380's and 390's Egypt seeking their instruction, so do Cassian's Gallic readers in the 420's attend to his *Conferences*, appropriately structured for this purpose according to the dialogic format of *erotapokriseis*.[12] With the "golden age" of Egyptian monasticism quickly receding since Theophilus of Alexandria's purge of Origenist monks from the desert in 399 (when Cassian likely left the desert himself), Cassian's dialogues both dramatize the way ascetic instruction took place and connect readers with the temporally and geographically distant *abbas* as exemplars for imitation of "behavior, attitude and orientation" in an age and locale in which such forms are actively constructed and contested.[13] The transmission of asceticism and its translation across the Mediterranean rely, in part, on representations of both ascetics successfully transformed and those in the process of formation.

Cassian's captivated and captivating ascetics show through their examples what systematic direct prescription cannot do: They dramatize the struggles and delights of ascetic life in the daily process of ascetic cultivation. Denied the benefits of training and experience through increasingly geographically and temporally removed pilgrimage, Cassian's readers are provided vivid *exempla* whose extraordinary personas can be imagined and progressively engaged by readers dedicated to ascetic transformation.[14] Cassian invites his readers to emulate the figures he describes, and yet often sets them up as too ideal in their exemplary embodiment of ascetic virtue. To mediate such daunting ideals to distant readers, his *Conferences* also stage the young John and Germanus as figures whose affects and behaviors model responses to the *abbas*. The *Conferences'* narrative framings bring to life everyday practices constitutive of ascetic formation. From descriptions of meals shared with Abba Moses to the sleeping practices urged by Abba Serenus to liturgical observances narrated with Abba Theonas, readers get a sense of what the ascetic life looks like in practice as well as through theoretical exposition. Through these narrations, the young companions consistently invite readers' affective and behavioral emulation of their own responses to the *abbas'* stories, opening these stories up to lived experience. From their sincere zeal in loosening Abba Moses's often mute tongue to their joy fostered through Abba Isaac's introduction to fiery prayer to their overcoming embarrassment to ask Abba Theonas about troubling nocturnal emissions, the young John and Germanus stage not moral lessons about right and wrong but the experience of forging an ascetic way of life.

In an extended reading of Cassian's ascetic *professio* (Latin for profession), I approach Cassian's construction of asceticism through attention to cultivation and an ethics of daily practice. Through historical-textual analysis, Cassian's practical view of humanity, divinity, and even demonology enables a view of human agency reliant on other human and nonhuman agencies. Cassian's works concern themselves with what humans *can* do, even as they are shaped and constrained by other agencies and influences—be they social, environmental, cultural, political, economic, physiological, psychological, or supra-human. Through contemporary theoretical analysis, Cassian's philosophical anthropology can be seen as involving a robust view of how embodiment, affectivity, and reflection constitute human subjectivity. Read through gender, feminist, and queer theories, Cassian's embodied, affective, and communal practices can be seen as basic to his asceticism and conceptualization of embedded human agency. This analysis contributes to a form of agency I designate *ethical agency*, where Cassian roots ascetic formation in the practical, daily cultivation of desired dispositions and the human effort required to commit to such practices despite their many challenges. I critically engage Cassian's distal historical and cultural formations as complementing Saba Mahmood's goal "to develop an analytical language for thinking about modalities of agency that exceed liberatory politics (feminist, leftist, or liberal)."[15]

In the process of bringing his training in Egyptian desert asceticism to bourgeoning monasticism in southern Gaul amid social, cultural, economic, and political shifts in the Roman Empire, Cassian writes texts rich in resources for adopting a pragmatic ethics as opposed to a rule-based morality. Robert Markus describes 380–430 as a "watershed" time of "great debates" in Roman society that "all revolved around the question: what is it to be a Christian?"[16] In this broader context, Cassian's attention to concrete, daily practices— eating, sleeping, working, reading, and talking (to God, to elders, to oneself)—allows us to take seriously the potential for late ancient Christian asceticism to involve not just renunciatory practices but also a transformative ethos. Cassian's pragmatism articulated at the edge of empire not only bridges forms of Christianity across the Mediterranean historically but, in accommodating the practices of the *professio* to one's capacities and contextually shaped possibilities, speaks directly to contemporary interest in the possibility of transforming selves in uncertain times.

"In Experience and Practice Alone"

"My plan," Cassian declares in the preface to his other monastic work, *De Institutis coenobiorum et de octo principalium uitiorum remediis* (translated in English as the *Institutes*), "is to say a few things not about the marvelous works of God but about the improvement of our behavior (*correctione morum nostrorum*) and the attainment of the perfect life, in keeping with what we have learned from our elders."[17] Dedicating his works to esteemed Christian leaders in Fréjus, Lérins, and the Stoechadic islands near Massilia, Cassian presents his writings as responses to their solicitations for his practical advice on monasticism, and his prefaces "indicate an active engagement with the developing monastic movement and its leaders in the West."[18] As Columba Stewart notes, such attention to behavior subtly indicts the legacy of Martin of Tours, whose bombastic tales of miracles and marvels drew the wrong kind of attention in southern Gaul at the turn of the fifth century. Cassian, by contrast, expresses central concern for the "dangers of emphasizing miraculous powers over goodness of life."[19] With even *Conference* 15, on divine miracles, stressing the futility of fixating on them, Cassian reinforces his concern for what humans can do in a world of contingency.[20] His tone is not polemic but paraenetic as he exhorts readers to take as examples the *abbas* with whom he trained, as well as his own younger self and Germanus in more nascent processes of formation.[21]

When reading Cassian's influential monastic *opera* with attention to theoretical constructions of asceticism, we see how he foregrounds practical questions about what the ascetic way of life looks like (materially and performatively), how it feels and is socially transmitted (affectively), and which symbolic economies sustain one's orientation (reflectively).[22] Cassian's desert *askesis* emphasizes experience so centrally that he thus defines the "profession" (*professio*), "occupation" (*propositum*), and "way of life" (*conuersatio*):[23] "For the whole of [the monastic life] consists in experience and practice alone and just as such things cannot be handed on except by an experienced person, so neither can they be grasped or understood except by someone who has striven to learn them with like zeal and effort."[24] "In experience and practice alone" (*in sola experientia usuque*) lies the heart of the monastic life, identifying both the true bearers and seekers of wisdom through their "zeal and effort" (*studio ac sudore*).[25] Valantasis stresses "practices of power" in his constructions of asceticism—and such dynamics are clearly basic to *sudore*, with the sweat and perspiration expected of toiling docile bodies. Yet focusing on power relations alone does not capture the force of ethics in ascetic practice and experience, so I argue that constructions of power need to be met with a corollary stress on constructions of ethics in asceticism, a theoretical move that I follow Michel Foucault in making.[26] With Abba John stressing "extended practice and superior experience" (*longo usu ac magistra experientia*) in *Conference* 19, Karl Suso Frank argues: "The key to [Cassian's] monastic writings lies . . . in (the terms) *experientia* and *usus*."[27] Where dogmatic prescription can drain practices of their force, stories bring them to life in their sweat and struggle, in their formative and transformative possibilities.

To preempt a focus on systematic and stringent rules, Cassian presents the stories of an array of *abbas* to dramatize psychological and physiological concerns as both part of ascetic development and open to modification instead of shamefully rejected as such. The characters of John and Germanus are themselves curiosities in their affective range, where questioning and confusion reflect how precepts and practices always require interpretation and critical judgment. Stephen Driver describes how Cassian puts his reader into his younger self's position through narrative use of the first-person plural, whereby the reader might "share the same perspective and suffer the same hopes, fears and difficulties."[28] Rebecca Krawiec further argues how Cassian "thus creates a relationship between past (biblical) foundations, past and present Egyptian abbas, and present Gallic readers, who are 'inserted' into this relationship."[29]

With experience, zeal, and effort foregrounded in the *professio*, we can use contemporary theoretical lenses to home in on bodily, affective, and reflective engagement as vital to the shaping of ascetic selves. In ongoing emulation of desert *exempla* who have advanced on this path, Cassian both reflects on traditions and doctrinal orthodoxies and exhorts the critical adoption, adaptation, and accommodation of such practices to one's own context.[30] Building on Teresa Shaw's analysis of the interdependence of physiology and psychology in Cassian's texts as influenced by Greco-Roman medical understandings, I analyze Cassian's practices by parsing bodily, affective, and reflective sites of formation, arguing for their possible integration through ascetic practices.[31] Cassian brings his acumen regarding the stark realities of being human by critically recognizing—and thereby opening up possibilities for negotiating—the challenges faced by ascetics as they work to produce forms of life.[32] Addressing such challenges requires a host of practices that engage different forms of subjectivity: (1) bodily practices of eating, sleeping, and manual labor highlight the work of the body even as affective and reflective attention are also needed to sustain such regulated and exhausting practices, (2) affective practices of scriptural *meditatio* and adoption of psalmic and desert voices highlight the work of the emotions even as bodily and reflective attention are involved in recitation and memorization, and (3) communal practices of emulating and adapting proximate and distal ascetic *exempla* require critical reflection and discretion even as bodily and affective engagement are required. Alongside challenges to endurance, motivation, and attention, these daily practices enable the formation of stable dispositions to action, feeling, and thought over time.

Dramatizing the process of formation, young John and Germanus illuminate an undertheorized component of ethics: the mechanisms of the process by which one goes about cultivating a particular way of life vis-à-vis daily practices and challenges, both as one is shaped as subject and also as one is self-shaping. Cassian's texts unfold the turbulent progression of ascetics new and old, showing how such cultivation requires urgent and ongoing engagement of the body, the emotions, and the mind in concert. Ascetic formation is arduous, communally rooted, and never complete. Ascetic subjects are both shaped by forms of power and can be self-shaping through daily practices and relations including maintaining intimate friendships, participating in communal celebrations, and being shaped by distant exemplarity. From the inculcated and ideological to the cultivated and ethical, ascetic living is shaped through tradition-producing power alongside self-transformation.

It will perhaps be surprising to some to see Cassian's texts on asceticism read for their transformative rather than their renunciatory potentialities. Readers of Foucault might identify Cassian with a stress on obedience, submission to authority, and self-renunciation in "'disciplines' of a monastic type, whose function was to obtain renunciations."[33] Foundational to my revised approach is Elizabeth Clark's analysis of asceticism in early Christian contexts, where "men and women are not slaves to the habitual, but can cultivate extraordinary forms of human existence," and Susan Ashbrook Harvey's stress on sensory experience of the divine as "transformative of the human subject."[34] When reading Cassian's texts through Clark's and Harvey's emphases on humans as "transformable," powerful possibilities open up for analyzing processes of transformation in the critical adoption, adaptation, and accommodation of ascetic practices. Abba Theonas emphasizes how the young John and Germanus need to exercise their own judgment and conscience through critical *discretio*, shaping their fasting practices with attention to their particular right time, character, and extent "in conjunction with other works."[35] Abba Daniel highlights the necessity of humans' willing to negotiate the tension between prideful temptations of the spirit and pleasures of the flesh, both extremes of which must be avoided.[36] By adapting practices through the hermeneutic principle of accommodation, the ascetic participates in self-cultivation.[37]

FROM RENUNCIATION TO CULTIVATION IN ASCETICISM

If it seems counterintuitive to read Cassian's early Christian asceticism as cultivation, this is also because of a scholarly tradition associating asceticism with renunciation. Ascetic cultivation as a formulation might seem incongruous, even oxymoronic, to readers since the publication of Friedrich Nietzsche's influential account of "ascetic ideals" in the *Genealogy of Morals* (1887). The well-known narrative juxtaposes active, happy, nobles with cunning ascetic priests whose physical weakness leads them to dominate the nobles by transvaluing virtues of physical strength with meekness. As Nietzsche laments, "what *bestiality of thought* erupts as soon as he is prevented just a little from being a *beast in deed!*"[38] Such ascetic ideals are not virtuous but simply vitiating, denying the life force that Nietzsche considers basic to human instincts before humans were domesticated like sheep within city walls.[39] Interiorizing the dominating instinct, the will to power turns inward as a perverse will to vitiate oneself through asceticism.[40]

Beyond philosophical parables, asceticism signals restriction and production for modern discourses of economics and religion through Max Weber's *The Protestant Ethic and Spirit of Capitalism* (1905), analyzing "the penetration of methodically controlled and supervised, thus of ascetic, conduct."[41] Differentiating forms of asceticism according to religious traditions, asceticism in Puritanism, for Weber, is oriented "towards the rational mastery of that world itself."[42] In the coincidence of rationality, labor, and productivity, Weber associates asceticism (at least *innerweltliche Askese*) with bourgeois interests of capitalist productivity.[43] Through the Protestant revision of economic and moral orders, asceticism becomes a means of maximizing the productive and consumptive activities of capitalist subjects in order "to remodel the world and to work out its ideals in the world."[44] As Geoffrey Harpham puts it, speaking of Weber, "a monastic ideology of restriction and deprivation can dilate into a worldly principle of consumption, power, and excess."[45]

According to Nietzsche's and Weber's constructions of asceticism, political and economic forces extol restriction and vitiation as means of controlling disciplinary subjects as the tools sustaining modern society. Such assumptions of asceticism endure in much of twentieth-century scholarship, as in Pierre Hadot's assumption of "the Christian—and subsequently modern—use of the word 'asceticism,'" accepting Heussi's definition of "[c]omplete abstinence or restriction in the use of food, drink, sleep, dress, and property, and especially continence in sexual matters.'"[46] Hadot describes asceticism as abstinence or restriction in dietary or sexual practices that "have nothing to do with philosophical thought-exercises" common to Greek and Roman philosophers when adapted by Christians, such as Justin Martyr and Clement of Alexandria.[47] The contrast heightens between Christian asceticism as self-vitiating and the spiritual exercises of ancient philosophers—located in "inner activities of the thought and the will"—as ethically transformative.[48]

Foucault, Asceticism, Ethics

Michel Foucault nuances these narratives as he gradually becomes invested in the discourse of asceticism for its ethical potential to contest power by forging subversive forms of life. Establishing a rigorous space for ethics—as a limited but necessary mode of action open to subjects discursively shaped but also capable of self-shaping—becomes central to Foucault's critical shift between 1976 and 1984, whereby he moves to ancient Greek and Roman texts in order to genealogize modern constructions of sexuality and disciplinary subjectivity.[49] What begins as his concern for disciplinary power encoded in the proliferation of discourses about sex in *The History of Sexuality*, Vol. 1: *The Will to Knowledge* (*La Volonté de savoir*, 1976) becomes recalibrated in *The History of Sexuality*, Vol. 2: *The Use of Pleasure* (*L'Usage des plaisirs*, 1984), and Vol. 3: *The Care of the Self* (*Le Souci de soi*, 1984), as attention to Greek and Roman sexual ethics whereby elite subjects can shape their lives through "an art of living" (ἡ τέχνη τοῦ βίου) and "care of the self" (ἐπιμελεία ἑαυτοῦ).[50] Analyzing practical philosophical texts, Foucault shifts his focus from power to ethics in an attempt "to think differently, instead of legitimating what is already known."[51]

Along with the texts of Greek and Roman antiquity, Foucault comes to appreciate forms of asceticism in Christian texts from the second through the fifth centuries. Foucault begins to theorize asceticism as a form of resistance to power in his 1977–1978 Collège de France lectures, *Security, Territory, Population*, describing the more insidious Christian pastoral power in the third through the sixth centuries as developing "to a not inconsiderable extent—against ascetic practices."[52] He sees asceticism operating as a form of "counter-conduct" to the Catholic ecclesial pastorate throughout the Middle Ages, characterized by "an individualizing tendency" and defining its challenge to power through "the exercise of the self on the self."[53] Diagnosing Christianity in its institutionalized forms as "fundamentally anti-ascetic," Foucault lauds the forms of asceticism internal to it as an "excess that *denies access to an external power*."[54] By his 1981–1982 Collège lectures, *The Hermeneutics of the Subject*, Foucault's ethics connects to his refined sense of ascetics: "Ascetics, that is to say the more or less coordinated set of exercises that are available, recommended, and even obligatory, and anyway utilizable by individuals in a moral, philosophical, and religious system in order to achieve a definite spiritual objective."[55]

Embedded in Foucault's reading of early Christian texts is a complex reading of ethical possibilities in asceticism. Ascetics' earlier anarchic forms prove to be in tension with the stress of monasticism's later institutionalized forms on obedience, subordination, and renunciation. As Mark Jordan illuminates, Foucault appreciates early Christian martyrs, matrons, and monks for bearing "human bodies that delimit power by scrambling language when they speak about the sacred or to it."[56] These ascetics who embody resistance to the institutions of power are tied to a transformative potential realized through exercises in particular forms of life, as a Greek or Roman philosopher "submits to a *forma* (a form)" rather than "obey a *regula* (a rule)."[57]

While Foucault's turn to Greek and Roman antiquity has surprised scholars for decades, the 2018 posthumous publication of *The History of Sexuality*, Vol. 4: *Confessions of the Flesh* (*Histoire de la sexualité IV: Les Aveux de la chair*) continues these possibilities for asceticism as an ethically transformative—and potentially transgressive—form of life. *Confessions of the Flesh* attends to forms of praxis linking regimes of truth and the constitution of subjectivity through the remission of sins in baptism, ecclesial penance, and examination of conscience, notably in third-century Christians like Tertullian, who reorganize the relation between subjectivity and truth through *exomologesis* (ἐξομολόγησις) as a ritual disclosure of one's status as a martyr and as a Christian.[58] In *Confessions*, Foucault also expands on the ethical potential of the arts of living, lauding Gregory of Nyssa for embracing the subversive potential of virginity and Augustine for his account of marital sex and the "duty of the spouse" to consummate and therefore curb male concupiscence.[59] Such readings are tied to Foucault's final lecture in 1984, with the possibility of Christian asceticism as an art of living that he movingly declares he wants to pursue, but which his death would preclude: "Maybe I will try to pursue this history of the arts of living, of philosophy as form of life, of asceticism in its relation to the truth, precisely, after ancient philosophy, in Christianity."[60]

Cassian, Asceticism, and Ethics

The reexamination of Cassian's ascetic ethics that I am proposing can contribute materially to this projected pursuit of an *ars vivendi*. Analyzing Cassian's late ancient texts in relation to transformative praxis brings together two Foucauldian discourses: that of the work of power and technologies of domination and the work of ethics and technologies of the self. Specifically, it can help make sense of Christian asceticism's complex status in the philosophy of religion by showing how, even where Christian asceticism is "limited, regulated, integrated, and almost socialized within cenobite forms," we find sites instituted for the realization of its "unrestrained and free aspect."[61]

Cassian's work is important territory for a critical ethical project precisely because of Foucault's unfinished engagement with the ethical potentialities of Christian asceticism. Foucault assigns Cassian a vital yet dogmatic role in propagating the mechanisms of confession in *exagoreusis* (ἐξαγόρευσις) as a verbalization of one's sins relying on the hermeneutics of the subject; that is, the means by which the subject subjects his or her thoughts to constant analysis.[62] The only previously published part of *Confessions* is the mostly unmodified "The Battle for Chastity," which reiterates Foucault's readings from 1978 to 1982, in which Cassian foregrounds obedience, submission to authority, and self-renunciation in the constitution of monastic subjectivity.[63] Foucault designates Cassian as the fulcrum between ancient self-formation and modern morality, inaugurating the western obsession with the "decipherment of interiority, the subject's exegesis of himself."[64] In Foucault's reading, Cassian anticipates modern disciplinary subjectivity as an outcome of monastic obsession with obedience, submission, and confession as producing the truth of oneself—stressing thought over action, interiority over exteriority—and renouncing one's sexuality as tantamount to renouncing one's self.[65] I find this reading particularly fascinating because even as Foucault deepens his textual engagement with Christianity over the years and comes to stress the transformative force of asceticism—for both subjects and societies—he maintains his reading of Cassian in an incongruously static way.[66]

To READ CASSIAN with Foucault's ethical emphasis on asceticism—without assuming the institutionalist and interiorizing reading to which Foucault reduces Cassian—involves embracing contemporary scholarly constructions of asceticism that recognize possibilities of transforming self and society. Through the influence of social and historical analysis on textual studies and the cultural depth given to late ancient studies, a shifting notion of asceticism in late antique Christianity has been informed by attention to embodiment, ritual practices, and performance.[67] Much of this recuperation of asceticism owes a debt to Foucault, who, John Behr notes, "direct[s] our attention away from the outward forms or codes of morality, to focus, instead, on how and why they were framed, what mechanisms were at work within them, and what the implications were either for the individuals whose lives took shape within this asceticism or, more generally, for the relationship between the individual and society."[68]

FORGING ASCETICISM IN LATE ANCIENT STUDIES

Beyond the privation and productivity we find in the vitiation models of Nietzsche and Weber, accounts of asceticism in late ancient studies foreground possibilities for social performance as well as spiritual pursuit with attention to embodied senses and forms of subjectivity that exceed economies of production or sexuality.[69] Richard Valantasis's definition ties the production of subjectivity to social relations and symbolic orders: *"Asceticism may be defined as performances within a dominant social environment intended to inaugurate a new subjectivity, different social relations, and an alternative symbolic universe."*[70] Susan Harvey stresses asceticism as a spiritual pursuit with a vital appreciation for the sensory, as "the practice of a disciplined life in pursuit of a spiritual condition. In late antiquity this discipline was exercised through a physical and mental process of ordering the self in relation to the divine."[71] George Demacopoulos focuses the ascetic perspective on Cassian's belief that "one could participate in one's salvation through ascetic discipline and a refocusing of one's soul toward God."[72] And Susannah Elm identifies monasticism as the "higher evolution" of asceticism, challenging elisions between institutionalization and conservatism through the force of late antique Christian women.[73]

Elizabeth Clark rejects interiorizing and renunciatory readings of early Christian asceticism, notably through her emphases on transformation and nuanced anthropologies:

> Early Christian ascetics assumed that humans were transformable: the human person could be improved by ascetic practice. The standard textbook approach to asceticism that dualistically pits soul against body is in urgent need of nuance, for early Christian ascetics usually claimed that soul and body were tightly connected, that the actions and movements of one had a direct effect upon the other. And this effect was not just in the direction of the soul reining in the body: rather, ascetic practitioners believed that attention to the body's discipline could improve "the self." Thus, despite the obvious ways in which asceticism can appear as a pessimistic movement in its alleged flight from "the world," there is a certain optimism at its heart.[74]

Clark articulates an optimism in asceticism that turns around its transformative possibilities, as early Christian ascetics contribute to their own constitution through this process. With no crosscultural essence to asceticism, Clark stresses that "asceticism has meaning only in relation to other behaviors in a given culture" and isolates "what ascetics give up and what they get, in various particular historical situations."[75] Affirming cultural particularity, as Vincent Wimbush and Richard Valantasis's volume illuminates, opens ways of considering category constructions today, and Clark's approach to late ancient sources forges a fulcrum between early Christian issues and their "contemporary resonance" in praxis and theory.[76]

These redefinitions of asceticism have been central to the shaping of late ancient studies since the 1990s, when attention to the body, gender, discipline, constructions of the self, and discourse analysis were intensified as theoretical approaches to the study of religious texts.[77] Attention to the disciplines of social history, cultural anthropology, and cultural studies, together with feminist studies, gender studies, and queer studies, sets the conditions for reading Cassian in transformative and not merely renunciatory ways. Patricia Cox Miller uses performativity to understand how ascetics are "enacting the spiritual body in the here-and-now" and asceticism as a form of spirituality "aimed at overcoming human instability."[78] David Brakke uses Judith Butler's challenge to the designation of sex/body and gender/culture, where "the concept of performativity questions the *apophthegmata*'s insistence upon the persistence of a 'natural' and 'true' gendered identity, female, grounded in a body impervious to the transforming power of performance."[79] Virginia Burrus describes a transformative politics of identity as enabling "a complex, fluid, and heterogenous society not only to subject itself continuously to internal critique but also to expose itself to unpredictable metamorphoses precisely at its sites of greatest vulnerability," linking "the ancient Christians" to our own "volatile age."[80] As David Brakke, Michael Satlow, and Steven Weitzman have expressed with regard to late ancient contexts, "the self was a religious concept."[81] There is no seat of "the self" like the early modern *cogito* or the phenomenological subject of consciousness; the reflexive pronoun that identifies "self" (Gk. αὐτός, Lt. *sui*) suggests a processual relation of self to self already shaped by a host of other agencies and formed through dynamic changes instead of as static substance.

Transformation is part of the world-ordering and subjectivity-shaping effects at the heart of asceticism in these late ancient texts and contexts. Just as Foucault comes to appreciate this in early Christian texts, so too can we extend this reading to Cassian. Asceticism, which at the turn of the twentieth century designates a perverse support for the economic and moralizing mechanisms shaping society becomes, at the turn of the twenty-first-century, an opportunity for thinking through and beyond economic and moral determinist frameworks by emphasizing the bodily, practical, and performative aspects of ritual, identity, and the critique of norms. Analyzing transformative possibilities in Cassian's asceticism holds the potential to critically inform ethics in the study of religion. In turn, the critical study of early Christian asceticism from an ethical perspective adds analytical clarity to the concept of asceticism, the call for which Wimbush and Valantasis put forward as a methodological goal in 1997 yet that continues to resist resolution.[82]

THINKING DIFFERENTLY THROUGH JOHN CASSIAN

To read Cassian's asceticism as ethical praxis allows us to use Foucault's construction of ethics as a "relation of self to self" without hewing to his interiorizing reading of Cassian, which obscures the work of embodiment and affectivity. Obedience, confession, and submission to authority all have a place in Cassian's ascetic *professio*, and selectively reading stories like those of Abba John and Abba Patermutus reinforces a renunciatory reading of asceticism. But, as Foucault indicates in his *Confessions*, even Cassian cannot be understood "without reference to the technologies of the self by which he characterizes the monastic life and the spiritual combat which it navigates."[83] Disciplinarily, my ethical reading of Cassian is an attempt to realize the potential of Foucault's appreciation for early Christians by foregrounding the technologies of self that he extols in antiquity but does not adequately engage in Cassian, including bodily practices, the construction of desire (as well as its social effects), and relations to others.[84] Such analysis shows how the deeper hues of lived experience and exemplary figures in Cassian help realize the ethical potential of early Christian texts to answer the questions motivating Foucault's late work.

To engage these possibilities of asceticism and cultivation over and against renunciation as an end in itself, in this book I analyze Cassian's texts to engage and extend Foucault's final philosophical task: to frame critical possibilities for ethical formation. Foucault himself turns back to ancient texts because he recognizes that even an unsalutary "morality" is in the process of "disappearing, has already disappeared. And to this absence of morality corresponds, must correspond, the search for an aesthetics of existence."[85] By reframing asceticism through Foucault's articulation of ethics, we can see in Cassian a view of asceticism not just through "constructions of power," as Valantasis memorably argues in 1995, but also through "constructions of ethics" that draw upon the resources that Foucault provides in his (previously inaccessible) later work, and we can do this while still subjecting his readings of Cassian's texts to critical analysis.[86]

Agency, Ethics, Affectus

The texts of Cassian provide an exemplary locus for a historically significant and theoretically productive view of ethical formation, partially because of Cassian's capacious but doctrinally suspect articulations of human *liberum arbitrium* (free will) and *uoluntas* (will) and his emphasis on transformational ascetic practices.[87] Cassian's influence on Christian discourses of monasticism and their impact on broader cultural movements unsurprisingly includes his controversial views on human ability. These views drew fire from supporters of his illustrious contemporary, Augustine of Hippo (354–430), who in the 410s fired missives at the British monk Pelagius for taking too generous a view of human ability, condemning Pelagian teachings at the Council of Carthage in 418 CE.[88] Between these two positions (though written a few years later) is Cassian's *Conference* 13, which has been read as a response to Augustine's increasing pessimism concerning human ability.[89] Though his association with "Pelagianism" would mute Cassian's greater legacy, Cassian actually focuses most of *Conference* 13 on the power of *divine* agency, framing his concern for human ability as preempting coercion by God and ensuring that humans can actively participate in their own cultivation.

Cassian illuminates a conception of ethical formation by calling attention to the daily work of the body, heart, and mind in ways that showcase their particular possibilities as well as their integrated force. Through his historical influence and textual transmission, we can also glean an account of social change that is linked to the cultivation of a particular *affectus*. This *affectus* is vital to conceptualizing asceticism not just through power but also through ethics. Correlating with both ἦθος and πάθος (*ethos* and *pathos*, respectively), the Latin *affectus* indicates the states of body, affection, and mind shaping one's disposition through "some influence" in Lewis and Short's standard definition.[90] *Ethos* unites Aristotle's Greek play in the *Nicomachean Ethics* on ἦθος as "disposition" and ἔθει as "by habit," and its Latin corollary *affectus* encodes both that done by habit in order to cultivate one's ethical disposition and the disposition itself.[91] Ascetics negotiate a host of influences—of one's body, emotions, and mind; of geographical, social, political, and economic environments; and of spirited agencies—which shape the possibilities for forging stable dispositions to act, feel, and think. Ascetic cultivation, then, must foreground the daily practices that one adopts and gradually makes closer to "second nature."[92] After all, Amy Hollywood reminds us: "Spontaneity takes work."[93]

Subject, Self, Subjectivity

Hollywood's analysis of forms of subjectivity—engaging bodily techniques that are social, performative, and constitutive of practical reason—informs my reading of Cassian, where spontaneity comes only through the cultivation of embodied, affective, and reflective forms of subjectivity. As Hollywood's *Sensible Ecstasy* stresses how affective work in late medieval women's mysticism might provide resources for thinking about "sites for more fully embodied practices" today, my reading of Cassian foregrounds analogous possibilities in late ancient asceticism.[94] Hollywood describes Cassian's mysticism through his attention to fiery prayer practices exceeding the everyday: "What begins as a physical, affective, and cognitive experience leads to an inner transformation Cassian calls fiery prayer."[95] Shaping an *affectus*, in mystical and ascetic discourses alike, requires recognition of how one participates in formation.

Analyzing Cassian's texts requires moving beyond conceits of "subjectivity" as either too "internal" and belief-oriented or too "external" and bodily. To speak about "interiority" or "the self" in this way is to misconstrue Cassian as sharing preoccupations with theoretical binaries more characteristic of modern thought.[96] For Cassian, the "inner" is not a psychological terrain that can be considered in isolation from physiological and socially participatory "outer" bodies. Contemporary discussions in the study of religion counter oppositions such as belief versus practice, the autonomous will versus the discursively shaped body, or renunciation versus cultivation. Cassian's texts provide a novel early challenge to such binaries in his robust constructions of subjectivity and ethics.

By teasing imputed emphases on ascetic self-renunciation from Cassian's own openness to self-cultivation, we gain a clearer understanding of the nuances in his late ancient asceticism. Thinking beyond the bounds of modern morality and constructions of asceticism, we can also refuse such modern oppositions such as interior selfhood versus exterior body. As Bruce Malina notes, "Anyone considering asceticism in antiquity quickly discovers a different sort of self, closer to the self as physical being than to the contemporary inner self."[97] To consider how human ability and the possibilities for transformation come together in Cassian's ascetic ethics, then, is to bring critical normative questions to bear in historically rigorous analyses of his texts. Looking at asceticism as a way of dynamically constructing subjectivity, "the subject," or "the self," we move closer to how Dale Martin argues ancient Greeks and Romans "by and large view the self as a continuum of substances which all, somewhat automatically, interact with and upon one another."[98] We can glean in Cassian's asceticism practices of ethical formation that work material changes to the body, emotions, and mind without the conceit of an "abiding self" or autonomous rationality. To Elizabeth Castelli's articulation of "the body as the site of religious self-formation," I extend the emotions and reflection as other sites of formation.[99] Reading Cassian's texts with attention to forms of subjectivity as multiple sites of formation that are dynamically linked helps us to articulate the transformative dimensions of asceticism.[100] At the intersection of historical and theoretical analysis of ethics and asceticism, distinctive forms of ethical possibilities open up, both for how subjects can change and how they shape societies in turn.

RADICAL ASCETICISM IN THE STUDY OF RELIGION

Through the enduring cultural influence of Greco-Roman medicine, physiology, and philosophy on Christian ethical practices noted by Clark, Cassian's texts help us to more fully theorize the ethics that Foucault himself pursued.[101] Asceticism as regulative practices of power operates in tandem with asceticism as ethical practices that operate beyond the strictly renunciatory. It encodes instead possibilities for resistance in subject formation, the capacity for a measure of ethical change, and the ability to affect society and shape traditions. It is through forms of asceticism as ethical self-relation that the philosophy of religion can consider not just resistance to power or forms of counter-conduct but also the "practices of the self" and modes of self-to-self relation, alongside "modes of veridiction" and "techniques of governmentality" in Foucault's late terminology.[102] The productive side of power can be seen as the excessive side of ethics, and I argue that Cassian's texts illustrate how practices of the self can be adopted, adapted, and accommodated with respect to the regimes of truth and forms of governmentality they critique.

This reading refuses to engage only the negative effects of asceticism writ in terms of social morality (Nietzsche), its instrumentalizing aspects in capitalist economies (Weber), and its marginalization from the ethical domain of ancient philosophers' "spiritual exercises" (Hadot). Noreen Khawaja insightfully frames the Protestant ethic as a "form of normativity that cannot be accounted for in purely ethical terms," figuring asceticism as "a form of conduct" or "action that is an end in itself (not instrumental) but is not in itself (spontaneously) good."[103] And this is, perhaps, the problem: that the Protestant ethic perverts the ascetic impulse, rendering it unmoored from visions of transformation and from one's particular art of living, which might actualize it by critically subverting dominant norms. Foucault himself was after the possibilities that open up when considering asceticism not as dictated by a particular normative vision of disciplinary formation but instead as capable of producing forms of life in agonistic relation to social norms.

With asceticism in Nietzsche and Weber hewing a troubling connection between capitalist production and subject formation, we can glean the danger of constructing asceticism primarily through power and vitiation—specifically, this framework makes it difficult to conceive of critique and resistance. Foucault comes to this very recognition by 1982, lamenting: "Perhaps I've insisted too much on the technology of domination and power. I am more and more interested in the interaction between oneself and others and in the technologies of individual domination, the history of how an individual acts upon himself, in the technology of self."[104] I therefore want to ask what happens when considering asceticism as a way of life that—as Hadot suggests of the ancients and Foucault stresses in turn—is able to contest cultural and political forms instead of merely recapitulating them. What happens if we do not assume a view of asceticism that is predicated on abstinence, restriction, or vitiation and that prioritizes "the thought and the will"? And how can asceticism open the possibilities for self-cultivation and follow Foucault's hope for resistance, as opposed to remaining tied to vitiation and the normalizing mechanisms of power? Finally, might the tie between self-cultivation and social critique illustrate how no formation is individual while also cultivating the ability to challenge vitiating and instrumentalizing mores?

I argue that a rigorous encounter with a figure central to the complex history of Christian asceticism will remind us that Weber's analysis is properly used as a critique of capitalism and not of Christianity as such. This is especially true in Cassian's emphasis on humans' self-transformative capacity. The very practice of challenging what normative forms of life might look like is part of an ethical project to not just *think* differently with Foucault but to *live* differently. As in the case of Foucault's *parresiast* ascetics, who capture the revolutionary potential of asceticism by speaking truth to power, it is not enough to change oneself.[105] One needs to live the philosophical life in word and deed, changing society through one's own example and forging traditions by critically adapting them, even when this puts one at odds with dominant powers. Cassian provides a variety of such exemplary ascetic figures to learn from, and his works have materially contributed to the communities whose forms of life we broadly refer to under the heading of Christian monasticism. Even the curbing of his broader doctrinal influence suggests that Cassian himself is an example of *parresia*. He insists on arguing for the vital role of human effort in a world of contingency and recognizing the myriad challenges that ascetics continuously face, even when his views put his influence at risk.

Cassian's works can help us to broaden our view of radical asceticism to include Christianity while also deepening our understanding of Christianity's role in redefining asceticism in the academic study of religion. I therefore reconsider contemporary debates about ethics and forms of subjectivity through an extended engagement with Cassian, whose stories of extreme asceticism and transformative religious experiences by desert elders help to establish Christian monastics' forms of life. With a focus on descriptions of lived experience and practical ethics, I analyze the shape of Cassian's ascetic *professio* to both critique and deepen our understanding of ethics and subjectivity in the study of religion and philosophy today. This reading of Cassian, on the one hand, challenges accounts of asceticism that imply an interior will renouncing the exterior body through its manipulations. On the other hand, it relies on readings of asceticism that emphasize the role of practices in the formation of subjectivity while productively pushing us beyond the "conflation of subjectivity and embodiment" as Constance Furey argues.[106] This reading of Cassian yields a view of ethical agency focused on an ascetic way of life (*cultus*) and the reflective, affective, and bodily aptitudes needed to engage it (*habitus*), without presuming that "interiority" becomes the primary site for subject formation and without abrogating agency.

In the process of demonstrating Cassian's acumen concerning the daily struggles that ascetics face, I make four interrelated arguments: (1) modern philosophical categories of interiority, notably a dualist split between internal and external, should not be applied to Cassian's texts; (2) attendant modern western views of "the subject" find a productive alternative in the integrating views of bodily, affective, and reflective sites of subjectivity; (3) ethical formation and human agency are productively understood through the daily practices of self-cultivation (themselves already made possible by social formation); and (4) daily practices constitute ascetic subjectivities and express ethical agency beyond either a volitional will or merely structural iterations. I push disciplinary boundaries by approaching Cassian's texts from a historically rigorous and theoretically rich dual perspective while shifting attention in the discussion of ethics to the most basic daily practices, theorizing human agency and ethical formation at the intersection of these sites of the ascetic self. Considering asceticism as an ethical practice and as a way of life can revitalize our theorization of ethical agency.[107]

A THREEFOLD PATH

To return to our original exemplar, Abba Pinufius highlights the discord between normative values and ascetic expectations. What to the former is but an old man is to the latter a paragon of excellence. The mores of the ascetic *professio* differ from those of the farmer, the sailor, or the soldier. However, like any *professio*, the ascetic negotiates a balance between a set of prescribed values and practices, on the one hand, and, on the other, one's adaptation of these practices to one's own strengths, aspirations, and social situatedness. There is no one-size-fits-all model that Cassian compels, but there are countless possible ways that one might take up the ascetic habit. This tension between being socially shaped and self-shaping yields a distinctive vision of the limits and possibilities of ethics. What results is an account of socially embedded agency expressed through the struggle in daily practices, unfolded in two parts.

Part I, *Constructions of Ethics in Asceticism*, starts with critical analysis of (1) theories of ethics as a way of life and (2) human agency, first in modern theories and then in Cassian's texts and contexts. Chapter 1 establishes the theoretical context and methodologies by which to reconsider agency and ethics in Cassian through engagement with discourses in the philosophy of religion and gender, queer, and feminist theories. Chapter 2 establishes the broader historical context for Cassian's texts and their ethical focus by considering Cassian's own situation as a monastic writer and the reception of his works alongside a reorientation of key categories in which he has been read. Chapter 3 then turns to Cassian's extended treatment of human effort as fundamentally reliant on a host of other agencies and material conditions, working out the contest between Cassian and followers of Augustine in their differing emphases on "the will" in their respective anthropologies. Part I therefore leaves us with the question of what it might look like to put such theory into practice, a question that Part II considers in the practical nuances of Cassian's works.

Part II, *Practices of Ascetic Formation*, textually and historically analyzes the daily practices constitutive of ascetic formation in Cassian's texts. Bodily practices, affective practices, and communal practices are read through critical theories of the body, affects and emotions, and intimate relationships drawn largely from queer and feminist discourses at their intersections with religious studies. Chapter 4 explores how Cassian's bodily practices, such as eating, sleeping, laboring, and praying, highlight the work of the body in concert with the emotions and beliefs. Chapter 5 considers Cassian's reading practices, in which the transmission of affects and modeling of emotions are central to the cultivation of salubrious dispositions modeled by exemplary personas through embodied and interrelational engagement. Chapter 6 analyzes social formation through the intimacies of friendship, spiritual directorship, and liturgical communities alongside beliefs, practices, and affects. The sites of Cassian's ascetic self are shaped and reshaped through daily practices at the intersection of the transformative and the mundane, where the force and sweat of ethics in asceticism becomes visible.

PART I

Constructions of Ethics in Asceticism

CHAPTER 1

Forms of Agency
and Ways of Life

Abba John of Lycopolis distinguished himself in the ascetic life with his unparalleled obedience. He subjected himself to the training of Abba Pambo so completely that Pambo advanced his trials to the point of absurdity. Given a nearly rotten stick, John unfailingly obeyed Pambo's order to water it twice a day, "so that it would take root with its daily waterings, come alive again as a tree, spread out its branches, and offer a pleasant sight to the eyes and shade in the extreme heat to those sitting under it."[1] Watering the stick required fetching water from two miles away every day, but this did not deter John. In winter chill or summer heat, in sickness or health, no excuse prevented John from carrying out Pambo's orders.

In Cassian's version of this story, the elder "silently and hiddenly observed this diligence of his day after day and saw him keep his injunction, as if it had been divinely issued, with a simple disposition of heart and without any change of expression or questioning of his reasons."[2] Pitying the youth his labors over the whole year, the elder asked John if the stick had grown roots yet. After a quick inspection, the elder plucked the branch out of the ground and threw it aside. The young John, Cassian notes, thereby "trained every day in exercises of

27

this kind, matured in the virtue of obedience and shone with the grace of humility, and the sweet odor of his obedience spread through all the monasteries."[3] John's obedience involves concrete daily practices of fetching water over miles and watering the stick twice a day, in addition to his other ascetic responsibilities. His virtue, manifested by "a simple disposition of heart" (*simplici cordis affectu*), is confirmed for the elder and olfactorily spreads to the community at large.

Another account of a stick-watering John figures in the *Apophthegmata Patrum* (*Sayings of the Desert Fathers*). This telling includes the *abba*'s injunction to take the stick and "water it every day with a bottle of water, until it bears fruit."[4] The distance of the water poses a particular challenge, as its source is "so far away that he had to leave in the evening and return the following morning."[5] This sleepless ascetic nevertheless perseveres in his discipline. After three years of watering, the wood sprouts into a fruit tree, miraculously rewarding John's efforts. His elder then carries this fruit to nearby communities, instructing: "Take and eat the fruit of obedience." Not the scent but the taste of John's obedience spreads through monasteries, confirming his exemplary virtue.

In both tellings of the story, John captures the imagination of ascetics across Scetis through sensory signs of his own excellence. While the actual practice of watering a long-dead stick might be absurd, the disposition John cultivates through his unfailing obedience to his elder is the fruit that it bears. John, the young ascetic, matures into a desert elder himself. The difference between the two accounts primarily relies on the miraculous plot twist: in the *Apophthegmata*, the stick takes root and fructifies; in Cassian's text, it is the story that takes root in the community's imagination. In the *Apophthegmata*, the fruit is the miraculous testament to John's virtue that overturns the natural world in the revification of a vitiated piece of wood. In Cassian's version, the *abba* throws the stick away and proceeds to test John through other trials, none of which result in a miraculous end. John simply moves to the next exercise, fortifying the disposition of heart (*cordis affectus*).

It is in the sensible ecstasy of Cassian's story that we can scent out his broader ethical objectives: exemplary marvels embodied in the improvement of one's behavior and way of life, not in superhuman feats and miracles. Instead of relying on miracles, the ascetic's form of life fructifies in his exemplary commitment to daily practices. He is an agent cultivating a disposition marvelous for its dedicated maximization, not its miraculous abrogation, of human possibility. His commitment both stems from his disposition of heart and fortifies this disposition itself. He expresses his agency in and through the daily practices of formation; not the spontaneous sprouting but the daily cultivation is most important.

Appreciating the force of human agency in Cassian's asceticism — notably in their daily practices — involves engaging two modern philosophical domains: (1) scholarly turns to antiquity in order to articulate alternatives to modern morality and (2) theories of agency that range from the rationalist to the embodied. Reading Cassian's texts in relation to these discourses counters the tendency to stress renunciation in asceticism, opening up ways of seeing Cassian's texts as more continuous with philosophical practices and ways of life in antiquity. This allows us to engage Cassian beyond Foucault's reading of him as obsessed with interiority and renunciation instead of attentive to transformative arts of living. In this chapter I set up the theoretical conditions for analyzing Cassian's texts with (1) attention to ethics as a way of life common to other practical texts in antiquity and (2) contemporary theoretical foci of embodiment, affectivity, and social formation as central to understand agency. Methodologically, I illustrate how contemporary theories can help illuminate historical texts and how historical texts can help challenge theoretical discourses to recognize the contingency of their own categories.

This chapter, therefore, lays the methodological and theoretical conditions for what follows in my reading of Cassian's asceticism and ethical agency. Attention to Cassian's historical context (chapter 2) and understanding of human effort (chapter 3) further extend and transform these claims by considering the late ancient world as one rich with potential for the transformation of selves in uncertain times. By bringing together ethics as a way of life with theories of agency that range from rational to embodied, I argue that a form of ethical agency is at the heart of Cassian's ascetic texts. Rooted in daily struggles of body, heart, and mind, such ethical agency produces not miraculous results but exceptional forms of cultivation. Analyzing Cassian's works in this way clarifies the strengths and limitations of modern theoretical frameworks taken up by scholars at the intersection of philosophy, religion, and history.

ETHICS AS A WAY OF LIFE

For philosophers and scholars of religion, Greek and Roman antiquity has come to offer a view of ethics as including one's whole way of life—through the dispositions one cultivates and the daily practices by which one shapes oneself—in an alternative to modern, code-based morality. Bernard Williams's turn to Socrates allows him to pose the question of how to live as the "best place for moral philosophy to start."[6] Like Foucault, Williams is concerned with the inability of modern philosophy and its stress on rationality and procedural morality to cope with contemporary challenges, arguing that "the demands of the modern world on ethical thought are unprecedented, and the ideas of rationality embodied in most contemporary moral philosophy cannot meet them; but some extension of ancient thought, greatly modified, might be able to do so."[7] Williams justifies engaging ancient thought for its opening of practical questions of how to live.

Related interests focus on societies' everyday practices, the challenges to living, and their ability to transvalue modern forms of morality from an alternative historical vantage point. Martha Nussbaum's engagement with ancient tragedies as a site for ethical reflection on the limitations of reason and the corollary confrontation of human vulnerability contrasts an Aristotelian focus on the cultivation of character with ratio-centric engagement of modern philosophers such as John Rawls.[8] For ancient tragedians like Aeschylus, "there were human lives and problems, and various genres in both prose and poetry in which one could reflect about these problems."[9] Pierre Hadot, who influenced Foucault as his colleague at the Collège de France, illuminates the everyday practices by which Greek and Roman philosophers articulate philosophy as "a way of life."[10] For Hadot, "spiritual exercises" (exercices spirituels) contour the daily domain of ethical action with the goal of self-transformation, accomplished by "mastering one's inner dialogue, and mental concentration."[11] Ethics as "aiming at a goal . . . that the common conduct of life hardly knew" requires the full reshaping of one's life in light of the commitments that one arrives at through reflection.[12] Through a genealogical analysis adapted from Foucault and Nietzsche, Charles Taylor moves away from deontology and toward the good life intertwining "selfhood and morality" in and since antiquity.[13] Taylor critiques moral philosophy's tendency to focus on "what it is right to do rather than on what it is good to be, on defining the content of obligation rather than the nature of the good life."[14]

In addition to an Aristotelian emphasis on *ethos* and a Platonic view of philosophy as *therapeia* (θεραπεία), Edith Wyschogrod describes the ethical potential of engaging narratives in medieval saints: "A postmodern ethic must look not to some opposite of ethics but elsewhere, to life narratives, specifically those of saints, defined in terms that both overlap and overturn traditional normative stipulations and that defy the normative structure of moral theory."[15] Engaging Wyschogrod's approach to life narratives as part of ethics, Cassian's texts become fecund sites for theorizing agency. Emphases on human vulnerability, the role of reflection in transformation, the centrality of doing over being, and the dialectical relation between conceptions of the self and ethics also illuminate Cassian's texts as practical and as defying "the normative structure of moral theory." Reading Cassian for such emphases extends attention to late ancient contexts alongside the ancient and medieval as another site where ethics is not primarily focused on moral judgments and rational conformity.

Such philosophical turns to pre-modern historical contexts help displace assumptions that descriptive and normative forms of inquiry need be (or even can be) separated. Following and extending these philosophical turns to the ancient Mediterranean, I argue that Cassian's early Christian asceticism might also help us think through questions of ethics and forms of life. As Foucault intimates in his late work, the domain of early Christian asceticism poses uncanny questions to our own understanding of resistance and subversion in an art of life. The desert ascetics who enchant Cassian's world and have informed monastic communities since are neither easily dissociated from modernity's utopian impulses nor neatly identifiable with its dialectics of individual and society. Exceptional human figures, demonic and angelic spirits, and dialogic considerations of the good proliferate in his work, offering us reflections, in a mirror darkly, of our own urgent ethical struggles to articulate ecosystems of self, community, and relationality.

Ethics in the Philosophy of Religion

The critical force of understanding Cassian's ascetic ethics as a way of life registers best when read in the context of recent iterations of the philosophy of religion that both critique modern western emphases on beliefs as centrally defining religiosity and open space for recognizing the centrality of practice, embodiment, and lived experience. Tyler Roberts establishes a frame for the philosophy of religion in the transition from "explicitly religious thinkers" using philosophical tools for their own theological ends, to philosophers who constructively reshape discourses in this encounter "in a way that blurs the boundaries between philosophical and religious thought."[16] Kevin Schilbrack describes how moving the philosophy of religion beyond traditional attachments to the "rationality of theism" opens up questions of agency in "the philosophical study of the experiential, practical, and institutional aspects of religions."[17] Stephen Bush frames experience as ideological and a vehicle for power and social formation, yet also as part of political agency and group identity, with "a role in the formation of bodily habits that have political implications."[18] Thomas Lewis foregrounds the methodological intersection between descriptive and normative, or historical and philosophical work, in texts across historical, geographical, and cultural contexts.[19]

My analysis of Cassian as a late ancient ascetic ethicist follows these scholars in engaging historical and textual inquiry not only for descriptive purposes but also to contribute to constructive theorization. I read Cassian's accounts of ways of life as tools for sharpening questions in the philosophy of religion today, notably through accounts of agency that are experiential yet practically formative and ——'tically salient. Cassian's ascetic ethics constructively suggest a theory of human agency to the point of nearly branding him a heretic historically. In this regard, his philosophical anthropology can be read meaningfully alongside Hollywood's rearticulation of the role of the philosophy of religion: "What if we understand philosophy of religion less as an attempt to justify or redefine belief than as an attempt to account philosophically for those aspects of human existence broadly characterized as religious?"[20] To "account philosophically" does not privilege theism and belief as special epistemic domains but focuses on practices, experiences, and normativity as also constitutive of forms of life. As I argue in Part II, Cassian's ascetic focus on human experience and human effort presents daily practices as the domain of individual and social transformation.

The subfield of religious ethics has undertaken a broadening of such categories by attending comparatively to historically specific forms of life through concern with "the close relationship between accounts of what human beings are and ethical ideals for what humans should do and become."[21] Focusing on practices, bodies, and emotions, scholars in religious ethics engage historical, textual, and ethnographic studies of religious praxis devoted to cultivating virtue. Elizabeth Bucar identifies how religious Catholic and Shi'i women use embodiment as a site of performative resistance to repressive clerical power vis-à-vis "creativity and conformity within the same act."[22] Aaron Stalnaker argues against neo-Aristotelians who privilege intellectualist virtues over more embodied forms of skilled practice, comparatively analyzing Confucian approaches to moral development and the cultivation of desired dispositions.[23] Analyzing rabbinic texts of late antiquity, Jonathan Schofer considers virtue and ethical formation through conceptions of the self, ideal traits and behaviors, and practices for attaining this ideal.[24] Lewis figures the practices of everyday life as constitutive of ethical formation by stressing G.W.F. Hegel's emphases on work.[25] Analytical attention to embodiment, skilled practices, orientation toward motivating ends, and everyday life informs my reading of Cassian's texts against assumptions of submission, obedience, and renunciation as ends in themselves. When read as historically and culturally embedded, Cassian's texts reflect Greco-Roman medical understandings of anthropology and do not assume separations between rationality and embodiment, nor do they privilege interiority over exteriority.

My reading of Cassian is predicated on the methodological claim that (1) historical, descriptive scholarship grounded in textual analysis and cultural contexts and (2) constructive, normative scholarship that critically interrogates categories and concepts in order to "think differently" can (3) inform each other in productive as well as critical ways, chastening the excesses of disciplinary assumptions. Philosophers and scholars of religion help us turn beyond modern western contexts for sites of not just historical knowledge but also ethical inquiry in their own right. Such methodological development engages the fraught question of what role normative inquiry plays in the study of religion and academic study in general. Ensuring the constructive production and critique of knowledge requires recognizing not just descriptions but also norms and their force. Recognizing how coimbricated descriptive and normative concerns are in Cassian's texts is necessary to glean the ethical force of his account of asceticism. We readers cannot understand what he is saying, descriptively, without appreciating why he thinks it is important, normatively.

While I certainly do not prescribe any of Cassian's practices for ethical formation today and am not a theologian urging Christian predicates for belief and behavior, I argue how critical analysis of his texts draws attention to embodied practices, contingency, and lived experience that has theoretical force for the contemporary philosophy of religion. When we take seriously the embodied, practical, and daily aspects of his asceticism, we can better grasp what Cassian views as the role of human effort and struggle in daily formation without assuming binaries of interior/exterior or reflectivity/embodiment. Recognizing the challenges of ethical formation opens up ways of thinking about ethics and agency, in and beyond the specifics of his asceticism.

SITES OF AGENCY

Cassian's ascetic ethics can be understood by modern critical theories not only within the framework of ethics as a way of life but also in relation to forms of agency and the constructions of subjectivity on which they rely. With accounts of agency that account for change through attention to different sites of subjectivity, I analyze Cassian's understanding of human effort as involving embodied, reflective, and social components.

At one end of the spectrum, Immanuel Kant locates human agency in the free exercise of human reason pitched in opposition to the fixed laws of the natural world. Kant focuses his attention particularly on the autonomy of the human will, human reason, and the freedom of the individual to engage in self-activity (*Selbsttätigkeit*). He extols the autonomy of the will for its capacity to act as "its own lawgiver."[26] Pierre Bourdieu, at the other end, describes human agency dialectically in relation to social structures without a significant account of rational deliberation, analyzing instead how social practices shape bodily acts.[27] Refocusing human agency on the social production of the body, Bourdieu expands Marcel Mauss's *habitus* as a set of learned dispositions enacting sedimented knowledge accumulated through social enculturation.[28]

Judith Butler resists both extremes in her rejection of conceptions of agency "as the capacity for reflexive mediation."[29] Similar to Bourdieu, she articulates human agency as a function of socially and linguistically produced bodies—but with a critical twist. Through a reading of Jacques Derrida's *différance*, Butler stresses *habitus* as a practical activity not deliberately engaged, yet one that can lead to variations in performance and structural change.[30] Invoking Foucault's paradox of subjectivation (*assujettissement*), she renders the social and cultural embeddedness of subjects as primary, describing agency "as a reiterative or rearticulatory practice."[31] The body, as the "site of an incorporated history," is both produced by and productive of the "embodied rituals of everydayness."[32] The agency of the subject is fully situated within, but not reducible to, relations of power.[33] Socially and politically constituted, loss and vulnerability are the very conditions of constitution.[34] Amy Hollywood extends Butler's account of performative agency by emphasizing how subjectivity is also constituted through "the bodily subject's encounters with other bodies in the world and by its practical or bodily citations."[35] Hollywood shifts attention away from Butler's overemphasis on linguistic performativity and toward bodily practices as constitutive of subjectivity. While Butler is "most interested in the movement between psychic and material bodies," Hollywood notes that something critical is missing in her account of agency because of a failure to foreground the materiality of the body and its constitution of practical reason.[36]

Agency is articulated at various sites: for Kant, it is reason against nature; for Bourdieu, the culturally responsive body; for Butler, the chiasmic relationship between language and the body; and for Hollywood, embodied subjectivity. The latter three accounts contest a Kantian privileging of rationality as the singular site of moral deliberation. For Bourdieu, structural determinants situate agency as an effect of spontaneous changes. Butler formulates agency as the capacity for resistance to determination by nature and social power alike. Hollywood's estimation of the operations of practical, embodied reason remind us that performance takes work and shapes who we are. Similarly, Saba Mahmood challenges liberal assumptions that human agency requires autonomy, recognizing instead the role practices and traditions play in the contours of human lives, looking beyond obedience and submission as ends in themselves.[37]

With emphases on embodiment, affectivity, and interrelationality, I argue for a view of ethical agency in Cassian that takes seriously the work of self-shaping even as subjects are already shaped by various determinants. This view stems from an appreciation of Foucault's subject formation and technologies of the self, his recognition of social power, and his aspiration toward ethical formation as a critical "aesthetics of existence." It also builds from views of human subjects as discursively produced as well as rational and experienced, refusing both models of structure as determinative and agency as autonomy. A view of ethical agency can recognize the roles of multiple sites of subjectivity, including the exercise of reason, the emotions, and the body. In Cassian's texts, transformation occurs not only through the unintentional and rote mimicry of social practices and forms, though this is part of formation. It also requires exercise of these different sites of subjectivity through daily practices that are arduous, rough, and never complete.

Limits of Lived Experience

Engaging multiple discourses on agency and ethics as a way of life, I read Cassian's texts through descriptions of practices, techniques, and goals adopted and adapted through everyday life. Following Wyschogrod, I analyze lived narratives to articulate a view of ethical agency that recognizes bodily, affective, and reflective labor, discipline, and intensity. Socially shaped subjects also adapt, accommodate, and transform themselves through the mundane and daily performance of everyday life.

The critical force of gender, feminist, and queer discourses embraces and extends Iris Marion Young's use of the "lived body."[38] Young critiques phenomenology for assuming "the subject as unitary and original to experience" even with an embodied view of consciousness.[39] Young's ethics refuse a unitary subject, an epistemic subject, and a detached observer by analyzing gender-based oppression in patriarchal social structures and the "liberating possibilities in them."[40] Young's emphasis on "lived bodies" helps me analyze how subjects are both discursively shaped and nonunitary in their formation, as lived experience contributes to a view of humans as subjects of experience and, to a limited degree, agents of change. Refusing to elide human subjectivity with either "interior reason" or the "exteriorly marked" body, Young supplements the theories of agency discussed above with a lived perspective.

Given that Young analyzes female lived bodies in patriarchal society, a question arises: How relevant can constructions of constrained agency be to Cassian's all-male texts? Cassian declares his direct audience is exclusively male, and yet it is a mistake to see in his texts modern elisions of masculinity and rationality. To make sense of the foregrounding of embodiment, affectivity, and interrelationality often coded as "female," I benefit from Virginia Burrus's vital reading of the gendered body where "a hypertranscendent masculinity incorporated characteristics or stances traditionally marked as 'feminine,'" usurping its social capital.[41] While the female subjectivity of medieval mystics requires rupture to forge its legibility—most notably through embodied and affective encounters in Hollywood's analysis—Cassian's model is one of particular and collective transformation, as opposed to disruption. Hollywood suggests the continuity of particular and communal formation in Cassian, even in times of excess: "The individual moves through the corporate recitation or singing of the psalms to a wordless exaltation, and then back to the measured voices of the community."[42] So while Cassian's patriarchal assumptions need to be critiqued, his concern for the body, the emotions, and interrelationality reflects a complex subjectivity capacious beyond gender binaries.

Engaging the constructive possibilities of queer readings of his texts requires that we also confront the clear misogyny of Cassian's texts and recognize this as one more reason not to prescribe Cassian's ethics as such. "A monk must by all means flee from women and bishops" is the oft-quoted declaration of Cassian and a testament to his propagation of the misogynist desert maxim.[43] Women and bishops with their attention to worldly values—including power and pleasure—prevent the ascetic from dedication "through insight into spiritual matters, to divine theoria."[44] Cassian warns that "the recollection of the female sex" leads to "wicked thoughts," advising ascetics not to think about even their female relatives or holy women, for such thoughts can expand to women in general.[45] Women are metonymic for temptation (though not for sin as such) in the example of Abba Paul, whose commitment to purity led him to flee even the sight of a woman as if "to flee from a lion or an immense dragon."[46] The joke is on Abba Paul, however, for mistaking this excessive abstinence for actual purity of heart. When he is struck with complete paralysis (including his tongue and ears), Cassian notes that only women can appropriately minister to his every need. Cassian's misogyny tends toward omission over invective, and women are barely present in his texts. They primarily exist as narrative occasions for male action, succumbing to temptation or resisting the power of their bodily suggestion.[47]

Cassian does not address female ascetics, yet his work is adapted by Caesarius of Arles, whose *Rule for Nuns* suggests the adoptability of Cassian's asceticism through adaptation and accommodation.[48] Reading Cassian through contemporary lenses from gender, feminist, and queer theories surprisingly illuminates the mechanisms at play in his asceticism, notably in its day-to-day labor, sweat, and challenges.

To understand Cassian's texts beyond the masculinist, rationalist, imperialist logics that articulate human agency in a hierarchical, interiorizing, and binary fashion, we need to look to the critical and theoretical resources illuminated by scholars who speak to the force of embodiment, emotions, and community.

Ethical Agency

Analyzing ethical agency in daily practice and laborious struggle requires unpacking the mechanisms by which subjects are both shaped and can participate in self-shaping. These include not just the practices that shape subjectivities as trained, shaped, and transformed—rather, it is necessary to maintain a reflective capacity to navigate competing social norms. As one shapes one's way of life, one can, in a Foucauldian fashion, potentially come to see and critique the mechanisms of power, in which "success is proportional to its ability to hide its own mechanisms."[49] The precondition for critiquing power is cultivating the ability to "think differently" enabled through processes of formation, as Foucault latterly describes.[50] Habituation in a disciplined yet nonnormative way of life is difficult and not just rote. Cassian's texts illustrate what ethical agency can look like by suggesting how this process works on a daily basis. These texts illuminate the fact that there is not just one source of ethical formation.

Analyzing ethics as a way of life requires a good account of these dimensions of subjectivity and lived experience, for only in the specific contexts of their production do ethics and agency become meaningful. Using these theoretical approaches to subject formation helps the modern reader overcome the interiorizing reading of Cassian, flattening views of interiority, renunciation, and obedience. These theoretical lenses allow us to understand aspects of Cassian that have been overlooked and to see the usefulness of thinking through these foci for reimagining ethics as self-cultivation and transformation today. From the ethical formation of ascetics to the social formation of late ancient asceticism, Cassian engages in the transmission not just of particular practices but of the lived narratives (as he constructs them, in any case) that help produce ascetic selves and society alike.

Cassian's asceticism provides a useful historical perspective on the question of agency both because of its structural resistance to binary logic and because it sits on the cusp of the interiorizing practices mistakenly identified as its primary drivers. Cassian's ascetic ethics involve the body, heart, and mind in intimate relations with others. Instead of privileging the interior, Cassian recognizes the complexity of ascetic formation as dependent on multiple sites of subjectivity, working together to cultivate dispositions or threatening dissolution through their division. Only through gradual habituation of body, heart, and mind can one transform one's life by integrating these sites. Cassian's focus on work, experience, and daily disciplines renders him a productive interlocutor for the articulation of asceticism not primarily concerned with sexual renunciation or with the renunciation of self through confession, but instead with the transformation of the self through ethical formation.

VULNERABILITY, CONTINGENCY, TRANSFORMATION

To analyze the operations of embodiment, affectivity, and reflection in Cassian's texts, I build from the work of Butler, Hollywood, and other theorists who recognize vulnerability and contingency as constitutive of subjectivity. This recognition of fracture becomes central to theorizing resistance to power and forms of agency while locating such agency neither in rationality nor in iteration alone but in the daily practices and efforts of particular subjectivities. I focus on the struggle, the effort, the work basic to the forging of subjectivities, especially beyond lukewarm inculcation of behaviors. To creatively participate in one's self-shaping—oftentimes in the face of, and as a counter to, how one has been constituted as a subject of power—is so difficult that it requires the reinforcement of multiple sites of formation working together over time in order to forge a way of life in dynamic relation with other agencies.

Recognizing the reality of suffering, fracture, and vulnerability, I am interested in how Cassian's texts present possibilities for practices of growth and transformation. His presentation of what I call ethical agency is not dissimilar from the model articulated by Holly-wood, where limitation and possibility emerge in practice. Indeed, his intertextual and character-populated writings demonstrate a deep engagement with the thorny processes of self-transformation and the citational practices that transmit and transform ascetic traditions. Through the everyday level of lived experience, Cassian offers a compelling picture of what this process of constitution through critical accommodation and habituation looks like.

In order to better understand the significance of Cassian's daily practices in Part II, I stress the potentialities of "discipline" in processes of self-formation. To read Cassian's asceticism as a way of life involves human agency as both provisionally capable of meeting the constant rigors of daily practice and adaptable to the various environments through which one is shaped. By engaging Foucault's late perspective of ethics as self-relation, we can open up ways of understanding ethics as a form of cultivation that situates agency materially, affectively, and reflectively in everyday practices. Recognizing how subjects are shaped through desire and constituted through practices, I highlight the reflective, affective, and embodied perspectives subjects can take toward their own ways of life beyond mere disciplinary coercion.

I proceed by analyzing the difficult work of constituting the subject not as unitary and detached but as fragmentary and dynamic. Human agency need not be merely an unintentional slippage in social formation, nor can it rest on mythical self-determination; it can be, as Thomas Pfau argues, "embodied, capable of intellectual self-awareness, constitutively related to other rational agents."[51] Following Theodore Schatzki's terminology concerning "agencies," an ascetic's agency does not preclude the influence of a vast network of agencies, some human, some social, some textual, some environmental.[52] Ethical formation relies not on a detached observer or interior consciousness but on lived experience that involves three elements vital to ethics and asceticism: the role of the body as transformative (not just an object of renunciation), the role of the emotions motivating the subject of action (not just the subject of knowledge), and the role of intimate social relations (not just subjection in confessional power plays).[53] I turn to these domains, respectively, in chapters 4 through 6.

Wyschogrod influences this book's foregrounding of Cassian's lived narratives. I begin each chapter with ascetic stories because of their pedagogical as well as performative power—these stories articulate a view of agency that is imaginable and experienceable on a daily basis. Ethical agency comes to life through stories that reflect theoretical commitments in action that constitute traditions in turn. As one learns how to navigate daily activities, one learns from the dispositions of other ascetics, dramatized in order to open ethical questions that each must answer oneself. Ascetic *exempla*, then, iterate through both similarity and difference.

All ascetics need to foster their own way of life—adopted, adapted, and accommodated from tradition and elders. Learning how to navigate their own struggles and foster their own stylized forms is basic to the lesson of the ascetic life that it consists "in experience and practice alone."[54] Recall Abba John, who distinguishes himself through his diligence in cultivating "a simple disposition of heart," which he commits to as if he was divinely ordered to do so. The miracle of John's obedience is precisely how unmiraculous it is—there is no divine intervention, and there is no miraculous outcome beyond this simple disposition. Yet his disposition would help guide other ascetics in turn, through both example and instruction.

CHAPTER 2

Cassian the Ethicist

In the closing decade of the fourth century raiding bandits massacred a group of Christian ascetics in the village of Tekoa near Bethlehem. On the report by Cassian, grief and lament over this massacre resounded through the lands of Palestine to Egypt. Living in Scetis in the Egyptian desert at the time and learning the ways of ascetic perfection under the tutelage of desert elders, young Cassian and Germanus were devastated when the news reached their community.[1] *Conference* 6 opens with the "considerably disturbed" (*non mediocriter . . . permoti*) young friends who go to Abba Theodore for advice on how to grieve and cope with the harsh reality of suffering in this world.[2] They ask how God could allow for his holy ones to be subjected to such evil.[3]

Cassian's contemporary, Augustine of Hippo, pens beautiful treatments on the question of evil, theodicy, and human suffering, philosophically arguing in *City of God* (*De civitate Dei*) that "evil has no positive nature; but the loss of good has received the name 'evil.'"[4] When pressed as to why "the Lord had permitted such a crime to be perpetrated on his servants," Abba Theodore similarly claims that evil does not exist and argues it as the privation of good.[5] However, Cassian differs from Augustine by quickly focusing on how adversity, just like prosperity, is an occasion for ascetic formation. Cassian reminds his reader that it is God alone "who possesses goodness not because of laborious effort but by nature."[6] Humans must work really hard to shape themselves for the better, contending with hosts of agents and influences.

Abba Theodore turns away from a theological discussion of theodicy in order to exhort ascetics to shape their own lives. This move captures the spirit of Cassian's work, where lived experience takes priority over theoretical distinctions and the focus is not on *why* things are the way they are but on *what* humans can do from here. Such attention to ethical formation contrasts with Gallic hagiographies of the time, which emphasize miraculous feats and shows of wonder, such as Sulpicius Severus's *Life of Martin of Tours* (*Vita Sancti Martini*).[7] Cassian expresses suspicion of such texts, writing instead "not about the marvelous works of God but about the improvement of our behavior and the attainment of the perfect life, in keeping with what we have learned from our elders."[8]

Orienting one's life toward the proximate goal of "purity of heart" (*puritas cordis*) and the ultimate end of "the kingdom of God" (*regnum dei*) does not come easily, Cassian recognizes, and is markedly less glamorous than the show of miraculous powers. As illustrated by Abba John, Cassian's texts respond to real human anxieties by locating human ability not in divine miracles but in everyday cultivation through rigorous practical training. Situating Cassian as an ascetic writer in historical context stages his experiential foci and prepares us for understanding the central role that practices and human effort play in his texts.

VITA CASSIANI

Cassian's life and works are open to some historical debate, since his biography is obscure.[9] This obscurity is notable because, although he features as a central character in his work, he offers little detail about his own life. His two main texts, the *Institutes* and *Conferences*, begin with his address to local Christian authorities in Gaul from 419 through the 420s.[10] Cassian is present in his works, both as an authority in his contemporary Gaul and as a novice around 380–399 in Egypt and Palestine. Cassian authorizes his construction of monasticism, while giving minimal details about his own life, requiring that we address the divergence between his literary presence and his own biography.[11] His legacy does not rest on a cult of his personality.[12]

Born around 360 CE, he was classically educated and from a family of some wealth in a region known as Dobrudja in modern-day Romania, between the Danube and the Black Sea, called Scythia Minor in antiquity; Gennadius notes that Cassian was "from the Scythian people" (*natione Scytha*).[13] This birthplace would accommodate Cassian's bilingualism in Latin and Greek.[14] He would go on to use Greek for at least twenty-five years in Palestine, Egypt, and Constantinople, although he would write his works in Latin when he eventually settled in Gaul after spending time in Rome. He went to Palestine in his twenties and underwent "initial training in the cenobium at Bethlehem."[15] He traveled with his companion Germanus, and the two continued to be close friends and lifelong travel partners.[16] At this cenobium, they roomed with Abba Pinufius, who captivated the young friends with stories of ascetics in the Nile Delta.[17]

This prompted the young Cassian and Germanus to set out for the Egyptian desert, probably in the mid-380s. There, luminaries such as Evagrius of Pontus and disciples of Macarius the Great trained the young friends.[18] The influence of Evagrius on Cassian is particularly pronounced, yet, as in the case of other Latin and Greek monastic writers of late antiquity and the medieval and Byzantine periods, "Evagrius' patterns of thought echo" without naming the condemned author directly.[19] Instead, Cassian expresses the highest praise for Abba Moses as having the "sweetest fragrance among the distinguished flowers" of Scetis.[20] He also praises Abba Paphnutius, in whose congregation they lived, who was famous for his humility and became the "Father of Scetis" after Macarius the Great.[21] In this context, struggle and spiritual warfare require that the ascetic exert significant effort with God's help. This enables progress toward "purity of heart" (*puritas cordis*), which Cassian bases on a fusion of Evagrius's *apatheia* (ἀπάθεια), becoming unperturbed by the passions, and the centrality of the heart in Macarius and Dorotheus of Gaza.[22]

Cassian and Germanus most likely fled Egypt in the 399 CE purge of ascetics provoked by Theophilus, the Archbishop of Alexandria, who turned against those he suspected of following the doctrines of Origen of Alexandria, foremost amongst them, Evagrius.[23] *Conference* 10.2 refers to Theophilus's written attack on Anthropomorphism dated to 399, but Cassian does not include how Theophilus would then turn against the Origenists with whom he was allied during the Anthropomorphite fight.[24] These associations with the Origenist controversy — and the pall over the legacy of Evagrius — likely contribute to Cassian's reticence to discuss his own life and friends.[25]

The two friends would eventually arrive in Constantinople around 402 and befriend John Chrysostom, then Archbishop of Constantinople, who would ordain Cassian deacon around 404.[26] Through the machinations of Theophilus in collaboration with the imperial Aelia Eudoxia, Chrysostom faced expulsion at the Synod of the Oak (403 CE), and Cassian would travel to Rome in the autumn of 404 to plead for Chrysostom after his second exile.[27] Speculation abounds regarding what happens between Cassian's arrival in Rome and his appearance in Massilia around 415, yet Geoffrey Dunn presents a compelling case for Cassian's going from Rome to Massilia but not to Antioch, Bethlehem, or Constantinople, as others have suggested.[28]

Cassian is said to have been commissioned by Pope Innocent I to put his practical, experiential knowledge of Egyptian desert asceticism to work in southern Gaul.[29] In Massilia, Cassian is said to have established monasteries for both men and women, with later tradition associating the male monastery with the Abbey of St. Victor and the female with St. Salvator.[30] Claiming in his prefaces to respond to requests of local authorities hoping for an ascetic program, Cassian pens twin works, the *Institutes* and the *Conferences*, between 419 and the 420s that were promptly distributed to monastic communities around southern Gaul.[31] Cassian would die around 435, having completed his third and final work, *De incarnatione Domini contra Nestorium (On the Incarnation of the Lord against Nestorius)* around 430; a work he claims was commissioned by Leo the Great (c. 395–461), archdeacon and future pope of Rome, whom Cassian had befriended while in Rome.[32] Cassian writes this doctrinal treatise against Nestorius of Constantinople's Christology in preparation for what would become the Council of Ephesus (431 CE), producing, as Thomas Humphries notes, "a treatise that links the Greek theology of Nestorius to the Latin heresy of Pelagius."[33]

CONFLICT AND CASSIAN'S QUIET LEGACY

During his lifetime, Cassian became associated with a number of controversies—Origenist, Nestorian, and Pelagian—but his status in the Pelagian controversy would be the one to shape the historical reception of his name most directly. Pelagius, a British monk, was formally condemned at the Council of Carthage in 418 for an overly generous view of human free will through the efforts of Augustine, along with Emperor Honorius and Popes Innocent I and Zosimus.[34] In 425, southern Gallic bishops were forced to profess their rejection of Pelagian views to Patrolcus, Bishop of Arles.[35] Augustine would then address his treatises *On Grace and Free Will* (*De gratia et libero arbitrio*) and *On Rebuke and Grace* (*De correptione et gratia*) (c. 426–427) to the monks at Hadrumentum, in modern-day Tunisia.[36] Cassian's *Conference* 13, *On God's Protection* (*De protectione Dei*) quickly comes to be read as a direct response to Augustine and his followers, despite its likely antecedent composition.[37]

Prosper of Aquitaine, a lay follower of Augustine who was suspicious of Gallic unorthodoxies, proceeds to attack Cassian in his work *De gratia Dei et libero arbitrio contra Collatorem* (432), with the title referring to Cassian's authoring of the *Conferences* (*Collationes*).[38] Augustinian anxiety over original sin and divine grace rendered Cassian and other eastern monks doctrinally suspect. That anxiety is amplified after Augustine's death in 430, even as Prosper's Augustinian theology shifts to a "mature explanation of the conversion of the will."[39] Augustine, in Stewart's characterization, turns his attack against all Christians whose "traditional theological anthropology, essentially eastern Christian in inspiration, was more open to natural possibility than Augustine's. Thus the issue was not really Pelagianism but Augustinianism."[40] Such Pelagian—or non-Augustinian—views come to be constructed as having too generous a view of human effort premised on an optimistic anthropology shared with eastern Christians. While this does not capture the richness of Augustine's own spectrum of views, their historical reception relies on the polemic opposition between human effort and divine grace.[41]

Cassian's role in this dispute—designated later in the seventeenth century as the "'Semipelagian controversy'"—continued until the Council of Orange in 529, where an Augustinian emphasis on divine grace would prevail.[42] Cassian, the ascetic affirming the necessity of human effort, was found suspect as a Pelagian who ascribed too much agency to humans.[43] As Rebecca Weaver argues, this is not just a matter of rejecting Cassian but of affirming Augustine's theology around the Mediterranean: "Pope Hormisdas, through his recommendation, however restrained, of Augustine's teaching over that of Faustus, had effectively enhanced the authority of Augustine over the monastic theology of Cassian and Faustus. Augustinianism was gradually becoming the Western tradition."[44] Augustine's later works' stress on human fallenness and human inability would become doctrinal orthodoxy, and Cassian's perspective would be doctrinally obscured through the spread of hyper-Augustinianisms.[45]

Cassian's Influence

What was threatening in Cassian's works? Or, to turn the historical gaze, what would prove powerful through Cassian's influence? It is significant that two damning controversies—those surrounding Origenism and Pelagianism—intersect in a shared optimism concerning the transformative capacity of humans. Cassian's emphasis on practical possibilities for human transformation proves influential across the Mediterranean.

Cassian is remarkable as a translator between eastern and western Christianities: he bridges geographies, languages, politics, customs, and friends. At an early stage, he was embraced by eastern Christianity, and his Latin texts were translated into Greek.[46] He is also the only Latin author included in the Sayings of the Desert Fathers (Apophthegmata Patrum), "a singular honor," William Harmless notes.[47] Cassian also directly influences many important figures of Gallic Christianity, with Christopher Kelley noting: "Names no less distinguished than Hillary of Arles, Maximus of Riez, Faustus of Riez, Vincent of Lérins, and Caesarius of Arles all fell under Cassian's influence. Dozens of monks were selected from Lérins and appointed to sees throughout Gaul. Cassian's thought and practice went with them."[48] There is historical benefit in spotlighting Cassian's role in the shaping of western Christian history, practice, and thought, for arguably "no other figure was as influential on the early development of monasticism in the west as Cassian."[49]

Cassian's immediate legacy is vital to medieval and Byzantine monasticism and theology, influencing Pope Gregory I, Cassiodorus, John Climacus, Nilus of Sinai, Alcuin, Rupert of Deutz, and Thomas Aquinas, among others.[50] For his historical influence, Cassian is important to study for both his fame and his infamy. These two aspects of Cassian's reception—proximate to heresy, yet practically formative—define his long historical profile and demand a corrective given his influence. Even when not named directly, Cassian would continue to exert a powerful influence over western monasticism.

His greatest influence comes through Latin monastic rules, where by the sixth century his influence is seen in the monastic legislation of Caesarius of Arles—the first section of the *Rule for Nuns* (*Regula Virginum*) depends on Book 4 of the *Institutes*, for example—other noted authors from Lérins, the author known as the Master, and Benedict of Nursia (influenced by both the Master and Cassian).[51] Cassian's influence on Benedict of Nursia's *Rule* (*Regula Benedicti*) is extensive, and Benedict recommends Cassian's *Conferences* and *Institutes* as required reading.[52] Pope Gregory I would recognize Cassian's significant influence, calling him "sanctus."[53] Due to his views on human effort, though, Cassian "hardly enjoys the title of saint in the West, despite his vast influence."[54]

Cassian in Historical Context

Cassian distinguishes himself with his geographically and culturally diverse experiences, living as an ascetic in the deserts of Egypt, as an advisor to John Chrysostom, and as resident sage of monastic communities in southern Gaul. Cassian becomes an authority by following the three stages of life that Claudia Rapp articulates as common to the educated Christian elite outside Egypt: "First came secular education, then spiritual formation in the desert, and finally a return to service in society by holding ecclesiastical office and by composing religious treatises."[55] Moving from secular (education) to spiritual (formation) to social (service) domains corresponds to broader social, cultural, and political changes in the fourth and early fifth centuries that shape the context for Cassian's work. The so-called Great Persecution pursued notably by Emperors Diocletian and Galerius (303–313) intensified Decius's mid–third century program of religious reform.[56] Persecuting Christians more pointedly, as Elizabeth Castelli argues, Diocletian's strategy requires "recognition of how thoroughly Roman law, civic identity, and religious obligation overlapped in the ideology of empire."[57] With imperial control no longer in the hands of the traditional aristocracy, a new "aristocracy of service" populated by military officers and administrators increased. Emperors Constantine and Licinius affirmed the legal status of Christianity in the so-called Edict of Milan (313), and forms of Christianity rapidly became political tools for social regulation and spread through the upper classes.[58] In 380, Nicene Christianity became the official religion of the Roman Empire in the Edict of Thessalonica of Emperor Theodosius I. Competition between cultural formations and religious experts — pagan, Jewish, gnostic, and Manichean; practitioners of various forms of Christianity and magic, and members of mystery cults — became increasingly fraught.[59]

A series of imperially sanctioned councils aimed to unify doctrine and regulate identity, constructing dangerous divisions between "orthodox" and "heretical" positions.[60] From the Council of Nicaea (325) to the Council of Chalcedon (431), the theological definitions of divinity and humanity polarized communities even as they reinforced political and ecclesial organization.[61] Meanwhile, the Mediterranean-adjacent Roman Empire was invaded by the Visigoths and Vandals and subjected to natural disasters, with imperial borders struggling to protect local economies and ways of life well before the final abdication of empire in 476 by Romulus Augustus.[62] This time of great imperial change and decay—and its use of Christianity as a tool—would have massive ramifications for late antiquity and beyond.[63] Cassian, accordingly, wrote in a time fraught with political, social, environmental, and economic challenges even as particular forms of Christianity were forged.[64]

CASSIAN'S TEXTS AND CONTEXTS

To William Harmless, "Cassian's advice is simple: follow the example of the East, above all the example of Egypt."[65] Cassian's *Institutes* and *Conferences* bring the threefold force of the Egyptian desert to Gallic communities, actively constituting the contours of their monasticisms.[66] Cassian's works do not present a history of Egyptian monasticism as such. As Jean-Claude Guy stresses, Cassian is not a historian but a theoretician of the spiritual life.[67] The *Institutes* (including the core components of monasticism) and the *Conferences* (including the details of challenging ascetic practices and doctrinal constructions) address asceticism in community, explaining features as basic as what to wear and as complex as ideals on unceasing prayer. From the literal and mundane to the spiritual and complex, Cassian presents a comprehensive framing for monastic ways of life. While the two texts differ in emphasis, they form a necessary unity.

Contexts

Cassian's epistolary exchange begins with Bishop Castor of Apta Julia (north of Massilia), whose purported request for guidance results in Cassian's dedication of the *Institutes* to him.[68] In the mid-420s, Cassian addresses *Conferences* 1–10 to Leontius, brother of Castor and bishop of Fréjus (the diocese of the monastic island center of Lérins) (c. 400–c.432/33), and the "holy brother" Helladius.[69] Cassian dedicates *Conferences* 11–17 to Honoratus (superior of the cenobium at Lérins) and to Eucherius, a monk of Lérins, writing so that they do not have to make the perilous journey to Egypt themselves.[70]

Cassian addresses *Conferences* 18–24 to four monks living on the Isles d'Hyères: Jovinian, Minervius, and Leontius, who support cenobitic and anchoritic ways of life and are unknown outside of Cassian, and Theodore, who would succeed Leontius as the Bishop of Fréjus.[71] Of these recipients, George Demacopoulos stresses that "Cassian knowingly identified and honored those men who were most capable of promoting his distinctively Eastern ascetic program."[72]

Dedicating works to such a "broad network of bishops and monks" suggests that Cassian has a level of authority and clout in both monastic and ecclesial circles, perhaps stemming from his association with Chrysostom.[73] Cassian's clerical and monastic goals are firmly intertwined, and it is a mistake to separate his texts into "for" cenobites or "for" anchorites. His texts reflect a fascinating tension between tradition and innovation, with Augustine Casiday noting: "The traditions not only train a spiritual guide for purposes of discernment in spiritual pathology, but they also provide a store of physical practices that can be prescribed like a regimen to the person who is spiritually unwell."[74] On the one hand, Cassian affirms the need for traditional rules, establishing a set order for the liturgy and system of psalmody. On the other hand, he urges ascetics to make the practices their own, adapted to their geographical, physical, and psychological particularities.[75] Neither exclusively cenobitic nor anchoritic, neither fully traditionalist nor revolutionary, Cassian's texts present issues and remedies for complex contexts.

Texts

In the *Institutes* and *Conferences*, Cassian addresses the myriad concerns that the male monk may encounter while pursuing the *professio*. He richly describes the everyday life of monks, from its dress to its food, from relations between fellow monks to the relation to God, from the reading of scripture to the contemplative practices of unceasing prayer. Addressing practical dimensions alongside ascetic anxieties, Cassian schematizes a way of life for Christian male monastics, using the desert elders to illustrate ideal ways of living while humanely recognizing their struggles.

Written over five years, the *Institutes* (*De institutis coenobiorum et de octo principalium uitiorum remediis*) engages the language of *instituti* deliberately, as Harmless notes: "The word means 'rules,' but more broadly, the sense is closer to 'foundational principles.'"[76] The first four books on the basics of monasticism were later disseminated as a free-standing *Rule of Cassian* (*Regula Cassiani*), with books on monastic dress (*Institute* 1), prayer and psalmody at night (*Institute* 2), prayer and psalmody during the day (*Institute* 3), and the heart of the ascetic life (*Institute* 4).[77] The following eight books detail the eight principal spirits or temptations that affect all humans, but that ascetics feel keenly as they struggle for formation. Such books mark a departure in tone and content for Ramsey, who stresses their subtitle, *The Remedies*.[78] These eight books include *Institute* 5, *De spiritu gastrimargiae* (*On the Spirit of Gluttony*); *Institute* 6, *De spiritu fornicationis* (*On the Spirit of Fornication*); *Institute* 7, *De spiritu filargyriae* (*On the Spirit of Avarice*); *Institute* 8, *De spiritu irae* (*On the Spirit of Anger*); *Institute* 9, *De spiritu tristitiae* (*On the Spirit of Sadness*); *Institute* 10, *De spiritu acediae* (*On the Spirit of Acedia*); *Institute* 11, *De spiritu cenodoxiae* (*On the Spirit of Vainglory*); and *Institute* 12, *De spiritu superbiae* (*On the Spirit of Pride*).[79]

In the *Conferences* (*Conlationes XXIIII*), Cassian introduces the voices of fifteen different desert *abbas* as the literary hosts of one to three conferences each, employing a ventriloquism similar to that Derek Krueger notes as common to hagiographers in late antiquity.[80] As the elder of the two companions, Germanus asks the *abbas* various questions, requesting clarification on earlier points or raising embarrassing or troublesome issues. Through the dialogue format, Cassian brings to monastics in Gaul the *abbas* "in their own voice," both delineating instruction for this Gallic audience and presenting the *abbas* as models to imitate.[81] Cassian performs *erotapokriseis* with a twofold paraenetic effect, both dramatizing the way monastic instruction took place and allowing Gallic readers to connect with the temporally and geographically distant *abbas*.[82] Filling the dearth of ascetic authorities in Gaul with the words of Egyptian desert figures, the *Conferences* help create "new *abbas* as they began to embody the texts in the same way as their desert counterparts."[83]

Opening the text's exhortations, Part I (*Conferences* 1-10) presents a complement to the *Institutes'* ascetic progression. These books cover the goal and end of the monk (*Conference* 1), the practice of discretion (*Conference* 2), the three renunciations (*Conference* 3), the relationship of the will between the flesh and the spirit (*Conference* 4), the eight temptations (*Conference* 5, a synthesis of the last eight books of the *Institutes*), the question of theodicy (*Conference* 6), the relationship between demons and humans (*Conference* 7), demonology in its cosmic origins (*Conference* 8), exegesis of the Lord's Prayer (*Conference* 9), and fiery prayer as the apex of the ascetic life (*Conference* 10). Written as an addendum to Part I, Part II (*Conferences* 11–17) covers an earlier time-period and different geography in the friends' travels. The themes covered foreground the pursuit of perfection and the cultivation of love (*Conference* 11), chastity in body, mind, and heart (*Conference* 12), the relationship between divine and human ability (*Conference* 13), the fourfold method of scriptural interpretation (*Conference* 14), divine miracles and humility (*Conference* 15), friendship and navigating anger in communal living (*Conference* 16), and justifications for promise-keeping and -breaking (*Conference* 17). Part III (*Conferences* 18–24) addresses other fundamentals, including the differentiation of three kinds of monastics (*Conference* 18), the goal of the anchoritic life and the cenobitic life (*Conference* 19), the utility of recollection in the work of repentance (*Conference* 20), the relaxation of kneeling and fasting during Pentecost (*Conference* 21), nocturnal illusions and the question of sin (*Conference* 22), sinlessness as only an aspiration (*Conference* 23), and the monk's orientation in body, heart, and mind (*Conference* 24). From cosmology to physiology, Cassian unpacks the practices and forms of life exemplified by his desert *abbas* for the edification of readers both proximal and distal.

VITA ACTIVA AND VITA CONTEMPLATIVA

In each conference, the *abba* treats an expansive set of ideas, at times seemingly unconnected to its central theme. *Conference* 16, on friendship, for example, focuses on how to negotiate the spirit of anger while living in monastic communities. *Conference* 22, on nocturnal illusions, has an extended treatment of Christology. *Conference* 13, on divine agency, is substantively a book exploring human effort alongside declarations of divine omnipotence. Reading themes and treatments across Cassian's monastic texts illuminates the constitutive role of both the active and contemplative, the practical and theoretical, and the exterior and interior in his *professio*.[84]

Constructing asceticism as "the arduous profession of their way of life" (*ardua conuersationis eorum professio*), Cassian identifies ascetics not by their spiritual excellence or moral superiority as much as by their dedication to a challenging way of life.[85] The ascetic is to use all tools and practices available, addressing inner (*interior*) and outer (*exterior*) concerns alike, to gradually forge a way of life. Ascetic living, understood as a profession like any other, requires engaging in specific practices, adopting certain norms, and holding certain aspirations. Abba Moses, host of *Conferences* 1 and 2, orients the text: "All the arts and disciplines . . . have a certain scopos or goal, and a telos, which is the end that is proper to them, on which the lover of any art sets his gaze and for which he calmly and gladly endures every labor and danger and expense."[86] To work toward the proximate goal (*scopos*) and the ultimate end (*telos*) of a given occupation requires commitment to its constitutive practices. It requires developing skills, habits, and dispositions while strenuously remaining oriented toward one's chosen goal.[87]

In *Conference* 1, Cassian illustrates how a farmer, a merchant, a soldier, and a monastic all order their lives with a shared rigor. Yet he also singles out the ascetic *professio* for maximizing human effort and for its superlatively motivating *scopos*:[88]

> Our profession also has a *scopos* proper to itself and its own end, on behalf of which we tirelessly and even gladly expend all our efforts. For its sake the hunger of fasting does not weary us, the exhaustion of keeping vigil delights us, and the continual reading and meditating on Scripture does not sate us. Even the unceasing labor, the being stripped and deprived of everything and, too, the horror of this vast solitude do not deter us. Without doubt it is

for its sake that you yourselves have spurned the affection of relatives, despised your homeland and the delights of the world and have journeyed through so many foreign parts in order to come to us, men rude and unlearned, living harshly in the desert.[89]

On behalf of this way of life, ascetics can withstand the physical and psychological challenges as they struggle to adopt, adapt, and accommodate these practices as their own. Through rigorous habituation, the pains of labor shift as one transforms one's daily life: "Then all the things that you used to do out of a certain dread of punishment you will begin to do without any difficulty, as it were naturally, and no longer with a view to punishment or fear of any kind, but out of love for the good itself and out of pleasure in virtue."[90] One renders such practices "as it were naturally" (*uelut naturaliter*), alleviating the difficulty and amplifying its root in "pleasure in virtue" (*delectatione uirtutum*). Habituation does not occur automatically or through rote repetition alone. Instead, rendering practices pleasurable and second-nature requires struggle and discipline. Practical understanding gleaned through "scenes of embodied instruction" requires reflective forms of attention in order to embody the disciplines basic to the *professio*.[91]

Praktike and Theoretike

Cassian's appreciation of the active life and the contemplative life draws from the relation between *praktike* and *theoretike* articulated by his teacher Evagrius.[92] Cassian reinforces the priority of wisdom culled through the arduous work of practical experience (*praktike*) instead of contemplative understanding (*theoretike*) alone.[93] As Luke Dysinger frames it, Evagrius renders *praktike* and *theoretike* two poles — "the ascetical ('ethical' or 'practical') life and the contemplative life" — in his ascetical and mystical theology: "As the *praktikos* makes progress he learns to perceive the work of asceticism from an increasingly contemplative perspective."[94] *Praktike*, as practical understanding, involves mastery of a particular discipline through training. Recitation and laborious memorization of scriptural practices, for example, involve a host of strategies that assist one with this labor. As Terrence Kardong describes it, *praktike*, the "active" life of purification from sin, "must be undertaken and brought to completion before one can hope to receive the gift of *apatheia* or purity of heart."[95] Contemplative knowledge, *theoretike*, is possible only through mastery of foundational *praktike*.

For Cassian, merging practical and theoretical concerns is necessary to fortify one's attention toward a single *scopos* and to advance in the ascetic *professio*. Otherwise, ascetics will be attracted and distracted by different directions they might take and by competing desires. Cassian allegorizes the mind as a tall ship in a tempest in which thoughts shove the ship around through gusts from different directions. The anchor of the body steadies the ship as the passions abate. Living the ascetic *professio* involves committing to practices that exhaust the body, shape the emotions, and steady the mind. Cassian presents these practices as not merely rote activities easily performed and discarded as one advances in the ascetic life. Instead the rigors of *praktike* require that embodied, affective, and reflective attention work together. In the continuum from the practical to the contemplative, daily practices are constitutive of the disposition necessary for theoretical understanding, and *theoretike* sustains and illuminates *praktike* (notably through scriptural understanding as we will see in chapter 5) in turn.

"Inner" and "Outer"

In order to cultivate the *scopos* of purity of heart and integrate *praktike* and *theoretike*, work on the thoughts (associated with the *inner* in modern thought) needs to take place simultaneously with embodied practices (associated with the *outer*). While Cassian engages the language of "*interior*" and "*exterior*," it is a mistake to import modern dualisms into his usage. Cassian's language of *interior* and *exterior* must be understood strategically, as forms of attention that relate to both his philosophical anthropology and the goals of his two texts.

In the opening to the *Conferences* that follows the *Institutes*, Cassian exhorts the reader to turn inward: "Let us proceed from the external and visible life of the monks, which we have summarized in the previous books, to the invisible character of the inner man, and from the practice of the canonical prayer let our discourse arise to the unceasing nature of that perpetual prayer which the Apostle commands."[96] Chadwick and other scholars read this as articulating a division between outer and inner and instituting a hierarchy between these modes of life as the ascetic moves from the "external and visible life" (*exteriore ac uisibili . . . cultu*) of the physical body to pursue spiritual perfection in the "invisible character of inner man" (*inuisibilem interioris hominis habitum*).[97]

However, as William Harmless urges, "this tidy division should not be overdrawn—as though the two works were intended for different audiences."[98] Both works advise ascetics in their collective and individuated pursuits of the holy life, and they should be read as companion pieces "since all monks must deal with both external patterns and interior states."[99] Of this change in focus, Philip Rousseau suggests that "the two modes of life might be more accurately considered as possible stages in the lives of individuals."[100] Cassian establishes a complex relationship between what we now flatly call outer and inner that demands the ascetic's constant attention to both *cultus* (external and visible life) and *habitus* (invisible character), the active life of bodily labor and the contemplative life of searching reflection. As Rousseau saliently notes of Cassian: "These two activities, 'thought' and 'labour,' (*cogitatio* and *opus*), form a real unity."[101] Practically, it is more accurate to conceptualize outer and inner as co-constituents of the ascetic *professio*, which only together enable the formation of ascetic dispositions.

Cassian's allegorical treatment of inner and outer in his discussion of chastity reflects how *exterioris hominis* and *interioris hominis* together constitute the ascetic. Cassian warns against the erroneous notion that "the whole of perfection and the height of purity consist exclusively in the asceticism of the outer man," arguing that attention to "outer" practices in the pursuit of chastity will fail without a simultaneous honing of the "discipline of the inner man" (*disciplinis interioris hominis*).[102] Even if one practices chastity of body but is stuck in unfruitful patterns of thought, one is far from purity of heart. So, too, if one imagines one's life as saintly without engaging ascetic practices. One cannot live either the "visible life" or the "invisible character" in isolation—only in their integration do they fully constitute ascetic progress.

Stewart forcefully argues this point, that bodily and affective practices are necessary for contemplation: "Cassian does not, however, oppose the 'practical' and 'contemplative' aspects of the monastic life. Monastic life is *always* both 'practical' and 'contemplative'; contemplation includes and situates action without eliminating its necessity."[103] The division between heart and intellect delineated by Irénée Hausherr illustrates the over-played distinction separating "the purported 'schools' of Eastern Christian spirituality, according to which schema Evagrius represented the 'school of intellect' and Macarius that of 'feeling.'"[104] Alexander Golitzin and Thomas Humphries express suspicion of such separation between affective and intellective schools, with Humphries arguing that Cassian "is distinct from both schools because he combines and synthesizes them."[105] Cassian sees the heart and thoughts as moving unpredictably, so he grounds the heart by "the weight of toil" in the body. Virtues of body, heart, and mind are practiced together and progressively reinforce each other.

In this relation between inner and outer, Cassian opens ways of analyzing how attention to multiple sites of the ascetic self—bodily, affective, and reflective—is necessary to forge purity of heart. Just as *praktike* is constitutive of the possibilities for *theoretike*, so is *exterioris hominis* also constitutive of *interioris hominis* and vice versa. In Part II I will analyze three domains of practice that foreground the work of body, emotions, or reflective social relations, respectively, while recognizing the gradual integration of these forms of subjectivity as constitutive of ascetics in their exercise of ethical agency.

THE HERMENEUTICS OF *ASKESIS*

Here I unfold the role of scriptural interpretation in the cultivation of *praktike* and *theoretike*. In this dialectic, advancing in practical meditative skill opens the possibility of advancing in contemplative understanding, which, in turn, illuminates one's reading of scripture and fortifies one's practice of *meditatio*. Cassian's method of scriptural interpretation, featured in *Conference* 14, guides not only a hermeneutics of texts but also a hermeneutics of ascetic formation as one learns to negotiate bodily, affective, and reflective aptitudes.[106]

Cassian's fourfold method of interpretation builds on a broader hermeneutical tradition. Philo of Alexandria sets the standard for allegorical interpretation of Jewish scriptures, reconciling Jewish scriptures with Greek philosophy in the first century.[107] Origen of Alexandria in the third century builds on Philo with an approach to Christian scriptures that counters views of Scripture he deemed heretical, engaging a threefold interpretation of Scripture with literal, allegorical, and spiritual levels.[108] By the late fourth and early fifth centuries, scriptural hermeneutics becomes central to how authority, tradition, and textuality are negotiated by ecclesial figures, most influentially Augustine of Hippo, whose *City of God* (*De civitate Dei*) and *On Christian Doctrine* (*De doctrina Christiana*) feature masterful scriptural interpretation using threefold as well as fourfold methods to reject accusations that Christianity weakened the Roman Empire.[109] Human history comes to be read as divine history in the order of time.

Cassian develops his fourfold hermeneutical method, engaging four senses or levels of Scripture, including the historical, tropological, allegorical, and anagogical.[110] With these senses codified in the medieval period, Nicolas of Lyra (1265–1349) cites Cassian as the originator of the mnemonic device: *Littera gesta docet, / quid credas allegoria, / moralis quid agas, / quo tendas anagogia.*[111] *Conference* 14 unfolds these senses: (1) the literal describes the historical account of events as they purportedly occurred, (2) the allegorical provides a narrative understanding of such historical accounts in relation to a broader history, (3) the tropological or moral helps one learn how to act, and (4) the anagogical orients the person toward the Christian's ultimate soteriological end.[112] These four senses of interpretation are neither separate nor stratified but are mutually enfolded. While the allegorical, moral, and anagogical senses are deemed "spiritual," these senses are incoherent without the first, "literal," historical sense that recognizes the material and historical reality enabling such spiritual interpretations. This integration is vital, as Fred Guyette notes: "Even the most sublime interpretation may remain outside the human heart and never be appropriated inwardly."[113] Far from both biblical literalism and abstracted spiritualism, this method reflects Cassian's understanding of Scripture and its historical, soteriological, and ethical framings.

Cassian describes these four modes of interpretation as opening up with the advance of scriptural *meditatio*, reflecting the influence of Origen and Evagrius, who stress its progressive nature. Elizabeth Clark argues that Cassian navigates the anthropomorphic peril of literally interpreting God as having body parts and emotions, on the one hand, and the "moral benefit" that can accrue from hearing such metaphorical language, on the other.[114] There are similar mechanisms at work in Cassian's Christology, navigating extremes of the materialism of Anthropomorphism and the spiritualism of Origenism. In the *moralis* sense, Cassian develops the ethical dimensions of scriptural knowledge as basic to ascetic practices and how to act. Weaver describes this as "an interaction between the sacred text and the sanctified heart."[115] This tropological sense guides the integration of *praktike* and *theoretike* through the practices of manual labor and scriptural *meditatio*.[116] As Cassian declares: "The upshot is that it is hardly possible to determine what depends on what here—that is, whether they practice manual labor ceaselessly thanks to their spiritual meditation or whether they acquire such remarkable progress in the Spirit and such luminous knowledge thanks to their constant labor."[117]

Constant manual labor and spiritual meditation involve working toward constant prayer, which Gedaliahu Stroumsa notes is "meditative in essence (*meletē, meditatio, ruminatio*)."[118] Reading Scripture properly requires cultivating the bodily, affective, and reflective practices that enact scriptural wisdom. Yet engaging *meditatio* alone is not enough, for bodily, affective, and reflective practices are needed to enable it. As Cassian writes: "The fact is that it is impossible for an unclean soul to acquire spiritual knowledge, no matter how hard it labors at the reading of the Scriptures."[119]

Cassian extends this tropological focus through stories by and about exemplary desert ascetics. Ethical praxis is central to Cassian's paraenesis, which relies on a threefold exemplarity.[120] First, desert elders take scriptural figures as exemplars to be followed. Second, young John and Germanus take desert elders as exemplars to be followed. Third, Cassian's Gallic readers take young John and Germanus as exemplars as well. Cassian's texts rely on exemplars at different stages of ascetic development to reinforce his constructions of Christian texts, practices, and traditions. Learning from scriptural and desert exemplars, practice and progress are inextricable for the ascetic life to "enter into the heart of Scripture or the hidden depths of spiritual meanings."[121] Scriptural hermeneutics involves ethical forms of imitation, cultivation, and contemplation that transform ascetic subjectivities in relation to other ascetic subjects. One gains a deeper understanding of the scriptural narratives and better participates in the Christian community, both scriptural and living.

Reading Cassian's texts through a tropological lens gives insight into the complex dynamics of ascetic formation. The ethical is central to Cassian's method of reading Scripture, and so, too, I argue, to how we can read his own texts. Marcia Colish argues that Cassian monasticized Stoicism in the west "more than any other single figure" and that his concern for ethics is connected to his understanding of anthropology: "He is interested in the genesis and dynamics of the vices, the virtues, and the passions as well as in practical guidelines for applying ethical principles in daily life."[122] Reading Cassian as an ethicist involves making central the themes and questions of ascetic formation and ethical practice in daily life. Extending Stewart's reading of Cassian as "a visionary and a pragmatist," we can better appreciate Cassian's attention to the mechanisms of transformation and the conditions for transmission of practices and traditions.[123]

CONTEMPORARY SCHOLARS OF early Christianity approach Cassian in a variety of ways, and I rely on their scholarship in my reading of Cassian. Columba Stewart gives the most sophisticated reading of Cassian as a monastic speaking to monastics and ecclesial figures in late antiquity, effecting his "own synthesis of monastic theology."[124] Rebecca Weaver illuminates Cassian as a deft navigator of doctrinal concerns over human and divine agency. Humphries argues pneumatologically:

"For Cassian the Spirit is both the author of scripture and the one who maintains orthodoxy in the tradition which authenticates and interprets scripture."[125] Christopher Kelley foregrounds Cassian's power as a scriptural exegete, while Rebecca Krawiec, Stephen Driver, and Conrad Leyser stress his reading practices and discourse analysis. A.M.C. Casiday argues for the doctrinal orthodoxy of Cassian, redressing claims of "Semipelagianism" in order to emphasize Cassian's relevance to contemporary Christian theology.[126] Philip Rousseau and William Harmless influentially analyze Cassian's historical impact in geographical, political, and social contexts as an inheritor and disseminator of Egyptian asceticism, while Richard Goodrich stresses Cassian's role as a political player in Gaul.[127] Teresa Shaw vitally situates Cassian's texts in cultural contexts shaped by Greco-Roman medical understandings of psychology and physiology.[128]

Work remains to be done to engage Cassian's texts from an ethical perspective, especially with attention to daily practices as central to ascetic formation. Building from these scholars' insights into Cassian's historical, theological, literary, medical, and exegetical work, I build a case for reading Cassian as an ascetic invested in treating the *professio* as a way of life, concerning all domains of practical action, affective negotiation, and rational reflection. The practical and contemplative dimensions of ascetic formation are continuous, reflecting Cassian's treatment of body, heart, and mind in dynamic relation. Cassian's ethical *askesis* involves a program including manual labor, physical fasting, scriptural attention, and unceasing prayer. Analyzing his texts with attention to these daily practices clarifies the range of human experience relevant to how to adopt and adapt an ascetic way of life. Cassian's *Institutes* and *Conferences* schematize the means to transform individual and community, stylizing self and society.

Just as Cassian believes that the active and contemplative—the practical and theoretical—dimensions of ascetic experience are both needed, so, too, do the literal and spiritual senses require each other. Not only do Cassian's texts describe the contours of asceticism as a way of life; they also narrate the daily life one seeks to adopt, adapt, and accommodate to one's capacities and contexts. Cassian masterfully merges direct prescriptions by the *abbas* with indirect prescriptions in the form of stories of the desert elders enacting the very activities prescribed. This reflects a philosophical commitment to the inextricability of word and deed, theory and practice, as constituting and sustaining ethical formation. As Terrence Kardong stresses regarding Cassian's view of monastic observance: "It is not enough to perform acts of askesis—one must experience personal transformation. One must become the value striven for."[129] Not performance, but the transformation it constitutes, is key.

Engaging scholars' readings of Cassian leads me to reject views of Cassian as mainly concerned with the "inner life." This assumption misses how more than being concerned with systematic development of theology, soteriology, or ecclesiology, Cassian's texts are ethical in focus. Cassian theorizes the ascetic life to help monastics in Gaul practice and live it in communities and as individuals. With contemplation "depending on the quality of our living and purity of our hearts," Cassian requires practically oriented asceticism in relation to the theoretically oriented views that were to become foundational for Catholic monasticism.[130]

CHAPTER 3

Cassian on Human Effort

In the early morning, after just a short sleep, the young Cassian and Germanus puzzle over the previous day's conference with Abba Chaeremon on divine grace and human chastity.[1] As the two friends wait for the *abba* in their cell, Germanus expresses his bewilderment and concern that the conference "nullified the value of human effort" even while inspiring the "highest desire for an as yet untried chastity."[2] Desire must be met with the ability to act on it, so human effort must play a role. Germanus wonders how Abba Chaeremon can suggest that the laborer's assiduous efforts are *not* integral to the pursuit of chastity.

Human effort and zealous toil are clearly central to the ascetic life detailed by Cassian. Abba Moses proclaims in *Conference* 1 that humans are subject to a multitude of thoughts—some of which are sent from bad spirits, others from God, and others produced oneself—but that humans must work tirelessly to decide which to embrace and which to reject. Recognizing this capacity to work is essential to *discretio*. "Otherwise," he says, "there would be no free will in a person, nor would the effort expended in our own correction be of any help to us."[3] He continues: "Free will" (*liberum . . . arbitrium*) and "effort expended in our own correction" (*staret nostrae correctionis industria*) are the preconditions for any progress in the ascetic life.

Cassian's most controversial conference, *Conference* 13, "On God's Protection" (*De protectione Dei*), opens with this question of human effort and how it is necessary but without divine grace insufficient for progress. Responding to the two friends' query, Abba Chaeremon shrewdly employs the metaphor of a farmer to explain how human effort and divine grace relate. The farmer works day in and day out tilling the soil, planting, and harvesting; he exerts a tremendous amount of effort and exercises significant discipline. Chaeremon has also seen "continual intense effort conferring nothing on the toilers, because it was not assisted by the Lord's guidance."[4] What, then, does the *abba* understand makes human effort effective through "the Lord's guidance" (*domini opitulatione*)?

In the metaphor, a good harvest is impossible "if adequate rainfall and a quietly peaceful winter had not played their part."[5] The environmental conditions have to be beneficial, not only with adequate rainfall, but also with good soil that has been nourished by a quiet winter that will enable vegetables and grains to grow. Without these proper seasonal and climatological conditions, Abba Chaeremon says, the material conditions for producing food simply do not exist. Human effort cannot *will* the organic growth of crops. At the same time, there is absolutely no chance of a good crop without the effort of the farmer and his diligence. Even in this effort Chaeremon identifies "the Lord's guidance," for the farmer can "endure all the burdens imposed by farming" because the Lord fortifies him.[6] God is also responsible for making the most basic implements of farming available: access to cattle, bodily strength and health in order to work the fields, and the tools needed to labor effectively.

A complex network of elements and agencies constellates in a successful farming venture: the farmer's physical strength, the quality of the soil, the labor involved in tilling the land, the strength of the cattle to push the plow, a good and sturdy plow, weather conditions that promote the right mixture of rain and a temperate winter, the absence of various pests, and the farmer's daily tending to the seasonally bound processes of farming which enable planting and harvesting at the right time. Chaeremon understands that all necessary elements are provided by God, who meets the efforts of certain people, enabling them to attain their desired ends. The farmer's strength and discipline enable good results if and only if the Lord enables felicitous weather patterns and forecloses "unexpected accidents" (*insperatos ... casus*). Yet the farmer must work if he is to yield produce at all.[7] Understanding the role of human effort turns on a twofold dependence on God. God both created human ability and enables the host of conditions that enable human effort to bear fruit when applied assiduously.

Cassian's texts produce a nuanced view of human effort and account for the ascetic capacity to produce effects in the world and in oneself. In this chapter I analyze human ability or "free will" in Cassian as not free in the sense of being unconstrained. Rather, such ability is the capacity to resist complete determination by other conditions, a capacity vital to any possibility for ethical transformation. Both freedom from complete determination and recognition of constituent constraints contribute to a picture of human ability that is contextually conditioned yet agential. Shaped by hosts of agencies and material conditions, the human ability to engage in ascetic formation requires recognition of subjects as embedded and interconnected. Human effort is still necessary, and the *abbas* exhort labor and assiduous exercise. This ability to engage in hard work, laboring day in and day out, and its promised returns, in turn, depend on elements and agencies beyond human control. Cassian understands these broader conditions—which we might today identify as environmental, social, cultural, economic, physiological, and psychological—as shaped by God. While "the laborer's toil can accomplish nothing without the help of God" (*nihil posse perficere sine adiutorio dei laborantis industriam*), Cassian theorizes an expanded understanding of how God enables and fosters human effort and its possible effects.[8]

The metaphor of the farmer suggests the twofold need to nuance Cassian's treatment of the relationship between human effort and divine grace beyond mere obedience and submission. First, on historical and textual grounds, to challenge, contest, and critique spurious readings of Cassian promulgated by doctrinal detractors since his own lifetime. I follow Rebecca Weaver's argument, for Cassian's complex view of agency is irreducible to the selective readings of his polemical partners.[9] Second, in an ethical reading of Cassian, human effort is crucial both to Cassian's view of divine-human interactions and to constructions of ethical agency in asceticism.

In this chapter I first address Cassian's historically controversial position on human effort and environmental synchrony in the ascetic *professio*. Then I analyze the hosts of agencies relevant for understanding human ability in a world of constraints, including agencies that hinder (demonic) and those that bolster (divine) human efforts. Cassian's view of human effort relies on a philosophical anthropology that belies substantial dualisms between "inner" and "outer" parts of the human, "active" and "contemplative" practices, and "practical" and "theoretical" concerns, as I set them up in chapter 2.[10] Part I thus frames for Part II a view of ethical agency located in the limited yet vital ascetic capacity to shape one's life through embodied, affective, and reflective engagement.

HUMAN WILL AND DIVINE AGENCY

Cassian infamously works through a complex account of how divine and human agencies relate in *Conference* 13. He clearly stresses the theological necessity of affirming divine agency above all.[11] Yet his practical focus also requires the human ability to commit to and sustain transformative ascetic practices. Cassian affirms the necessity of both divine grace and human free will, noting that they only *seem* opposed: "These two things—that is, the grace of God and free will (*id est uel gratia dei uel liberum arbitrium*)—certainly seem mutually opposed to one another, but both are in accord, and we understand that we must accept both in like manner by reason of our religion, lest by removing one of them from the human being we seem to contravene the rule of the Church's faith."[12]

For Cassian, divine grace is all-powerful and absolutely necessary for any activity in the world. Cassian pointedly situates the activity of human "free will" within the orthodoxy respecting "the rule of the Church's faith" (*ecclesiasticae fidei regulam*). Just as God needs to be recognized as all-powerful, so must humans be recognized as made with freedom of choice. Human choice does not abrogate divine power; rather it relies on divine grace for its efficacy while exercising its own agency. Human "free will" (*liberum arbitrium*) and divine grace are at best cooperative and "in accord" (*concordant*), even though they can "seem mutually opposed" (*inuicem uidentur aduersa*).

Human free will is definitional of how God created humans, with Abba Chaeremon arguing that such creation is a characteristic of a good God: "It must not be believed that God made the human being in such a way that he could never will or be capable of the good. He has not allowed him a free will if he has only conceded that he will what is evil and be capable of it but not of himself either will the good or be capable of it."[13] Cassian's logic is salient: if God created human beings with free will, such a will cannot be compelled to choose only bad and evil things. Human will must be able to choose the good, since freedom of choice involves having the ability to choose different courses of action. Human nature bears the potential for good action precisely because it "has been bestowed by the kindness of the Creator."[14] Without inflating human ability at the expense of divine grace, Cassian renders human will a feature of God's good creation, situating human agency in dynamic relation to other agencies. As humans have the capacity to change, they also have the capacity to cultivate particular ascetic ways of life.

Cassian warns against attributing everything good to God "in such a way that we ascribe nothing but what is bad and perverse to human nature."[15] For Cassian, it is blasphemy to claim that God created human nature to pursue sin, for that impugns God's goodness. Humans can desire "the grace of good health" (*sanitatis gratiam*) only because God designed them as capable of such well-being.[16] It would be cruel for God to impart the desire for health without the ability to attain it.

Human effort can pursue good or ill actions alike, which correspond to either harmony or discord with God. As Abba Chaeremon articulates the relation, "There always remains in the human being a free will that can either neglect or love the grace of God."[17] Chaeremon visualizes this tension in *psychomachia* (ψυχομαχία), in which a good angel perches on one shoulder of a person and a bad angel on the other, each counseling opposing behavior.[18] Humans have the ability to choose between competing paths. Movements away from God are guided by demonic lures or the machinations of one's own thoughts, while one's own thoughts can also propel one toward God. As Weaver argues of Cassian: "Human agency is of crucial significance for human life and destiny. Persons can direct and order themselves toward God even to the point of exercising control over their thoughts."[19] Human nature was not created damned, and free will allows for people to act without coercion. The ethical implication is that it is not a deficient human but the freedom of human choice that blocks ascetic progress and pursuit of the good.[20]

Liberum arbitrium signifies the human ability to choose between different courses of action through the exercise of one's judgment in ways not determined in advance by God or any other influence. Cassian's dynamic conception of *liberum arbitrium* does not associate choice and judgment with an interior faculty of "the will." Indeed, as Abba Daniel explains in *Conference* 4, "the free will of the soul occupies a somewhat blameworthy middle position and neither delights in the disgrace of vice nor agrees to the hardships of virtue" (*animae uoluntas in meditullio quodam uituperabiliore consistens nec uitiorum flagitiis oblectatur nec uirtutum doloribus adquiescit*).[21] Between the urgings of the spirit and those of the flesh, the "free will of the soul" (*animae uoluntas*) is insufficient to best the spirits in any absolute way, rendering the struggle to fight against them ongoing.

Cassian's language, and Ramsey's translation, further foreground the grammatically plural extension of this willing to humans as a whole with *Conference* 13's "power of our will" (*arbitrii nostri facultas*), "our free will" (*liberum arbitrium nostrum*), and "their free will" (*liberum eorum . . . arbitrium*).[22] Cassian carefully designates divine agency as the source of human judgment in *liberum arbitrium*. Simultaneously safeguarding divine power and human choice, Cassian notes, "[God] stirs up, protects, and strengthens, but not so that he removes the freedom of will that he himself once granted" (*ut incitet, protegat atque confirmet, non ut auferat quam semel ipse concessit arbitrii libertatem*).[23]

So what does God help if he does not determine what the human will wills? Cassian clarifies this in *Conference* 13: "Not only does he graciously inspire holy desires, but he also arranges favorable moments in one's life and the possibility of good results, and he shows the way of salvation to those who are straying."[24] God can inspire good desires in the human that one must choose to cultivate; God can create the conditions for salubrious actions to reach maximal effect; and God can provide occasions for reorientation toward "the way of salvation."[25] Cassian notes in the *Institutes* that divine aid also comes through "the daily exercise of his providence."[26] The farming metaphor, for example, illustrates how God controls the material conditions of the environment and all factors needed to produce these arrangements. Cassian also describes humans as children under the care of a metaphorical nurse, as the best nurse expresses loving kindness toward a child and yet allows the child to endure "some burdens and hardships by which he will not be oppressed but exercised."[27] As with the farmer and childcare metaphors, human effort cannot yield successful development alone but requires a host of other factors and material conditions. Cassian stresses the goodness of God to chasten ascetics against believing in their own autonomous abilities and to curb the spirit of pride. Despite a couple of textual exceptions in which even undeserving humans can be assisted by God, human effort, choice, and labor are vital.[28] Only given divinely supported conditions can one successfully face the challenges of rigorous training. Divine grace thereby operates on humans in two central ways: it both creates human nature in general as having free will and provides the conditions for a specific human to cultivate ethical dispositions.

CHALLENGING AUGUSTINE AND HIS FOLLOWERS

Cassian's views on the goodness of human nature contradict neither Augustine's influence on Cassian nor the Augustinian alternative articulated at this time. Yet his stress on the necessity of human effort challenges aspects of Augustine's later doctrines.[29] As Peter Brown notes regarding Cassian's *Conference* 13, "He had attempted, with the utmost tact, to modify what he thought was a dangerous denial of the freedom of the will implied in Augustine's notion of grace and predestination."[30] As Weaver describes it, Cassian's is the "first well-developed alternative to the Augustinian logic of grace."[31]

Philosophical Anthropologies in Cassian and Augustine

Cassian's and Augustine's views of the human being come to be bifurcated by how they conceive of human effort. Peter King notes that for Augustine, "the key to moral action is found in the agent's possession and exercise of free will—the psychological faculty of choice and volition."[32] As I have been arguing of Cassian, the key to ethical formation is found in the ascetic's attention, exertion, and labor—in what we might follow Peter Brown in calling his "practical anthropology"—which involves psychological and physiological attention alike. By contrast, Augustine "had placed sexuality irremovably at the center of the human person" and had come to emphasize "*poena reciproca*—an exquisitely apposite and permanent symptom of Adam's fall."[33] Augustine's view of human nature shifts across his corpus, and Cassian contests his later views of the fallenness of human beings as instigated by the original sin of Adam, who condemned the whole human race. In Augustine's late view, grace alone can instigate human good actions or good will precisely because humans are so fallen.[34] Contrasted with Brown's critique of Augustine's "drastically limited vision of a complex phenomenon," Cassian's view of human nature seems optimistic.[35]

Augustine's view of such fallenness relates to his view of sexuality as central to the human condition. Cassian, however, does not share this stress on sin and fallenness, nor does he foreground sexuality. Being human is rife with challenges and struggles, and Cassian does not consider sexuality its defining feature. Instead, he reconceives sexuality as one way that desires attach to insalubrious objects and practices—a characteristically human struggle to be worked through but not moralized as such.[36] Sexuality is not a condemnation but rather provides a litmus for the strength of one's orientation in one's *professio*. Ascetic formation contextualizes sexuality in the shape of one's whole way of life, stressing the continuous toil of human effort. Ramsey describes how some monks in southern Gaul were not drawn to Augustine because "his pessimism concerning human effort and his doctrine of predestination undercut the whole possibility of conversion and the necessity of the ascetical practices that were at the heart of monasticism."[37] By contrast, for Cassian the "desire for chastity" motivates one to commit with constant effort to asceticism as a *professio*.

Ramsey highlights a key tension between Augustine and Cassian, despite a lack of recognition of how Augustine's thought changes over time. In his own treatment of divine grace and human effort, Cassian does not stress human fallenness as overcome only by divine grace — instead, he affirms both the goodness of human nature and the necessity of free will to choose one's way of life in the midst of constraints. Cassian also refuses to undercut the necessity of divine grace. Both divine grace and human free will are required to realize good actions or desirous outcomes. Because Cassian refuses to compromise human agency, as Weaver frames it, the issue becomes "the result of the interaction of grace and human effort, an effort that was always constituted by a struggle."[38]

Prosper and the Pelagian Controversy

As I introduced in chapter 2, Augustine's follower Prosper of Aquitaine was unhappy with Cassian's account of human ability and attacked it as a threat to divine grace.[39] Prosper's selective reading of *Conference* 13 sees it as a polemical response to Augustine on the possibility of free will and human effort.[40] In one famous passage, Cassian's Chaeremon notes: "When [God] notices good will making an appearance in us, at once he enlightens and encourages it and spurs it on to salvation, giving increase to what he himself planted and saw arise from our own efforts."[41] God created humans with a good will, and when human effort fosters this will, God encourages its growth in turn. Cassian infamously connects the divinely created good of human nature to the generation of a good will: "But so that it might be still more evident that out of a good nature, which has been bestowed by the kindness of the Creator, the beginnings of a good will sometimes spring up, although they cannot attain to the perfection of virtue unless they are guided by the Lord, here is the witness of the Apostle who says: 'To will is present to me, but I find no way to perform the good.'"[42] Since God created humans with the possibility of a good will (*bonarum uoluntatum*), "the beginnings of a good will sometimes spring up" (*nonnumquam bonarum uoluntatum prodire principia*). This seemingly spontaneous springing up can be read as suggesting action against the divinely created natural order of things. Alexander Hwang explains of this *uirtutum semina* model: "A person is either inspired by God for the beginning and the completion of the good will, or a person alone begins the good will and is then assisted by grace, which does not occur as much as the former case."[43] To Prosper, then, "the beginnings of a good will" in the human suggest inordinate human power at the expense of divine agency.

Prosper makes the Pelagian tendencies he reads in Cassian's writings his focal point in *On God's Grace and Free Will against the Conferencer* (*De gratia Dei et libero arbitrio contra Collatorem*). Calling Cassian only "the Conferencer" (*Collatorem*), Prosper influentially argues against Cassian's view of human will.[44] To his mind, Cassian's affirmation seems suspiciously similar to that of Pelagius, who claimed that humans have free will even apart from divine grace.[45] Augustine had, after all, won the contest against Pelagius in 418 CE at the Council of Carthage, where Pelagius was formally condemned, which set the predicates for the Council of Ephesus (431 CE). Yet, as Harmless indicates, Prosper was not immediately successful in Gaul, for "by the early 430s, the main body of Gallic monks and bishops stood closer to Cassian, for all their genuine respect for Augustine, and Prosper had to back off from his campaign."[46] In the following century, however, Prosper becomes key for Augustinians in Gaul, with the Council of Orange (529 CE) "insisting that the fallen human will is incapable of choosing the good without prior grace."[47] Tied to the negative legacy of Pelagius, Cassian comes to be doctrinally maligned even as his influence in monasticism remains.[48]

Mediating Extremes

However, is Cassian truly so tied to Pelagian views? As A.M.C. Casiday argues, *Conference* 13 is a response not only to Augustine's overemphasis on divine grace but also to Pelagius's overemphasis on human effort.[49] Against Prosper's "deeply and systematically flawed" reading, Cassian can be seen to argue against both extremes: "These things are mixed together and fused so indistinguishably that which is dependent on which is a great question as far as many people are concerned—that is, whether God has mercy on us because we manifest the beginnings of a good will, or we acquire the beginnings of a good will because God is merciful. For many who hold to one of these alternatives and assert it more freely than is right have fallen into different self-contradictory errors."[50] Acquiring the beginnings of a good will requires divine grace, yet human good will requires significant effort to meet the extreme challenges of ascetic transformation. Divine grace and human will both need be recognized, "mixed together and fused so indistinguishably" (*indiscrete permixta atque confusa*).[51]

Prosper and Augustine promote one line of tradition and Cassian another, the former that of bishops and ecclesial authorities and the latter that of desert ascetics—even as Cassian influences the Gallic bishopric as well.[52] As Weaver identifies, Cassian follows Origen and Evagrius, for whom "grace was understood not in terms of its sovereignty or predestinating decrees that unfailingly effected their determinations in human life but in terms of its multi-faceted character, its innumerable adaptations to the condition of the human person."[53] As humans bear the potential for transformation, Cassian reflects his Origenist and Evagrian influences, as Brown says, "convinced that the very depths of the person could shift."[54]

The particular capacities and contexts of each human call for different forms of adoption and adaptation in their ascetic ethos; so, too, does grace adapt to each human, yet it does so effortlessly. Human progress in ascetic formation requires adaptation as well as human toil and effort, and Cassian notes that divine protection goes "together not with a lazy or careless person but with one who labors and toils" (*non otioso neque securo, sed laboranti ac desudanti eam cooperatam*).[55] Human labor and toil are invariably required, and human nature has the seed of goodness, which can develop through the synchrony of one's toil and the material conditions given by God, whereby one learns "by disposition and virtue and his own experiences."[56] Such cooperation between divine grace and human effort reflects the necessity of both, even as divine conditions can promote or preclude human flourishing.[57]

AGENCIES, DIVINE AND DEMONIC

Cassian's account of human effort invites rigorous engagement, posing an alternative to a willed submission model. As William S. Babcock notes, Cassian's insistence that humans *can* change rests on the fact that they "are capable of opposites, that they may now pursue the good and now the evil."[58] The "subtle and inextricable mix of human effort and God's grace," as Harmless puts it, does not imply that human choice simply submits to divine grace. Of the complicated relation inhering between divine and human agencies, Weaver describes "interacting agencies, each with the power of self-initiation, both of which must be held together in a necessary tension in order to do justice to the complexity of the church's faith."[59] Marcia Colish analogously argues of this relation: "What Cassian proposes is the synergistic interaction between God and man typical of the Byzantine Church Fathers and the eastern orthodox tradition as a whole."[60] Cassian reinforces the interdependence between agencies without assuming autonomy. He refuses to view "the human contribution to this ethical enterprise . . . as ethically autonomous either in a strictly Stoic or in a Pelagian sense."[61]

When oriented toward shared ends, there is not just accord between divine and human agencies but a deeper synergy of their operations.[62] Cassian describes the relation between divine grace and human free will as aspects of a divine gift:

> Therefore it is understood by all the Catholic fathers, who have taught perfection of heart not by idle disputation but in fact and in deed, that the first aspect of the divine gift is that each person be inflamed to desire everything which is good, but in such a way that the choice of a free will faces each alternative fully. Likewise, the second aspect of divine grace is that the aforesaid practice of virtue bear results, but in such a way that the possibility of choice

not be extinguished. The third aspect is that it pertains to the gifts of God that one persevere in a virtue that has been acquired, but not in such a way that a submissive freedom be taken captive.[63]

Human choice is encoded in the conditions of divine grace, because human choice is a divine gift in three registers. First, even for the subject who fervently desires the good, one still perceives alternative courses of action, as "the choice of a free will faces each alternative fully."[64] Not blind submission but critical awareness is at the heart of one's desire when inflamed for that which is good. Second, "The possibility of choice [is] not extinguished," even as one progresses toward "perfection of the heart."[65] Only with God's assistance can one's practices produce results. The road to holiness is not straight, nor is one led down it like an ox; one must learn through the messiness of experience, not the orderly logic of disputation. Third, one cultivates virtues through the formation of stable dispositions, preventing virtue from hardening into mere laws that bind one's conduct.

Cassian describes ascetic cultivation as forging dispositions to act virtuously without rendering such dispositions compulsory. One "perseveres in a virtue" but "not in such a way that a submissive freedom is taken captive" (*ita ut captiuitatem libertas addicta non sentiat*).[66] Human choice must be continuously active, laboring through the practices that habituate one in good courses of action, feeling, and thought. Cassian affirms human choice as central to ascetic training, yet the exercise of choice and effort never preempts or circumvents divine incitement to good action. Instead of a binary opposition, Cassian stresses the necessity of both grace and free will at all times: "What does this all mean except that in each of these cases both the grace of God and our freedom of will are affirmed, since even by his own activity a person can occasionally be brought to a desire for virtue, but he always needs to be helped by the Lord?"[67]

Agencies, Human and Demonic

Such cooperation between human and divine agencies acts as the precondition for the monastic *professio*. Asceticism relies not just on divine agency, however, but also on negotiation with another class of agencies: the demonic agencies that tempt and torment particularly, but not exclusively, the solitaries of late ancient desert asceticism.[68] Cassian adapts the "eight principal vices" (octo principalia uitia) or "passions" (passiones) to Latin monasticism from the "eight danger-ous thoughts" (thoughts as λογισμοί) of his teacher Evagrius and the Stoic-related goal of curbing the passions in ἀπάθεια.[69] Challenging the daily practices central to ascetic formation, these spirits tempt ascetics to linger on titillating thoughts, to crave luxurious foods, and to engage in petty jealousies. No human being is exempt from the chal-lenges "found in everyone" as "the kinds of passions lying concealed in our heart" (latentium in corde nostro passionum) and "the seething emotions of burning desire" (concupiscentiae flagrantis aestus).[70] Far from the ambiguity of the Greek daimon, David Brakke argues that the ancient encounter between the demon and the monk itself gave rise to "the new religious identity of the Christian monk—in Greek, the monachos, 'single one,'" precisely because the daimon becomes "the unambiguously evil demon."[71]

Instead of fleeing demons, the ascetic must "learn to triumph by endurance and by doing battle."[72] Doing battle is no mere meta-phor, for in the tradition of desert ascetics since Antony the Great, the ascetic engages in constant warfare against the demons and their leader. As Cassian relates in Institutes 4 and 12, the devil introduced the disease of pride into himself and into humanity through his influ-ence. His mistake was "his belief that he could attain to the glory of the Godhead by his own free will and effort" (gloriam deitatis arbi-trii libertate et industria sua credidit se posse conquirere).[73] Asserting autonomy of free will entails the abrogation of the conditions enabled through God's grace. The devil broke the pact, and so "he lost even that which was his by the grace of the Creator."[74] The devil's example warns the ascetic to recognize human effort as reliant on the grace of God for both its origin and its sustenance.

As the devil indicates the negative peril of assuming autonomy in free will, his demons become the very agencies against which humans fight, for "the wily serpent is ever at our heels—that is, he lies in wait for our end, and he seeks even to the close of our life to overthrow us."[75] These demons would become known as the seven deadly sins through Gregory the Great, but are better understood in Cassian's texts as subtle-bodied spirits also referred to by Cassian as *spiritus* and *uitium*. In *Conference* 5 (*De octo uitiis principalibus*), Cassian does not use "*daemon*," referring instead to the eight "*spiritus*" from *Institutes* 5–12 as "*uitia*" and "*passiones*" in *Conference* 5. By contrast, *Conference* 7, "*On the Changeableness of the Soul and On Evil Spirits* (*De animae mobilitate et spiritalibus nequitiis*) and *Conference* 8, "*On the Principalities* (*De principatibus*), feature "*daemones*" influencing human "*passiones*" as well as their "*mentes*" (minds) and "*cogitationes*" (thoughts).[76]

Demons are real agents, yet they cannot penetrate the minds or hearts of humans. Demons can only discern the ascetic's susceptibility to a particular vice through the person's visible behavior and signs, the *exterioris hominis*. From Evagrius, who gauged by external signs if an ascetic was susceptible to demonic manipulations, Teresa Shaw notes that "John Cassian likewise stresses that demons are able to detect by outward signs what is hidden in a monk's soul. . . . This emphasis on external signs of internal conditions is significant because it further highlights the importance of the external presentation of the ascetic body."[77] As demons are constantly waiting for opportunities to prey upon humans, Cassian describes them as acute readers of the human psyche, inferring a human's mental state through other behavioral patterns. The *interioris hominis* and the *exterioris hominis* are fused instead of dualized, and different observable signals attract different demons: looking at the last morsel of food signals that the time is ripe for the demon of gluttony, or listlessly flipping to the end of one's text to see how much more one has to read lures the demon of *acedia*.[78] As Charles Stewart notes of the Evagrian flavor, this "provides one example of a demonic thought that allied the irascible and sensuous parts of the soul and 'suffocated the intellect.'"[79] Demons are perilous because they distract human attention: gluttony focuses one on sensory pleasure, anger focuses one on petty responses to others, and *cenodoxia* as vainglory obsessively curries other people's approval.

Many demons can assault a person in quick succession, so learning how to negotiate some of the easier ones—gluttony and fornication in Cassian's schema—is necessary to focus on defeating the more difficult—*cenodoxia* and pride. To fight the incursion of such demons, establishing more "basic" virtues is crucial for progressing on the spiritual path. Cassian emphasizes, for example, fasting as a necessary counter to gluttony. In *Conference* 14, Cassian describes the causal chain between the eight virtues: "With this concatenation of virtues he very obviously wished to teach us that one proceeds from watching and fasting to chastity, from chastity to knowledge, from knowledge to long-suffering, from long-suffering to gentleness, from gentleness to the Holy Spirit, and from the Holy Spirit to the reward of unfeigned love."[80] With the practical cultivation of virtues as necessary for coping with vices, Cassian schematizes ascetic counters to demonic temptation. Yet as the virtues become more difficult to ensure, divine grace becomes foregrounded.

Understanding demons is crucial to understanding the interaction of agencies in Cassian. Demons cannot penetrate the inner spaces of the human, and yet they are one of three sources of thoughts, along with the human and God.[81] This interplay of agencies requires the ascetic to consent to or reject thoughts, meeting them with pleasure and sustaining them or rejecting them as undesired. The human is porous to both divine and demonic influence, and Cassian does not assume that a singular fixed identity or an autonomous will determines one's actions. To best demonic agencies and harmonize with the divine requires the negotiation of competing desires and influences through the formation of stable dispositions. To analyze how ascetics can cultivate such dispositions over time requires appreciating the role of ascetic orientation alongside Cassian's philosophical anthropology.[82]

Ascetic Agencies

Negotiating demonic, human, and divine agencies, Cassian extols practical intelligence over and against worldly knowledge. Of exemplary ascetics, he declares: "They did not receive it in a worldly spirit by way of dialectical syllogisms and Ciceronian eloquence; rather, by their experience of an unspoiled life and by the most upright behavior, as well as by the correction of their vices and, to speak more truly, by visible indications, they learned that the nature of perfection is contained in it, and that apart from it neither the love of God nor the cleansing of vice nor the improvement of behavior nor the perfection of virtue will be able to be laid hold of."[83] Not in the didacticism of classical rhetoric but in the experience of the ascetic life can one cultivate the ascetic *professio*. The sweat of experience integrates bodily, affective, and reflective attention, stabilizing ascetic dispositions against competing desires and demonic distractions.

Cassian's view of *liberum arbitrium* and *uoluntas* reflects how experience and transformation are at odds with an intellectual or voluntarist notion of human "free will" as determining human actions. For Cassian, cultivating ascetic dispositions requires the critical discernment of *discretio* and the practices of everyday life one adopts and adapts. Not an interior faculty of will legislating a course of action, *liberum arbitrium* more closely designates the capacity for the ascetic to reinforce his orientation toward the goals of the *professio*—in body, heart, and mind—through the daily practices that constitute it.[84] One's orientation toward the ascetic *scopos* and *telos* motivates one's commitment to ascetic practices, despite their challenges: "For we do not keep to solitary silence or strict fasting or intense reading by our own will even when we are able to, but even against our own will we are frequently distracted from beneficial practices by conflicting interests, so that we are obliged to beseech the Lord for ample space or time in which to carry out these things."[85]

The practices of silence, fasting, and scriptural meditation that contribute to the *professio* are difficult to maintain even under the best divinely given conditions. To have "ample space or time" depends on the practical conditions of one's day, and "conflicting interests" can include everything from demonic intrusions to visits from fellow monks requiring hospitality. Curbing distractions requires practices of concentration and discipline within stable environmental conditions that are necessary but not sufficient for living the ascetic *professio*. Just as the conditions for agency need to be divinely provided and humanly exercised, the ascetic must commit to the necessary practices in order for the environmental conditions to yield the right fruit. Committing to daily ascetic practices expresses one's ethical agency and ability to shape one's life in confluence with the divine, despite the daily struggles and the threat of regression.

Cassian's view of agency is more complex than a model of "willed submission," which accounts neither for the nuanced synergism between divine and human agencies nor pays adequate attention to the challenges of training in the ascetic *professio*. This synergy of human and divine agencies reinforces the double orientation of the ascetic, who needs to be oriented toward the ultimate end of the kingdom of God in order to pursue the proximate goal of *puritas cordis*. The distal goal amplifies commitment to the proximate goal, fortifying the ascetic's motivations in the daily *professio* despite its challenges. Cassian's asceticism thus includes both reflective engagement with the divine good and practiced resistance to the demonic. Human choice and free will are not interior faculties—they are exercised through everyday practices bringing bodily, affective, and reflective forms of attention together as the ascetic pursues the motivating end. Conditions, agencies, and forces beyond individual control shape ascetic selves—yet ethical agency is also vital to formation in the ascetic *professio*.

PHILOSOPHICAL ANTHROPOLOGY
AND ASCETIC FORMATION

To analyze the mechanisms of ascetic formation in Cassian's texts also requires analysis of the philosophical anthropology that renders such formation possible. Since no one faculty of "the will" determines one's actions, feelings, and judgments alone, the interplay between embodied, affective, and reflective attention needs to be analyzed. Ion-Valeriu Hiu analyzes Cassian's anthropology as a citadel: "The soul can be reinforced as a citadel. Senses are the gates of this citadel, or its walls. And through them either the good or the bad can enter a soul's life."[86] Instead of Hiu's citadel, I follow Cassian's allegory of a household as an *oikonomia* (οἰκονομία; economy) for its stress on managing its constituent agencies together.

Cassian describes the human allegorically:

For as long as the man who is strong and armed—that is, our spirit—keeps watch over his house and secures the depths of his heart by the fear of God, all his property will be safe—namely, the profits of his labor and the virtues that he has acquired over a long period. But if someone who is stronger comes upon him and overcomes him—namely, the devil, through the assent of our thoughts—he will take away the arms in which he trusted—namely, the recollection of Scripture and the fear of God—and he will divide his spoils, which means that he will disperse the deserts of his virtues by the contrary vices, whatever they may be.[87]

Just as the householder is responsible for the overall functioning of the household, the spirit (*spiritus*) of the human being regulates the operations of the human as a whole.[88] The householder *spiritus* both keeps the household in order and protects the treasures in the metaphorical depths of his heart (*cordis sui*) from the thievery of the devil. Because they can be led astray, thoughts (*cogitationes*) must be placed "in the scale of our heart" (*in nostri pectoris trutina*), and the "heart" (*cor*) adjudicates between "whatever our thoughts suggest that we should do" (*gerendum cogitatio nostra suggesserit omni*).[89] Cassian urges the weighing of thoughts through critical *discretio* to a fourfold end: to assess the veracity of thoughts, to reject illegitimate thoughts, to see through faulty interpretation of Scripture, and to identify thoughts that stem from vanity.[90] Because "the assent of our thoughts" is needed for demonic thieves to plunder the sanctuary of the heart, *discretio* is vital to safeguard the heart's treasures and to thwart thieves.

Thoughts can both consent to or reject demonic advances; they are morally neutral, tending naturally in no particular direction. Like hired guards, thoughts have the power to protect or to undermine the security of the household, following the commands of the spirit or accepting the demonic lure of greater rewards. Scriptural recollection and fear of God provide the allegorical armor that helps the heart adjudicate between thoughts and work to protect the whole household.[91] Maintaining this focus requires strength that comes from an accumulation of labors and virtues developed over time in practices that Cassian correlates with manual labor, bodily fasting, and unceasing prayer.[92] The spirit benefits from the labor of the body, because physical engagement requires so much attention, there is less room for other demonic temptations to gain purchase.[93]

Through bodily labor and affective recollection of Scripture, the mind becomes "slimmed down" and, with fewer errant thoughts, is more able to turn to heaven.[94] Scriptural readings and fasting likewise serve the "useful purpose" of "purifying the heart and punishing the flesh" through bodily practices.[95] Yet the excesses of the flesh and the spirit are both to be avoided through the common attention of body, heart, and mind, allowing for the purification of the heart and integration of the whole ascetic. To "the connection between heart, mind, and soul" stressed in Cassian's texts by Humphries, it is necessary to add the body.[96] Repeating Plato's tripartite conception of the soul in *Conference* 24, Cassian stresses how the rational (λογικόν), irascible (θυμικόν), and concupiscent (ἐπιθυμητικόν) require a "heartfelt disposition" (*cordis adfectu*) for stability.[97] Harmonizing the competing desires of rationality, irascibility, and concupiscence helps integrate the ascetic in mind, heart, and body.

Through the conjunction of the ascetic's practice and the work of divine grace, the human is dynamically transformed.[98] Demacopoulos stresses that "one could participate in one's salvation through ascetic discipline and a refocusing of one's soul toward God."[99] Attention of the heart works with that of the mind and that of the body, integrating exterior and interior sensibilities.[100] William Harmless's account of how *puritas cordis* involves the body, heart, and mind is vital:

> For Cassian, purity of heart touched not just the heart (in the modern sense) or the body (in an extended sense), but also the mind. He routinely links purity of heart with tranquility of mind. The connection is not obvious to us. We tend to distinguish heart from mind, emotion from thinking. But Cassian, like many early Christian theologians, treats the biblical term "heart" (*cor* in Latin) as a synonym for "mind" (*mens*). In the ancient view, mind is much more than the locus of thinking; it is the conscious center of our experience as human beings, what we tend to call the

self. And Cassian saw the mind — at least, the mind as it is now enfleshed in the physical world — as singularly unstable.[101]

The heart as synonymous with mind as the "conscious center of experience" involves the body, emotions, and thoughts — and the goal is to stabilize the human by integrating these sites of the ascetic self. Health and stability of the heart-body-mind, in Cassian's Greco-Roman milieu, requires quelling the passions, tempering bodily excitations, and reducing the distractions of thoughts.[102] Of this ascetic economy, Teresa Shaw notes that "in order to achieve a life in accord with nature and to maintain a healthy condition in the soul, one must not only apply techniques of self-examination and evaluation, but also make practical, daily steps toward virtue. Training or *askesis* toward virtue and autonomy involves the whole person. . . . Thus soul and body are in a dynamic, mutually dependent relationship."[103]

In his attention to the mutual dependence of body, heart, and mind, Cassian not only respects Galenic medical along with Platonic philosophical views but also synthesizes theological traditions. To the well-noted influence of Origen and Evagrius Cassian incorporates the practical elements of Macarius and the desert tradition of heart-centered *askesis*.[104] Diadochus of Photike's definition of prayerful knowledge captures the essence of Cassian's Pseudo-Macarian inflected spirituality — "knowledge: not to know oneself while with God in ecstasy."[105] Cassian's emphasis on *puritas cordis* involves a relation to God that exceeds an abstract intellect or interior will, even as he builds from Evagrius's account of *apatheia* as "freedom from domination by the passions."[106] Bodily, affective, and reflective attention integrate and intensify to render oneself ecstatically present to God.

Laborious practices require human effort, as the cultivation of the ascetic life integrates the activities of the body, the heart, and the mind.[107] The body is not sinful or to be renounced in itself, depending instead on the "will and command" of the heart. As the heart is purified, the body tends toward salubrious behavior; when the heart is overrun by vices, it tends toward negative behavior, defaulting to the flesh (*caro*) when operating in an economy of constant misdirected desire.[108] The heart, when purified of the excessive wants of the flesh, embraces salubrious thoughts and allows for the body to follow the governance of the spirit without overzealously pursuing virtue.[109] Curbing both the excesses of the flesh and its temptation toward gluttony and fornication, along with the excesses of the spirit and its temptation toward vainglory and pride, the ascetic balances both extremes.

Facilitating the integration of body, heart, and mind involves practices that produce, sustain, and transform ascetic subjectivities.[110] The body cannot be renounced and forgotten; if the body is not given sufficient sustenance and care, the ascetic cannot function.[111] Aspiring toward the spirit alone threatens the integrity of the ascetic body, as the example of old man Heron shows. Effort and care for the body contribute, in turn, to the cultivation of the mind. Cassian notes that "whatever is assimilated gradually and without too much bodily labor is always more effectively grasped by the heart."[112] The body needs to be cared for so that it can support the heart and mind. The heart fortifies one's motivation to commit to the ascetic life. And the mind directs the attention toward the double orientation of the *professio*.

CASSIAN'S VIEW OF the ascetic as constituted and transformed through these multiple sites enables a view of ethical agency attentive to what humans can work on gradually if ploddingly: "The sum total of our improvement and tranquility . . . comes, rather, under our own power."[113] Bodily practices steady reflective awareness and affective engagement, affective engagement motivates flagging bodily practices and reflective awareness, and reflective awareness orients bodily practices and affective awareness. The practices ascetics engage in—the way they fast, their means of controlling thoughts, their warring with demons, and their cultivation of dispositions—transform particular selves as they help shape traditions in turn.[114]

Cassian's philosophical anthropology and estimation of human ability suggest an integrative model that does not rely on oppositional categories like interiority and exteriority or mind apart from body. Transformation requires that modes of action, feeling, and thought harmonize and gradually forge a unified disposition in the ascetic *professio*.[115] For Cassian, the inner ascetic is not separable from the embodied and socially participatory outer ascetic. Cassian's anthropology not only enables but even requires a robust view of ethical agency that operates in concert with myriad agencies and in the environmental and social conditions that shape one's possibilities for action and development. And although his affirmation of human effort proves controversial, Cassian does not reject or minimize human dependence on divine grace or other agencies. Cassian views the ascetic not in terms of domination or freedom but with a subtle view of agency that belies any binary of determination versus free will.

PART I OF this book has set up the theoretical framework and textual contexts for ethical agency and ascetic formation. Part II addresses domains of daily practices and the mechanisms of formation in Cassian. Each chapter opens with a narrative of a dangerous spirit that presents daily challenges to one's commitment to fostering ascetic ways of life. With dangerous agencies impinging on ascetics—not to mention the vagaries of chance, the harshness of the environment, the political struggles with clerical intervention, and the threat of invading barbarians—Cassian presents a set of strategies to battle the spirits, to embrace one's path, and to forge one's way of life. Through attention to daily practices, Cassian's texts provide ways to fight against ever-present spirits, as well as the fickleness of mind, the exhaustion of body, and the instability of emotions. Ethical agency involves not freedom from constraints but rather the daily means of negotiating such challenges.

In Part II I engage three domains of practices to analyze the mechanisms of ascetic formation using theoretical frameworks from gender, feminist, and queer theories at the intersection with religious studies. Through attention to embodiment, affectivity, and communal formation, I analyze Cassian's dynamic accounts of change and agency, with each chapter treating a different yet connected domain of formation. Chapter 4 engages contemporary discourses on embodiment in order to appreciate the significance of manual labor and other bodily practices in Cassian's asceticism and to give a clear picture of what an ethics without an ossified mind/body dichotomy looks like. It juxtaposes *acedia*, as spiritual torpor, with the manual labor and bodily practices needed to negotiate the struggle with paralyzing thoughts. Chapter 5 engages critical discourses of affects and the emotions in order to understand the play of contingency and cultivation in Cassian's reading practices and the role of exemplarity in the formation of ascetic dispositions. The negotiation between vainglory, as one's desire to be perceived as a rigorous ascetic, and the disciplined work of cultivating an ascetic *affectus* is integral to advancing asceticism. Cassian's texts do not support solipsistic, merely individual self-betterment but work toward a broader program for the transformation of selves and society. Chapter 6 foregrounds the social dimension in Cassian, reading community not just as a disciplinary force but as constitutive of both selves and the intimate relationships that forge them. Such communal relations, in turn, influence the transmission of social practices and construct traditions. This chapter juxtaposes pride, in which one mistakenly believes in one's own self-sufficiency, with the interrelational practices at the heart of Cassian's asceticism.

PART II

Practices of Ascetic
Formation

CHAPTER 4

Bodily Practices

Cassian describes how "a wearied or anxious heart" (*taedium siue anxietatem cordis*) and an "irrational confusion of mind" (*inrationabili mentis confusione*) testify to the presence of ἀκηδία (*acedia*), the sixth dangerous spirit that is "the peculiar lot of solitaries" (*solitariis magis experta*).[1] Early Christian ascetics hypostasized this spirit as the noonday demon, attacking a person in the middle of the day, "rushing in upon him like a kind of fever at just this time and inflicting upon the enfeebled soul the most burning heat of its attacks at regular and set intervals."[2] Evagrius says of the demon, "He instills in the heart of the monk a hatred for the place, a hatred for his very life itself, a hatred for manual labor."[3] Cassian believed that the spirit of *acedia* "renders him slothful and immobile in the face of all the work to be done within the walls of his cell or to devote any effort to reading."[4]

The ascetic sighs continuously and glances anxiously around the cell, eager for distraction.[5] He has difficulty concentrating on the reading at hand, skipping ahead to the end of the passage and superficially skimming over the words. If trying to write, he convinces himself that just one more walk outside his cell or a visit to a neighbor will recharge his creativity. His talents are being wasted in isolation, and he would clearly be better off spending time teaching and instructing others.[6] He grumbles to himself that he would make so much more progress if only he had a more supportive community, better equipment, more sleep, less labor, adequate food, and peace of mind.[7] If one does not ardently resist the spirit's machinations, one succumbs to them, fleeing the suffocation of the cell or falling asleep for a quick nap.[8]

The solitary succumbing to *acedia* risks more than productivity — once one lets such distracted thoughts into one's heart, spiritual listlessness settles over every operation.[9] *Acedia* casts its influence "like a foul mist" (*uelut taetra . . . caligine*) in the ascetic, who becomes "so disengaged and blank" (*otiosus ac uacuus*).[10] The aspiration toward "the vision and contemplation of that divine purity" is at risk.[11] Cassian brings exceptional psychological acumen to his articulation of this spirit, declaring that the best antidote to *acedia* is manual labor, in which, by "the fruit of their hands," ascetics engage in spiritual warfare. Refocusing attention on daily bodily practices challenges the seemingly hopeless task of raising one's thoughts from the thick torpor of despondency. The rigors of manual labor in conjunction with other bodily practices help temper the influx of thoughts, steady the emotions, and shape the ascetic self.

Cassian's early Christian ascetic commitment to work is directed at a specific set of difficulties and toward a specific set of goals. Cassian even extols Egyptian ascetics for their superlative integration of labor, meditation, and prayer: "For they are constantly doing manual labor alone in their cells in such a way that they almost never omit meditating on the psalms and on other parts of Scripture, and to this they add entreaties and prayers at every moment, taking up the whole day in offices that we celebrate at fixed times."[12] The Egyptian desert ascetic does not merely observe ritual practices at prescribed hours but imbues the whole day with forms of bodily, affective, and reflective attention typically associated with intense moments of ritual. Influenced by Greco-Roman medical views of physiology and psychology, Cassian's bodily practices invite reflection on the mechanisms involved in shaping ascetic subjectivities.

This chapter focuses on the bodily practices ("constantly doing manual labor") and continuous ritualized prayer ("celebrated continuously and spontaneously") that shape one's whole day.[13] I have already suggested that to read Cassian's ascetic ethics as inaugurating interiorized subjectivity imposes a modern dualism of self that his works are well positioned to help us think beyond. Here I elaborate what that contribution looks like by reading his texts through contemporary theories of embodiment formed in reaction to modernity's interiorized, rational theory of the subject. Cassian's practical treatment of embodiment resonates with his optimistic views on human agency, especially in his advocation of manual labor to combat the spirit of *acedia*. Cassian uses nocturnal emissions and tears to dramatize how the everyday operations of the body form and transform selves through the cultivation of dispositions that depend on the coimbrication of physiology and psychology.

BODIES IN RELIGIOUS STUDIES

Engaging with contemporary theories of embodiment, practice, and performativity allows me: (1) to better analyze Cassian's practices with attention to relevant bodily foci and (2) to situate Cassian's production of the body as a site of subjectivity shaped through the daily operations of ethical agency. From gender, feminist, and queer theories, discourses of embodiment have productively moved theories of religious subjectivity beyond traditional attention to beliefs, rationality, and intentionality.[14] Influenced by Michel Foucault, theorists like Catherine Bell and Talal Asad analyze bodies, rituals, and practices as central to the construction of religious subjects and importantly render practices primary to beliefs.[15] With attention to the body and social power informing theoretical discussions since the 1970s, these discourses have been vital to the construction of religious studies as a discipline. This theoretical shift provides the necessary lens by which to read Cassian as Constance Fury says of the study of religion, not in terms of "the Protestant-style tendency to equate religion with interiority and belief," but instead to emphasize "the body, gender, emotions, or praxis."[16]

Such attention draws from a century's rich theoretical engagement with embodiment. Marcel Mauss, in the early twentieth century, helps reverse the priority of interior belief and exterior body, analyzing how bodily techniques are socially shaped and transmitted through practical knowledge.[17] Through habituation in social and cultural techniques, embodiment focuses the intersection between physiology and cultural embeddedness. Pierre Bourdieu stresses bodily constitution through its practices: "The body believes in what it plays at: it weeps if it mimes grief. It does not represent what it performs, it does not memorize the past, it *enacts* the past, bringing it back to life."[18] Framing the accounts of *habitus* of Mauss and Bourdieu, Asad amplifies attention to the body "as an assemblage of embodied aptitudes, not as a medium of symbolic meanings" or as brute physicality unshaped by culture.[19] The body is not, as Sarah Coakley frames it, "a 'natural' datum of uncontentious physicality upon which religious traditions have then spun their various interpretations."[20]

Shifting the discourse from belief to the body notably when analyzing the religious subject is insufficient in itself, however. "The 'body,'" Coakley notes, is "what is left" when attempts to overcome Cartesian mind/body dualisms grow too suspicious of the mind.[21] This overcorrection has recapitulated similar disjunctions, setting up "the body" as a site to be passively manipulated.[22] The body as too determined by social formation undermines human agency, however, as Judith Butler assiduously corrects in her affirmation of bodily speech-acts in the iterative process of contesting social norms.[23] At this intersection between embodiment and agency, Saba Mahmood describes embodied practices as a locus of agency for religious subjects in the Egyptian piety movement of the 1990s, troubling the western conceit that women's liberation comes from resisting the constraints of religious practices and other traditional forms.[24]

Focusing on bodily practices as constitutive of religious subjectivities counters interiorizing readings of religious praxis and assists in a rereading of Cassian's texts. I pursue this reading in part through the influence of Foucault's stress on the technologies of the self and ancient ethical attention to dietary, sexual, and economic practices as vital to theorizing the body. Susan Ashbrook Harvey gives a dynamic account of how embodied subjectivities contribute to soteriological epistemologies, where humans change through their encounters with the divine sensorium.[25] Patricia Cox Miller articulates the ascetic body as a "perceptual construct" allowing the audience to see an emergent angelic body.[26] Both critical points help us frame Abba John's sweet odor of obedience from chapter 1. Such emphases are necessary for understanding bodies both as social constructs and as capable of engaging in ascetic formation as sites for imitation and transformation, beyond an interiorizing reading.[27]

EAT, WORK, PRAY: THREE DOMAINS OF BODILY PRACTICE

Cassian gives a rich sense of the ascetic *habitus* and the performances ritualizing daily life. Yet he does not gloss over their difficulties or ongoing challenges to the body's abilities. From grueling physical labor to spare dietary consumption, Cassian imbues his *Conferences* and *Institutes* with a range of physically intensive activities as the backbone for an ascetic way of life.[28]

The first four books of the *Institutes* depict the framing practices of cenobitic monasticism, from the type of dress monastics wear to the parameters of diet to the number of services they observe. *Institute* 1 (*De habitu monachorum*) designates the dress monastics wear every day, each garment of which Cassian gives a "spiritual" meaning reflecting the *professio*'s layers of scriptural and historical significance. Cassian describes such practices as contributing to the "regulation of behavior" (*morum formulam*), beyond caring for the "well-being of the body" (*curam corporis*).[29] Shaping dispositions and protecting the body are both central. *Institute* 4 continues to distill the ascetic life, presenting in concentrated form the themes that span the twenty-four books of the *Conferences*. With the first four books of the *Institutes* later disseminated as the "Rule of Cassian," the spread of these texts suggests their practical efficacy.[30]

Specifications of bodily practices populate the *Conferences* in a double respect, whereby the *abbas* both prescribe specific practices and enact these practices with the young Cassian and Germanus. Cassian does not treat daily, concrete practices in a cursory or merely preliminary way. Rather, these practices are constitutive of the ascetic *professio*. Taking these many dimensions of practice into account, Cassian schematizes a rich way of life using the elders of the Egyptian desert to illustrate exemplary ways of living while frankly addressing the anxieties common to all humans cultivating virtues and mitigating vices. Cassian describes many of the relevant practices as "virtuous things" (*uirtutes*) by which people are ascetically formed and transformed, noting that "fasting, vigils, scriptural meditation, nakedness, and total deprivation do not constitute perfection but are the means to perfection."[31] With perfection always deferred, the disciplines of bodily cultivation foregrounded in Cassian and featured in this chapter include fasting (*ieiunia*), manual labor (*labores*; *opera manuum*), and holding vigil (*uigilia*). Cassian rounds out his regimen of care by recommending between three and four hours of sleep per night.

Dietary Practices

While Cassian does not prescribe a diet for his readers in southern Gaul, he does represent dietary customs of Egyptian desert ascetics, outlining typical and exceptional consumption patterns.[32] Young Cassian and Germanus discuss the daily regimen of two pieces of hard bread (*paxamatia*), a drop of oil, a mixture of salt and water (*muria*), and minimal intake of water.[33] Abba Moses, in *Conference 2* (*De discretione*), discusses these norms directly and also narratively closes with Moses, Germanus, and Cassian engaging in this dietary practice. *Conference 8* (*De principatibus*) opens with Abba Serenus offering hospitality to the young Cassian and Germanus in an elaborate feast, providing each with salt, three olives, five ground chickpeas (*trogalia*), two prunes, and a fig.[34] Cassian describes this as the maximum amount one could consume in the desert without being looked down upon.[35] *Institute 4* (*De institutis renuntiantium*) discusses food preparation in communal contexts and in other references to social hospitality.[36] Yet the majority of the references to food accompany discussions of fasting, the means of moderating one's intake, and the imperative to adjust Cassian's suggestions to the capacity of one's individual body. Columba Stewart wisely questions "how literally Cassian's descriptions of desert meals were meant to be taken: writing for monks in southern Gaul where both foods and climate were different from Egypt, these certainly were not sample menus."[37]

Cassian's many references to food both give insight into desert dietary practices in late antiquity and also reflect the various anxieties concerning consumption. Not sex, but food, as Peter Brown writes, is the primary anxiety for desert ascetics and requires one to deliberately shape one's consumptive practices.[38] Teresa Shaw analyzes Cassian's view of the connection between dietary and sexual practices with reference to the cultural and geographical contexts of his own formation. With Greco-Roman medical views informing late ancient cultural milieus, Cassian correlates bodily humors with libido, where consuming too much fluid or food increases the libidinous fluids as well. The Egyptian monastic diet that figures most prominently in Cassian's texts stresses dried and uncooked foods because they have a drying and cooling effect on the bodily humors according to Galen of Pergamon's humoral theory.[39] The ascetic's goal is to dry and cool the body in this context.[40]

Excess as such is the problem, remedied best by an "evenhanded abstinence" avoiding rich foods and minimizing intake of even common foods.[41] What one eats contributes to one's humoral makeup, and if one tends toward heavy foods or foods that do not agree with one's constitution, an excess of one humor destabilizes the constitution of the whole person. Only by balancing one's diet can humoral excesses be curbed. Stewart notes that Cassian supports a moderate diet because he is "wary of the physical and psychological enervation that comes from alternating severe fasts with excessive eating."[42] He rejects excessive fasting, urging the regulation of dietary consumption by geography and climate as well as the particular constitution of the individual. Dietary needs and possibilities in Gaul differ from those in Egypt, and knowing this context of his publication, we can reasonably read this as a suggestion to exercise discretion in adapting practices to different climates in order to forge stable dispositions. Although Cassian's individually accommodated ideal of balance still includes extreme fasting practices, Cassian ascribes a positive and necessary function to these consumptive practices.[43]

Such dietary practices reflect important assumptions about the correlation between physiology and psychology. Shaw stresses how "it is simply artificial and somewhat dangerous to apply modern distinctions of physiology and psychology to the ancient formulations—at least without careful definition."[44] Not simply reducible to a "body" or "mind" issue, dietary formation is a discipline of both, and Shaw keenly notes that physiology and psychology are continuous for Cassian. "Medicine and ethics," Jackie Pigeaud describes, "are not developed as two independent techniques, they are deeply connected by a certain understanding of the human."[45]

With Greco-Roman medical theory, physiology, dietetics, and philosophy setting the context for early Christian ascetic practice, one's formation is "displayed in the body and its activities."[46] Navigating the connection between vices of gluttony and fornication, Brown notes, "Cassian deliberately chose the medical terminology of his age."[47] Cassian develops the link between gluttony and sexuality clearly in *Conference 22* (*De nocturnis inlusionibus*), where overeating is seen as the first of three causes of nocturnal emissions (the second is an unfocused mind and third is the work of the devil). Without curbing gluttony one can never curb incitement to fornication; to progress in the ascetic *professio*, one must start with fasting.[48]

Cassian exhorts monastics to watch that "the purity of body which we have acquired may long remain in us and imitate in some respect our inviolate chastity of spirit."[49] In a recursive logic, one must balance bodily humors to quell negative and enhance positive psychological functioning. Negotiating the demons of anger and sadness, the ascetic cultivates a chaste spirit that, in turn, reinforces the stability of bodily appetites. Cultivating physiological and psychological stability together enables one to see how "the chastity of the inner person is discerned by the perfection of this virtue [of dietary restraint]," due to their coimbrication.[50]

Manual Labor Practices

Along with bodily formation through dietary regulation, Cassian reinforces the necessity of manual labor.[51] Such toil in late ancient Egyptian desert communities could involve collecting timber, making rope from reeds, and weaving baskets and the mats on which ascetics sit. Farming is also no mere metaphor for Cassian, and the monk's practices in that regard include farming the land near one's cell, cultivating the land, planting seeds, watering the earth after procuring the water from a distance, and harvesting the products.[52] Daniel Caner notes of such bodily practices, "Manual labor was not just a spiritual discipline but a virtue of necessity."[53] Cassian, Augustine, Chrysostom, and Basil all follow Paul in emphasizing this necessity as well. Producing enough food for one's community as well as visitors requires constant labor. Figures like Evagrius made writing their trade, composing treatises and guidelines for local communities and pious supplicants.[54] The *Apophthegmata Patrum* (*Sayings of the Desert Fathers*) also represents ascetics weaving ropes and baskets as part of "a communal work ethic developed that eventually became normative in Egyptian tradition."[55]

Such bodily exertion involving the work of the hands is the cornerstone of *askesis*. As Maria Doerfler analyzes in Augustine's treatise *De opera monachorum*, physical marks of asceticism in the form of long hair are inadequate for spiritual progress without the attendant labor.[56] By *studio ac sudore* we see labor and sweat as central to Cassian's texts, as the standard by which elders evaluate novices' ascetic development and "measure the state of their heart and their progress in patience and humility by their eagerness to work."[57] Even one's desire to work reflects one's spiritual state and proves an ongoing testament to one's progress or regress as one negotiates physiological and psychological challenges. Only with such tireless work can the threat of malaise—intensified as *acedia*—be combated with constant vigilance. Eagerness to work is not merely preliminary. Instead, work is constant and daily and is performed by monks at all stages of the ascetic life.

Cassian's Abba Paul exemplifies such continuous and daily manual labor. With plenty of food from nearby date palms, Paul does not need to work in order to grow more food. Nevertheless, he labors tirelessly every day, storing up its fruits and at the end of the year burns up the entire lot of food. Abba Paul commits to manual labor even when it is not necessary for sustenance because manual labor is a constituent part of the ascetic *professio*: "And so, although the obligation of earning a livelihood did not demand this course of action, he

did it just for the sake of purging his heart, firming his thoughts, persevering in his cell, and conquering and driving out acedia."[58] Continual
labor is necessary for ascetic transformation as it helps unify affective,
reflective, and embodied attention, purging the heart of errant desires,
centering one's thoughts, and reinforcing one's physical perseverance
despite tedium. Paul's industry, discipline, and commitment to manual
labor not only signal his virtue but are also constitutive of the exemplary ascetic way of life.[59]

Focusing one's hands, heart, and mind on manual practices importantly helps the monk negotiate *acedia* and its distractions from the
spiritual life. One is not as susceptible to *acedia*'s proliferation of
thoughts and anxieties when one's attention is drawn to bodily practices and the exhausting exertion of manual labor. When the monk is
focused on physical labor, he is less prey to an onslaught of demons
because his attention is rapt. The idler is easily distracted by any
demonic threat, lacking both the affective drive and the reflective orientation toward the *scopos* and *telos* required to meet the challenges of
manual labor. As Cassian warns, "A monk who is working is struck
by one demon, whereas an idler is destroyed by innumerable spirits."[60]

Prayer Practices

Manual labor is vital as a focusing activity that unites the attention of
body, heart, and mind. It also enables and is accompanied by constant
prayer and, as Stewart says of Cassian's traditional attitude, "Prayer
and manual labor are natural partners."[61] Cassian conjoins manual
labor and scriptural *meditatio*, rendering the body busy with manual
labor, the mind reflecting on texts, and the heart oriented toward
divine entreaties. Cassian's constant prayer is not imposed by the
canonical hour but imbues all of one's actions that engage embodied,
affective, and reflective attention together.[62]

In addition to imbuing one's daily life with prayer, Cassian
describes canonical hours and offices for prayer, notably throughout
Institutes 2 and 3 and *Conferences* 9 and 10, the latter of which provide "the most extensive single treatment of prayer in early monastic
literature."[63] Bodily engagement remains basic to canonical prayer

practices as one stands with arms outstretched in the *orant* posture. At intervals, one drops quickly to one's knees and bends one's head to the ground in a supplicating position. One immediately gets up and continues to pray standing up with arms outstretched, Cassian stresses, for such a quick supplication ensures that no one falls asleep on the ground.[64] Spoken prayer involves the recitation of psalms and short personal prayers, as well as memorized excerpts from the Scriptures.

The intersection of canonical prayer and constant prayer informs the performance and *habitus* of the exemplary ascetic life. To establish constant prayer as present in one's every action, feeling, and thought requires intensive training and ongoing struggle. The arduous bodily practices of dietary regulation and manual labor are continuous with the intensive bodily practices of prayer. This continuity tends toward integration as one cultivates forms of attention through dietary and manual practices that shape the quality of prayer itself. As Cassian says in his treatment of the Lord's Prayer: "Hence we must prepare ourselves before the time of prayer to be the prayerful persons that we wish to be."[65]

Cassian's point is profound: Prayer is not separate or extricable from everyday practices. The quality of one's prayer practice relates directly to the quality of one's other bodily practices. Orienting one's contemplation toward God helps sustain commitment to arduous bodily practices, better deflecting demons and the proliferation of anxious thoughts. Brouria Bitton-Ashkelony indeed argues how the omission of prayer as a "spiritual exercise" in Hadot and Foucault also obscures the relationship between demons, prayer, and the construction of self in early Christian discourses.[66] Just as fasting and manual labor support the struggle against distraction through bodily exhaustion, honing one's prayer practices reinforces one's reflective and affective orientation toward the ascetic *scopos* and *telos*.

Discussing the possibilities of unceasing prayer, Cassian describes the fortification between bodily labor and prayer practices: "The upshot is that it is hardly possible to determine what depends on what here—that is, whether they practice manual labor ceaselessly thanks to their spiritual meditation or whether they acquire such remarkable progress in the Spirit and such luminous knowledge thanks to their constant labor."[67] Cassian's stress on the coimbrication of manual labor and spiritual meditation highlights the integration of such practices in ascetic formation. Instead of a hierarchy of spirit or thought over the work of the body, Cassian describes an integrated dynamic between bodily practices focused on sweat and effort in manual labor and bodily practices focused on meditation and reflective orientation toward God. "What depends on what" (*quid ex quo pendeat*)—a formulation Cassian also uses in *Conference* 13.11—stresses an integration of forms of attention, labor, and practice. As Stewart argues, for Cassian prayer "is of a piece with his eschatological orientation, his integrative view of the human person, and his spiritual understanding of the Bible. All come to bear on the practice and experience of prayer."[68] With habituation in bodily practices and the formation of stable dispositions, one can transform one's entire way of life.

THE IMPORTANCE OF diet, labor, and prayer practices favors a reading of Cassian's asceticism as constituted through habituation in bodily practices—and this *habitus* is informed both by the project of self-transformation and by its own transmission within the community. Bodily practices are necessary to anchor the ascetic's attention and prevent the incursion of other desires and distractions. Regulating consumptive practices and engaging laborious practices remains necessary and, in a humoral medical perspective, helps to eliminate excess fluids. Such practices transform one's way of life by instilling disciplinary focus and preempting the free play of other distractions. Physiological imbalance correlates with psychological imbalance, and ascetic transformation requires struggling to integrate both effectively and sustainably.

TRANSFORMING PHYSIOLOGY AND PSYCHOLOGY

Foregrounding bodily practices in Cassian's asceticism, we can see how physiology and psychology integrate as they come to regulate everyday behavior. We can also better analyze the mechanisms involved in formation, arguing a view of asceticism as a means of self-cultivation as opposed to self-renunciation. Cassian's treatments of nocturnal emissions and tears offer two ways to analyze such formation.

Nocturnal Emissions

Cassian offers frank and detailed treatments of nocturnal emissions, both as the central theme of *Conference* 22 (*De nocturnis inlusionibus*) and as the heart of *Institute* 6 (*De spiritu fornicationis*), on fornication, and *Conference* 12 (*De castitate*), on chastity. Such frankness contrasts with English-language translators of Cassian's work. Terrence Kardong publishes the books with the *American Benedictine Review* in 1979, and Boniface Ramsey renders a full translation only in 1997 (*Conferences*) and 2000 (*Institutes*).[69] Edgar C. S. Gibson's Nicene and Post-Nicene Fathers editions do not translate *Conferences* 12 and 22 and *Institute* 6 at all, simply noting that the translations are omitted.[70] In his 1950 classic on the life and texts of Cassian, Owen Chadwick avoids reference to *Conference* 22 completely. When references to nocturnal emissions occur in the texts (*Institute* 6 on fornication, for instance), Chadwick employs loose euphemisms instead.[71]

Beyond the prudery of some modern English scholarship, this omission signals issues with how Cassian's texts have been read. By rendering sexuality taboo, Cassian's texts could be read with the assumption that sexuality, the flesh, and renunciation of the self are overwhelmingly important. Indeed, Foucault's use of Chadwick's *John Cassian* could have contributed to his own assumptions concerning Cassian's views on renunciation.[72] Analyzing these three books, however, offers a view that is remarkably unmoralizing and uninvested in castigating the flesh.[73] Cassian discusses the body and what he considers its natural functions in order to quell (not intensify) anxiety over its operations. Obfuscating the experiential and pragmatic foci of Cassian's texts also obscures how his view of the body stresses its practical possibilities, not its sinfulness.

Cassian treats nocturnal emissions as natural processes of the body that should not simply precipitate shame. The physical erection as a "movement of nature" is not morally problematic in itself. Rather, the problem arises when desire is involved. Cassian sees the physical movement of the body as natural but the impulses of the flesh as not: "This is incumbent upon us, then, and we must fight against the movements of the soul and the impulses of the flesh until the condition of the flesh submits to the requirements of nature and does not arouse pleasure, expelling excess matter without any harmful wantonness and not doing battle with chastity."[74]

Instead of a "battle for chastity"—from Foucault's important reading of Cassian—that foregrounds the fight of flesh against a purified virtue, Cassian counsels recognizing the bodily "requirements of nature" without succumbing to the spirit of *fornicatio* by desiring the act. The movements of the spirit and the impulses of the flesh are *both* prey to demonic influence as I analyzed in Part I, and the ascetic can focus too much on either extreme. Cassian reflects on nocturnal emissions in relation to the ideal of chastity conceived as a refashioning of desire, not a renunciation of the body.[75] He states of such an achievement: "It will be a clear sign and a full proof of this purity if either no unlawful image occurs to us as we lie at rest and relaxed in slumber or at least, when one does surface, it does not arouse any movements of desire."[76] Through habituation, the ascetic can control his desire to indulge in lusty images, even as his penis moves and expels emissions according to the "requirements of nature." Far from a condemnation of erections or emissions, Cassian recognizes the neutral status of the body, locating the issue in desire oriented toward sexual pleasure and bound by the flesh.

Progress in *puritas cordis* and the ascetic life involves two related signs. First, seductive images will abate in frequency as the ascetic sleeps. Second, even if the images do occur, the ascetic does not desire to dwell on these images. That such images occur is an inevitability; humans cannot control this.[77] What does come under one's control is one's response to them. As in any negotiation with Cassian's three sources of thoughts, one need exercise *discretio* to evaluate which thoughts to embrace and which to deflect by gleaning which come from demons, from oneself, or from the divine. Cassian exhorts ascetics to emulate others who establish "a similar degree of purity through lengthy toil and effort and by way of integrity of mind and body, and who do not feel the stings of the flesh in the form of an onslaught of base desire but only in the form of a movement of nature."[78]

In his stress on "lengthy toil and effort" (*laborem longum et industriam*) and on "integrity of mind and body" (*integritate mentis et corporis*), Cassian warns ascetics against mistakenly thinking that "the whole of perfection and the height of purity consist exclusively in the asceticism of the outer man."[79] Cassian vehemently rejects exclusive attention to outer practices as a measure of chastity, arguing the simultaneous necessity of the "discipline of the inner man."[80] In order to cultivate purity of heart, work on inner thoughts and feelings needs to take place in tandem with outer practices. David Brakke elegantly captures this inner and outer dynamic in relation to the problem of nocturnal emissions: "Nocturnal emissions are problematic, then, because they suggest the persistence of boundaries between a person's 'inside' and 'outside,' a distinction that precludes an entirely visible self."[81] Transforming oneself so that one no longer experiences nocturnal emissions reflects the continuity of inner and outer forged through ascetic formation. This transformation (not renunciation) is of an interdependent, porous, nondichotomized, and integrating ascetic self.

Cassian stresses the limits of human effort, noting that the full quelling of nocturnal emissions can be obtained only through divine grace. What one can control is how one focuses one's attention: one occupies one's body, heart, and mind with salubrious pursuits and practices to distract them from harmful thoughts and the enticements of demons, coming to embody them as second nature.[82] Cassian's exemplary *abbas* move from the experience of "corruption" (as susceptibility to base desires) to the inverse of purity through the efforts of the ascetic who effects the "integrity of mind and body." *Puritas cordis* is neither an intellectual purification nor a renunciation of the body or the emotions. These bodily practices are necessary for the transformation of the whole ascetic, integrating inner and outer.

Tears

The example of nocturnal emissions stresses the difficulty of integrating sites of the ascetic self. Tears become corollary markers for gradually achieved integration. A simultaneously psychological state and physiological event, tears have performative force and indicate progress in the ascetic *professio*. In fiery prayer, tears partially constitute the referent of *conpunctio*, which includes the spontaneous expression of tears and sorrow. Tears are not a physiological signifier for a more important psychological state. Stewart describes Cassian's *conpunctio* as "a multivalent term, signifying both state and event."[83] Cassian's *conpunctio* is simultaneously the state of sorrow and the event of tears, refusing the diremption between psychological "state" and physical "event" or between inner state and outer event. The multivalence of *conpunctio* dynamically illustrates the coconstitutive relation of psychology and physiology in Cassian.

Tears encode a variety of propositional attitudes, ranging from "tears not from bitterness over his sins but from the delight of eternal joy."[84] Cassian accordingly reflects a fourfold progression in *conpunctio*. First are tears from remembering past sins.[85] Second are tears anticipating the glory of the afterlife, characterized by "unbearable joy" (*intolerantia gaudii*) and "tremendous liveliness" (*alacritatis inmensitas*).[86] Third are tears spawned by fear of hell, which prompt opposing emotions of terror and repentance. The second and third are best suited to forms of canonical prayer outlined in *Conference* 9.15. Fourth are tears of sorrow for the sins of others, precipitated especially in those who have advanced in *puritas cordis* as part of their unceasing prayer as described in *Conference* 10.11.1.

Cassian describes *conpunctio* as a manifestation elicited from the recesses of the soul through the work of divine illumination. Prompted by a singular infusion, compunction can take many forms. The "fruits" of compunction can be characterized as joyous and exultant as well as silent and stuporific. Three expressions are typical: One is rendered stunned, or groans excessively, or handles this experience only by excessive tears. While these sound like characterizations of grief, tears are never expressions of grief particular to Christ, as Irénée Hausherr notes in his study of the doctrine of compunction in eastern Christianity: "Weeping for Christ is not Christian. Monastic *penthos* will never be found related to the death of Christ."[87] Remembrance, anticipation, terror, and sorrow for others become a fourfold way of categorizing tears in their typical expressions. The integration from surfaces of the body to the depths of the psyche constitutes the phenomenon as a whole. Tears when the mind is "filled with such an abundance of compunction and with such sorrow that it cannot deal with it except by an outpouring of tears."[88] Spontaneous physical release of tears is part of the intensity of the experience of compunction.[89] In fiery and wordless prayer, compunction is a bodily, affective, and reflective state both propositionally directed and involving physical tears.

As in the case of the cessation of nocturnal emissions, only divine agency can precipitate the tears constitutive of *conpunctio*.[90] Instead of the privative movement in nocturnal emissions, the productive movement in the shedding of tears has not three sources (demons, oneself, or God) but only one—the divine.[91] Trying too hard to weep reflects the spirit of vainglory (*cenodoxia*); showing off one's tears to others renders an ascetic's efforts moot. Or such effort can lead to an acedic despair in the effects of asceticism and intimate one's defeat in the *professio*. Even when one sincerely sheds tears, the threat of pride continually lurks, and, as Evagrius cautions, one can forget why one is crying and become prideful of these tears as marks of divine favor. The presence of decoy tears can illustrate just how many vices are still rooted in the ascetic, in that false tears are not divine gifts but distractions sourced by demons or human hubris and therefore do not involve *conpunctio*. *Conpunctio* is not "left behind" after one has attained a level of perfection, indicating instead the fullness of ascetic experience. As Stewart notes of tears, "Like all ascetical disciplines, they were never left behind . . . weeping for sins was seen not as a phase of the monastic life but as a way to characterize the whole of it."[92]

TRANSFORMATION THROUGH EMBODIED PRACTICES

Cassian's account of tears illustrates *puritas cordis*, where the fruits of deepest compunction are experienced in terms of divine delights. The ascetic *professio* involves a view of human agency participating synergistically with divine agency as one cultivates one's way of life through dietary, manual, and prayer practices. Such practices are the preconditions for cessation of fleshly lusts in nocturnal emissions, as well as divine illumination and the *conpunctio* it elicits. Both active and contemplative, as Thomas Merton describes, "contemplative life on earth is the *skopos* which we must seek by active asceticism."[93]

Nocturnal emissions and tears reflect how, from bodily practices to prayer practices, the integration of physiology and psychology enables the transformation of the ascetic self. Advances in contemplation rely on the quality of one's practices and the degree to which one has been transformed. Describing ascetics' everyday practices, Cassian illustrates how integrated contemplative and bodily practices are in this perspective: "For they practice equally the virtues of body and of soul, balancing the profit of the outer man with the gain of the inner. On the heart's slippery movements and thought's unstable undulations they fasten the weight of toil as a kind of steadying and immovable anchor, and, once the shifting and roving character of the heart has been fixed to it, it can be kept within the confines of the cell as if in a most secure harbor."[94] Virtues of "body and soul" (*corporis animae que*) are practiced equally and in tandem in that the state of the "outer human" (*exterioris hominis*) relies on the state of the "inner" (*interioris*), and vice versa. Cassian sees the heart and thoughts as moving unpredictably in part because of demonic temptations, so there can be no advance in contemplation without daily manual toil that counters demons like *acedia*.[95]

Far from a disjunction between the exterior and the interior, between action and contemplation, Cassian affirms a continuum and mutual reliance between them. While the proverbial difference between Mary and Martha is that of choosing the contemplative life or the practical life, Cassian affirms both ways of life.[96] This is no division between labor of the body and labor of the mind. Instead, the focus is on how ascetics think about their own actions, how they order their own daily activities, and how they understand the simultaneously spiritual and material significance of any given practice, from the way they dress to their participation in fiery prayer. Attending to Cassian's texts with such attention, separation between the contemplative interior life and the practical exterior life proves itself untenable.

Puritas Cordis

These aspirations are realized in Cassian's account of *puritas cordis* as the proximate goal of the ascetic *professio*, building from the *apatheia* of Evagrius, as "freedom from the inner storm of 'passions,' irrational drives which in their extreme forms would today be called obsessions, compulsions, or addictions."[97] From the beginning of *Conference* 1, Abba Moses helps stage how habituation in prayer practices enables an orientation of the whole ascetic and trains one's attention on an ultimate good. Cassian's double imperative involves both the ultimate objective of reaching the "kingdom of God" and the proximate objective needed in order to successfully pursue it.[98] This consists of "the reintegrative process he calls 'purity of heart,' 'perfect chastity,' or 'unceasing prayer.'"[99] As Stewart affirms of Cassian, "He was no dualist: the most intimate and private realms of bodily and sexual experience were drawn into the project of transformation through grace."[100]

The development of purity of heart through these practices involves the coordinated progress of the body, heart, and mind. Humphries identifies Cassian as weaving together "an intellect-centered asceticism with a heart-centered asceticism" and says that this philosophical anthropology oriented toward *puritas cordis* shapes his ascetic pneumatology.[101] Having the resources to combat the onslaught of demons, the ascetic *scopos* is *puritas cordis*. As one engages these practices, one opens the possibility of experiencing unceasing prayer, quelling the frequency of nocturnal emissions and other forms of sensual desire, and experiencing the tears that manifest as part of divinely granted experience.

Hosting *Conferences* 9 and 10, Abba Moses discusses the centrality of prayer practices in two stages. Book 9 is primarily dedicated to an analysis of the Lord's Prayer, which is recognized as authoritative and extends treatments like that of Origen. In transition to Book 10, Cassian introduces "fiery prayer" or "wordless prayer" (*ineffabilem orationem*).[102] This stage is "known and experienced by very few," and it is neither a common occurrence nor a requirement of the ascetic *professio*. Described as illuminated by "heavenly light," this moment of fiery prayer is wordless, and yet "the mind" (*mens*) "gushes forth as from a most abundant fountain and speaks ineffably to God."[103]

In Cassian's account, this intense and prayerful communion with the divine is experienced as an infusion of divine light in the ascetic still engaging in the practice. Not "beyond" the body, this form of prayer does not differ from constant prayer in physical gesture or articulation. Yet at times it surpasses human comprehension and exceeds what the "self-conscious mind is able to articulate easily or to reflect upon."[104] One experiences the fullness of prayer as an achievement of perfect integration between bodily, affective, and reflective forms of attention informed but ungoverned by discursive reflection on one's state. The mind, the body, and the heart are united and their integration is maximized in their intensified experience of the divine.

Accommodation, Habituation, Formation

To engage ascetic practices is to work to transform one's life in every way, cultivating one's potential instead of renouncing one's self. Ascetics work physically to help purify their hearts, redirecting their desire toward God and their reflective attention toward *puritas cordis* and *regnum dei*. The disposition cultivated through such laborious practices realizes the ascetic's aspirations. Cassian thereby describes the key features of the ascetic life—to mirror Hadot's account of the practices of ancient philosophers—in terms of a disposition to act, feel, and think in habituated yet challenging ways. Such action can start with bodily kneeling in the Pascalian adage, yet one makes practices second nature through the work of not just the body but also the heart and mind. By engaging in practices that regulate one's behavior each day, one becomes habituated in these practices, like those elders who had "celebrated continuously and spontaneously throughout the course of the whole day, in tandem with their work."[105] Instead of daytime celebration of the monastic offices, exemplary ascetics do not require the ritualized hours set aside for prayer. One engages in continuous and spontaneous celebration at every moment, and one changes the quality of one's life where advances in contemplation firmly rely on the quality of one's practices.

Cassian stresses the need to accommodate practices to one's capacity, suggesting that different physiological and psychological constitutions as well as geographical, cultural, social, and environmental conditions need be considered. One cannot perform the same practices with the same intensity in the cooler climate of Gaul as do the elders in the heat of the Egyptian desert. Monastics in Gaul also have different dietary needs and possibilities than those in the desert, so ascetic emphasis should remain on attaining balance and supporting the integration of physiology and psychology.[106] By adapting practices in order to make them one's own, the ascetic is both constituted and transformed through them. Particular ritual moments are no longer set aside as exceptional moments of attention and intensity. Instead, one's whole life is turned into an intensification of constant prayer in body, heart, and mind.

Cassian affirms that through such habituation one can continuously and spontaneously perform the practices that are vital to the monastic life. One does not act out of blind adherence to a rule but continually adapts such practices to oneself and makes them one's own.[107] Making these practices one's own, in turn, reflects how one commits oneself to a "voluntary service (*uoluntarium munus*)" that "is more pleasing than functions that are carried out by canonical obligation."[108] Cassian sees that "what is unceasingly offered is greater than what is rendered at particular moments," and the goal of training is to become habituated in dispositions to continuously act in desired ways.[109]

ACEDIA INDICATES AN advanced asceticism, with the first five spirits having been provisionally bested. To best this sixth insidious demon requires manual labor along with bodily practices drawing the ascetic's attention away from recursive, destructive thoughts. Readings of Cassian focusing on interiority miss that it is precisely the pleonexia of interior thoughts battling themselves that Cassian hopes to curb. Instead, the bodily practices constituting Cassian's asceticism include dietary practices, manual labor, and prayer practices as structured, stylized, and integral forms of self-transformation. Cassian emphasizes the lived body and its constitutive practices as necessary for shaping the ascetic *professio* in *cultus* and *habitus*. The body does not act as a mere sign of the substantively more significant inner, intellectual referent. The external body cannot be considered as only a symbolic structure or a discursive site, nor can the interior life totalize subjectivity.

What is relevant to ethical agency when considering Cassian's asceticism is not a singular faculty but an orientation of the whole ascetic to the daily practices that reinforce the integration of one's physiology and psychology. Such practices shape the ascetic through a combination of labor, exertion, and attention. Cassian's discussions of nocturnal emissions and tears and his discussion of how human physiology and psychology mutually constitute each other in concert with demonic and divine agencies illustrate the outcomes of this rich, pragmatic view of embodiment. At the same time, he recognizes how transformation requires continuous struggle—and describes this in a more realistic and sympathetic way than we often find today, when ethics quickly tips over into moralization.

Analyzing bodily practices through contemporary theories of embodiment, Cassian's asceticism helps frame how bodily aptitudes require care and attention for their transformation and transmission. And it helps to undercut theoretical assumptions of interiority as the privileged site of subjectivity. Embodiment, affectivity, and reflection play discrete and coconstituitive roles in formation. Like the monastic garment, the ascetic *habitus* both inculcates ascetic dispositions and cares for the formation of the ascetic through manual labor, eating, sleeping, and dressing. Stressing the body's role in ascetic formation enables reflection on how training the body requires the cooperation of the emotions and the mind to participate in self-cultivation.

CHAPTER 5

Affective Practices

"Disturbed by carnal impulses" (*carnalibus incentiuis . . . inquietari*), a young ascetic seeks advice from an elder.[1] Hoping to get encouragement and help, the young man is met with derision and rejection: "Instead the old man reprimanded him in the harshest language and declared that anyone who could be titillated by this kind of sin and desire was a wretched person."[2] The young man leaves "in a state of terrible hopelessness, disconsolate to the point of deadly sadness."[3] Seeking empathetic support leads instead to judgments of his sinfulness, reinforcing the suspicion that he is damned.

Cassian's story then takes a twist. Abba Apollos, a venerable elder, comes along and finds the despairing young man seated on the road, contemplating departure from the ascetic life and setting off for the local town to find a wife and fulfill his urges. Unlike the other ascetic, Apollos consoles the young man, declaring that he himself constantly has such thoughts and persuades the novice to defer his departure. Apollos then pursues the old man and, through prayer to God, sends a particularly potent demon of fornication against him. This demon thrusts lewd missiles into the old man's heart, overwhelming him with the same sexual fantasies he had just castigated; "his mental unbalance and intellectual confusion had been caused by unbearable seething

113

emotions" (*confusionem mentis ac perturbationem sensuum intoleran-
dis aestibus operari*).[4] Despairing, he finally repents.

Apollos chastises the older man for communicating negative
affects and showing little compassion to the youth who is struck by
sadness when faced with disgust. If you haven't experienced such
struggle, Apollos reprimands, it is because of the tepidity of your
asceticism: "Return . . . to your cell and realize at last that up until
now you have either been ignored by the devil or disdained by him,
and that you have not been counted among those against whose progress and zeal he daily struggles and fights."[5] Far from ascetic excellence, the old man was ruled by vainglory, κενοδοξία (*cenodoxia*), and
its dangerous preference for the "external" appearance of holiness
without the "internal" sincerity and attention—*exterioris* split from
interioris. He engaged only a lukewarm asceticism without the intensity and true "progress and zeal" required to pursue the ascetic *professio*. As Abba Apollos inspires in the novice, models for imitation are
necessary, both exemplary in their ascetic rigor and relatable in their
own ongoing struggles.

With demons transmitting their destructive affects and "seething
emotions" to ascetics, corollary constructive affects are transmitted
through the positive *exempla* of excellent ascetics. Cassian's texts
reflect a host of affective practices centered around reading, recitation,
and imitation of exemplary figures, including scriptural heroes and
desert champions. Reading practices and *meditatio* become privileged
loci of affective formation through both psalmic recitation and Cassian's textual construction of exemplary *abbas*.[6] Cassian's narratives
both mediate and model the reader's imitative relationship to the desert *abbas*, as his textual depiction of his younger self and Germanus
models the training of emotions.[7] As one shapes one's disposition
in imitation of heroic exemplars, one adopts their emotions, makes
them one's own, and fortifies one's way of life through the fire of their
motivation. Like the young Cassian, one can become a model in turn,
helping to transmit affects and shape societal formations.

To appreciate the role of affective practices in the daily possibilities of ethical agency, I analyze Cassian's texts in relation to contemporary theories of affects and emotions. Bringing together the affects

and the emotions can be difficult insofar as philosophical treatments of the emotions tend to reinforce the individualized subject who experiences these emotions, and affect theories foreground the impersonal transmission of affects, chiding psychological accounts for transforming feeling into a form of property. Cassian, to my mind, helps to reframe this debate with his ethical emphasis on emotional cultivation, figured in its complexity by his exemplary *abbas* and his struggling novitiates and affective transmission figured in both the attacks of dangerous spirits and the effects of his texts. Reading the *Conferences* involves an inculcation of affects through sometimes privative and sometimes positive examples. Abba Apollo's own excellence contrasts with that of the old man conquered by vainglory, evoking in the reader the desire to embrace not the appearance of virtue but its arduous production.

Here I parse three types of affective imitation in the reading practices vital to Cassian's asceticism, all of them relevant to both individual cultivation and the transmission of desert asceticism. First, the *abbas* prescribe imitation of scriptural figures, notably in the Psalms, by adopting their emotions. Second, the *abbas* endorse *imitatio* of other *abbas*, extoling behaviors stemming from positive emotions and proscribing negative ones. In the *Conferences*, Cassian has the *abbas* discuss these first two types through direct discourse. A third type operates in indirect discourse, where Cassian narrates from the position of his younger self and companion Germanus's reactions to the *abbas* and their struggles to develop ascetic dispositions. Cassian's texts thus provide an affective and effective matrix for the transmission of the ascetic *professio*.

Affects and Emotions in Religious Studies

Like discourses of embodiment, theoretical attention to the emotions and affects contributes to a reading of Cassian's texts against interiorizing emphases and assists analysis of the mechanisms of ascetic formation and transmission. The emotions have been relevant to studying religious subjectivity since the nineteenth century's philosophical

challenges to the priority of reason. This includes Friedrich Schleiermacher's German Romanticist embrace of emotions as exceeding the
work of the intellect and G.W.F. Hegel's German Idealist critique
of forms of determinate religion because they remain attached to
"natural feeling."[8] In a pronounced denigration of feeling, Immanuel
Kant juxtaposes the rational formation of subjects in *Moralität* with
Affekten as an emotional and unreflective response that compromises
"inner freedom."[9] *Affekten* later comes to define William James's
view of emotion as "a general seizure of excitement."[10] Correlating
emotions with the unreflective, the physiological, and the religious
demeans religious subjects as lacking moral autonomy and inade-
quately self-legislating.

The conceit of the autonomous subject's having been long since
dismantled by the late twentieth century, Fredric Jameson characterized postmodernity in terms of its "waning of affect," arguing that the
postmodern "'death' of the subject" discards psychological depth and
leaves only affects, emotions, and feelings as surface-level "intensities."[11] Ann Pellegrini and Jasbir Puar note how Jameson's declaration,
however, has precipitated renewed critical interest in affect.[12] Theorizing affect involves recognizing affects as not belonging to a particular
subject but as operating via extended networks of influence. "Affects
are no longer feelings or affections; they go beyond the strength of
those who undergo them," Gilles Deleuze and Felix Guattari influentially claim of works of art.[13] Building from Baruch Spinoza's relation
of excessive states of mind and body like joy (*laetitia*), sadness (*tristitia*), and appetite (*cupiditas*) to feeling and emotion, Deleuze identifies
affect as "every mode of thought insofar as it is non-representational."[14]
In his translation of Deleuze and Guattari, Brian Massumi defines
affect as not a personal feeling but "an ability to affect and be affected.
It is a prepersonal intensity corresponding to the passage from one
experiential state of the body to another and implying an augmentation
or diminution in that body's capacity to act."[15] Inhabiting the inter-
val between physiological and psychological experiences, affect is an
embodied and precognitive suffering of other influences.

Even across different epistemes, emotions and affects both indicate
forces that exceed the particular experience of the subject while also

giving insight into how the subject is shaped, whether via metaphysical forces or discursive formations. Accounts of subject formation and social critique deployed by feminist and queer theorists raise important political questions about the transmission of affects. Affects might be pre-personal, but they have real effects on how subjects are shaped and treated, from being demonized to being humanized. As Lauren Berlant argues, forms of cultural politics like the fantasies proffered by financial capitalism inculcate affects that reinforce behaviors that blindly work against, not toward, flourishing.[16] Eve Sedgwick analyzes the affective force of shame, which socially marks queer genders and sexualities as deviant, becoming a structuring part of nonnormative identities.[17] And Teresa Brennan frames the tension between social formation and biological explanation, framing the transmission of affect as "once common knowledge" that becomes a problem only with the modern rise of scientistic identification of individuals that assumes an "affective self-containment."[18]

Common to these approaches is how affects affect subjects in ways that exceed our discursive resources for naming, and therefore taming, them. The political hope for change remains, however, with Berlant naming the *disorganization* of the everyday, Sara Ahmed the *disorientation* effected by contingent "willful subjects" (instead of autonomous voluntarist subjects) through a queer phenomenology, and what Eugenie Brinkema identifies as "the not-yet vitality of both form and affectivity" that opens when greater formal specificity is brought to bear in the "the Episteme of Affect."[19] Donovan Schaefer builds on the "materialist shift" toward "religion as it is lived by human beings" articulated by Manuel Vásquez by bringing "the multidirectional vectors of influence between embodied emotions and politics" to the study of religion.[20] And Biko Mandela Gray powerfully theorizes how humans—notably African Americans—are dehumanized by racist social scripts that construct black bodies as transmitting negative affects and enable state violence against black lives.[21]

Like theories of practice and turns to embodiment, affect theories helpfully displace the centrality of cognition and language, giving insight into the social, biological, and nonrepresentational dimensions of subject formation.[22] But they do so with attention to the specific ways in which socially constituted subjects transmit affects, giving insight into the political stakes of recognizing affective force in order to counter the dehumanization encoded within discourses of shame, of being rendered less human and more expendable because of one's race, gender, sexuality, ability, or class. Such views challenge the conceit that emotions "belong" to subjects.

When reading historical texts like those of Cassian, the trick is to isolate the force of this nonrepresentational shaping without, according to Ruth Leys's warning, rendering affect altogether "independent of signification and meaning."[23] Historians engaging ancient and medieval texts insightfully point out the necessity of maintaining a role for representation. At the intersection of affects and meaning, we can see attention to the emotions in historical texts by philosophers and historians such as Martha Nussbaum on the relevance of emotions for the production of judgments in Stoic philosophy, Richard Sorabji typologizing the emotions from antiquity through the medieval period for their synchronies and differences, and Barbara Rosenwein analyzing the emotional constitution of medieval communities.[24] As Robert Davis argues in the domain of medieval mysticism, not only are emotions tools for management and manipulation, but also, on a potent level, *affectus* "describes the way things are affected—not just the way we touch others but also the ways we are touched, acted, and impinged upon."[25] Resonant with this twofold engagement, my reading of Cassian brings together attention to emotions with their propositional content and the transmission of affects as both necessary to illuminate possibilities for ascetic formation.

MEDITATIO, PSALMIC RECITATION, IMITATION: THREE FORMS OF AFFECTIVE PRACTICE

The central contrast between affects as nonconscious ("prepersonal intensities" in Massumi's language) and emotions as intentional (bound to reflective subjects) is troubled in the *affectus* of Cassian's texts. Closer to the "common knowledge" episteme Brennan suggests, there is no binary between external affects as nonconscious and observable and internal emotions as conscious and unobservable. Instead I share Davis's account of *affectus* as "the privileged site of transformation that it represented on a spiritual level for many medieval writers. For medieval writers and their modern interpreters, affect is axial."[26] The ascetic cultivates an *affectus* as a disposition that integrates bodily, affective, and reflective forms through affective practices.

Meditatio

Meditatio as a daily exercise of reading sacred Scriptures involves "careful and sustained meditation on the Word of God."[27] Such daily practices of recitation and memorization also involve embodied and reflective capacities.[28] While recitation is typically oral, textual evidence points to silent as well as oral *meditatio*.[29] "Meditation," as Douglas Burton-Christie describes it, "was not, as the word has come to imply today, an interior reflection on the meaning of certain words."[30] Reading is very rarely silent or "in one's head," in part due to typographical technologies lacking spaces between words in unseparated text (*scriptura continua*).[31] Above all, for Cassian, "The successive books of Holy Scripture must be diligently committed to memory and ceaselessly reviewed."[32] As one memorizes parts of Scripture, this allows for silent expression, vocalization, and understanding to be linked in performance.

Central are the character archetypes in the Hebrew Bible and the New Testament, "whose lives and actions, aspirations and personalities are interpreted as epitomizing the goals and requirements of the monastic life."[33] Famously related in Athanasius's *Epistula ad Marcellinum*, ascetics in the desert milieu engage a host of scriptural readings daily, notably recitation of the Psalms.[34] The Psalms permeate Cassian's texts in several ways. Through the *abbas*, Cassian cites the Psalms directly in the *Conferences* more than any other scriptural text.[35] He also repeatedly refers to the practice of singing the Psalms, from the correct number of psalms to sing in *synaxis* to keeping vigil at night with a psalm's protection. Cassian cautions against angrily singing psalms out of annoyance at other worshippers or distractedly singing psalms while thinking about other things, like pagan poetry.[36] The salubrious effects of singing psalms are felt when one is fully focused on this activity—with body, heart, and mind—which becomes paradigmatic of how "meditating on it should consume all the days and nights of our life."[37]

Psalmic Recitation

Reading the Psalms in order to "form" or "model oneself" is a technology of the self and a form of *meditatio*. Similar to Hadot's description of "self-realization and improvement" at the heart of Hellenistic spiritual exercises, it is a way of "attending to" or "caring for oneself."[38] In this formation of self, one adopts and adapts the words of the Psalter as one's own, forging a Christian identity through the therapeutic logic undergirding *meditatio*. "The daily chanting of Psalms then," Paul Kolbet argues, "is a therapy that gradually heals the human person. The language of the Psalter progressively 'counters the instability of selfhood' with the stability of a written text that becomes a second nature when it is written in the soul."[39] Cassian also promotes psalmic practices as a means of identifying normative Christian asceticism, where the manner of psalmody identifies Christians as much as do ways of fasting and manners of dressing.[40]

Meditatio operates in a therapeutic register when one actively approaches the emotions conveyed in the Psalms, gradually making it "second nature when it is written in the soul." While cenobitic communities engage daily set offices in which psalms are recited and sung, Cassian describes desert ascetics as exceeding these set offices with "perpetual and unceasing continuity of prayer."[41] Learning psalms "by heart" and reciting them until one makes the words one's own contributes to the *affectus* necessary for ascetic transformation: "When we have the same disposition in our heart with which each Psalm was sung or written down, then we shall become like its author, grasping the significance beforehand rather than afterward. That is, we first take in the power of what is said, rather than the knowledge of it, recalling what has taken place or what does take place in us in daily assaults whenever we reflect on them."[42] Memorization is not the end of the practice but a means by which one adopts the emotions of the psalmist through "long habituation and meditation" (*longo usu ac meditatione*).[43]

This process is both empathetic and disciplinary and shows how exemplarity operates. Cassian links one's everyday struggle with various emotions to the dramatic renderings of the psalmist, which becomes an opportunity to reflect on one's daily experiences for analogous sources of experiential knowledge. As one reflects on one's daily experiences, one gains access to the laments and hymns, the woes and joys, dramatized in the psalter. Cassian is by no means alone in this foregrounding of experience and bodily practices, as Kolbet says this of Athanasius: "Not unlike contemporary Hellenistic philosophers, Athanasius believed that personal practice convinced the mind as much as any proof. He, therefore, advised Marcellinus to adopt a regime of physical actions that occupy the mind and train the body."[44] The transmission of psalmic affects occurs so that with the right receptivity and personal practice, one takes in the nonrepresentational power of what is said before the discursive knowledge of it.

There is a gradual merging of the bodily practice of recitation, reflection on one's emotional struggles, and the fortification of motivation to adopt these exemplary dispositions. As Amy Hollywood economically describes Cassian's view, one must learn to live the Scriptures: "For Cassian, the entire body and soul of the monk is affected; he is transformed by the words of the Psalms so that he lives them and through this experience he comes to know, with heart and body and mind, that God is great and good."[45] To live the Scriptures involves what Duncan Robertson refers to as the "ethical internalization" of scripture through *meditatio*, where one repeats scripture until the texts are part of the ascetic.[46] "It has," Robertson suggests, "a sacramental efficacy—a capability of placing the reader in a live presence and in communion with the church—on the same level as participation in a full 'ecclesial' liturgy."[47]

Conference 10 features a powerful account of the focus of heart (*cordis intentio*) involving *meditatio* on a single verse of Psalm 69 (70): "O God, incline unto my aid; O Lord, make haste to help me" (*domine ad adiuuandum mihi festina*).[48] Cassian situates this verse at the heart of psalmic recitation as the means by which "to leave behind all the limits of the visible by reflecting on a single verse."[49] This psalm includes "the dispositions of every prayer in a brief phrase" (*affectus orationum cunctarum breui sermone*) and "takes up all the emotions that can be applied to human nature and with great correctness and accuracy it adjusts itself to every condition and every attack."[50] It is, for Cassian, a one-size-fits-all psalm, with beneficial application to any scenario. If challenging, it is meant to have God come to one's aid; if virtuous, God is invoked to preserve one in such a state.[51]

Persevering in this recitation can lead to constant *meditatio*, to the extent that Cassian exclaims: "You should not stop repeating it when you are doing any kind of work or performing some service or are on a journey. Meditate on it while sleeping and eating and attending to the least needs of nature."[52] One's whole life is to become a continual exultation of this psalm that gives sustenance to any activity. Psalmic exemplars like David show how to act, how to feel, and how to believe in tandem, with the emotions guiding individuals to make the texts' lessons their own through resonance with their own experiences.[53] Between the moments of recitation and reflection, one's feeling and one's specific emotional ties to the text foster an experiential understanding that is embodied and affective as it is reflective.[54] One is thereby able to "take in the power of what is said, rather than the knowledge of it," the nonrepresentational before the representational content of the words.[55] At its most advanced, singing the Psalms with *cordis intentio* becomes an occasion for fiery or glowing prayer, in a maximization of the ascetic life.[56]

Exemplary *Abbas*

In addition to scriptural figures' emotions adopted through recitation, Cassian permeates his *Conferences* with *abbas'* emotions, transmitting affective force through their examples beyond direct prescription. Their examples inspire, perplex, inflame, and even dispirit the patient reader. In the *Institutes* Cassian stresses that it is necessary "to set out by way of example some of the deeds of the elders in which they shone forth in virtue."[57] Not just emotions or deeds represented in texts, these historical, literary, and ethical constructions affect readers beyond their particular emotions. Rebecca Krawiec argues that Cassian creates a monastic literary culture in the image of Greco-Roman rhetorical education, rendering monastic learning a continuation of pedagogical processes, and I extend this cultural production to the training of the emotions.[58] In both registers, exemplary *abbas* teach the novices the "spiritual knowledge" (*scientia spiritalis*) attributable "solely to purity of heart" (*soli cordis tribuit puritati*).[59] The elders' own experiences affect ascetics, motivating them forward and consoling them in their challenges.

Three types of narratives feature the elders. First, Cassian the writer reflects on the biography of the elder hosting the conference stressing their exemplary virtue. Such sensational stories both authorize the elder's wisdom and show an example of how to act, feel, and think in both orthopraxy and orthodoxy. Second, the elders discuss hortatory examples of *abbas* within the conferences' dialogues. These figures behave heroically and virtuously, providing positive examples for imitation. Third are the cautionary tales of monastics who went awry, told by the *abba* hosting the conference.

Cassian presents the credentials and characters of the host *abbas* in order to authorize their spiritual and practical discussion of the issue at hand. He introduces Abba Serenus of *Conference 7*, for instance, as "a man of the greatest holiness and abstinence and one who reflected his own name, whom we admired with a unique veneration more than we did the others."[60] Cassian discusses how Serenus managed to attain such purity through ascetic exercises in communion with God: "With prayers day and night, then, and with fasting and vigils, he pleaded tirelessly for internal chastity of heart and soul."[61] Cassian introduces Abba Theonas, the host of *Conferences* 21, 22, and 23, with the "beginning of his conversion" to the ascetic life.[62] Although married at his parents' insistence, Theonas heard the words of Abba John and became increasingly "inflamed with an inextinguishable desire for gospel perfection," coming to renounce social life and his wife.[63]

Cassian introduces Abba Pinufius, the host of *Conference* 20, in a narrative prehistory by which the young Cassian and Germanus found him in Bethlehem. Pinufius fled the large cenobium near Panephysis, rendered himself anonymous, and submitted himself as a novice to a cenobium in Tabenna where he was received with much derision due to his age.[64] Cassian presents Pinufius as an exemplary interlocutor who inspired Cassian and Germanus to seek out wisdom in the Egyptian desert.[65] Evincing "obedience characterized by utter simplicity and faith," Pinufius remains both spur and lodestar in Cassian's monastic writings.[66] All the host *abbas* evoke adoration and a desire for imitation in the auditors, opening their hearts to being changed by the message imparted.

Beyond Cassian's descriptions of exemplary *abbas*, the *abbas* also describe other ascetics as salutary examples or as cautionary tales. Their stories sometimes inspire with their heroism and sometimes shock with their negative consequences—they always move John and Germanus, indicating how the reader should be moved in turn. In *Conference* 8, for example, Abba Serenus narrates how Abba Antony prevails over a multitude of demons sent by two wicked philosophers tutored in magic.[67] This story's miracles and fantastic feats are meant to reassure the reader of Cassian's ascetic and ethical point, that for all their fearfulness, "demons are utterly unable to get into a person's mind or body."[68] Abba Antony as a teacher figures into *Conference* 2, where Abba Moses refers to his childhood spent in the Thebaid where Antony movingly taught on perfection and discretion.[69]

Cassian's negative examples include figures like old man Heron, whose extreme asceticism led him to the apex vice of pride. Considering himself already among the angels and able to fly, Heron fell down a well instead and soon thereafter died from his injuries.[70] Abba Moses also refers to two brothers who foolishly vowed to eat only what appeared before them as gifts of God as they delivered figs to friends across the desert. Upon getting lost and nearing death by starvation, one brother ate a fig and lived until he was rescued, while the other one perished instead of consuming the fruit meant for another. Cassian thereby warns against the extremes of obedience.[71] Issues of doctrinal orthodoxy also feature, as when Cassian refers to the Anthropomorphite controversy prompted by Theophilus, Bishop of Alexandria, who expelled ascetics whose view of Christ was too anthropomorphic. Serapion, said to be ensnared in the error of the Anthropomorphites, woefully cries, "They have taken my God from me, and I have no one to lay hold of, nor do I know whom I should adore or address."[72] Serapion is portrayed pitiably missing his bosom friend, as he must adopt the orthodox position or risk expulsion (and eternal damnation), and so, too, is the reader cautioned to mind the doctrinal line.

The reader is introduced to a vibrant cast of characters, many as exemplary elders whom all should strive to emulate. Other elders depict how imbalance and excess reflect affective discord that makes ascetics prey to dangerous spirits and point out that those ascetics provide examples the reader should think about. The elders become extrabiblical sources of wisdom, and their stories reflect what it is to be an ascetic and a Christian as these categories were being constructed. Stressing experience and practice as well as the *exempla* Cassian paints so vividly, affects are transmitted in excess of the prescriptions and descriptions of the narrative, shaping the behavior of readers in turn. With both hortatory and cautionary tales, Cassian culls stories from the *abbas* and presents them in a format both transmissible and amenable to canonical status like that of Athanasius's *Life of Antony* and compilations like the *Apophthegmata Patrum*.[73]

Such exemplarity also authorizes Cassian's texts, for the elders stand on a continuum with scriptural figures as the "living exemplars" preserving ways of life described in the scriptural record. Cassian describes Elijah and Elisha, for example, as the inaugurators of monasticism.[74] He claims John the Baptist as the first anchorite, as does Jerome. Establishing this illustrious lineage, Cassian both justifies ascetic practices through their scriptural origins and promotes monasticism as a scriptural ideal to be continuously maintained in southern Gaul. In *Conference* 24 Cassian explicitly constructs the addressees of his *Conferences* as monastics to be emulated in turn, provided that "the precepts of the greatest and most ancient fathers confirm what you yourselves teach by your living example, not by the dead sound of words."[75] He situates these Gallic monastics on a continuum with the elders of the Egyptian desert, as they themselves are impacted by and take up the practices of these *abbas*. These monastics, in turn, might become exemplary to the members of their respective *cenobia* and transmit the force of these traditions in Gaul.

TUTORING THE EMOTIONS WITH YOUNG CASSIAN AND GERMANUS

While the *abbas* present sterling exemplars, they can appear so incredible that it is difficult to imitate them. To bridge this divide, Cassian narrates the emotional development of his younger self and Germanus, illuminating their experience of ascetic formation in the Egyptian desert and affectively shaping his own Gallic readers. Three stages sketch the ascetics' emotional path as they move from awe to despair to expectation. The desert elders exhort the "incitement to perfect life" (*incitamentum ex his uitae perfectae*) and the "outline of our chosen orientation" (*propositi forma*), but the young companions show how to emotionally approach and engage asceticism.[76]

Enthusiastic *Professio*

The *Conferences* begins with a scene familiar to desert literature: Two novices—our John and holy Germanus—seek out an esteemed elder for instruction in the ascetic life. "Together," the young Cassian says, "we were tearfully begging for an edifying word from that abba."[77] Begging for an edifying word amplifies the typical Greek request in the *Apophthegmata Patrum* to "leave them a concise and salutary saying as their inheritance," passed from elder to novice, with the expectation that it would be lived with a similar intensity.[78]

"Worn out by our pleading" (*fatigatus precibus nostris*), Abba Moses consents to speak to them about the ascetic life.[79] Cassian sets up his and Germanus's encounter with the desert *abbas* in an intense yet sincere fashion. Abba Moses, in this narrative, is willing to speak to the young novices because they both "faithfully desired" (*fideliter desiderantibus*) this wisdom and sought it with the appropriate attitude of "utter contrition of heart" (*omni cordis contritione*).[80] Cassian thus opens the *Conferences* by stressing to the reader the right attitude and intensity with which to pursue ascetic wisdom, and he registers the emotional labor even of listening to these stories as he unfolds them.[81]

Particular precipitating emotions are needed in order to gradually develop the monastic dispositions enjoined by Cassian's protagonists.

With the necessary openness to affective shaping, the reader sees the way Moses's words affect the young companions. Responding to Abba Moses in *Conference* 1, the friends are struck by "amazement" (*obstupescentibus*) and "greatly stirred" (*ualde permoti*).[82] So moved by these words, they become "inflamed with an insatiable love" (*inexplebili ardore succensos*) for this profession and way of life described by Abba Moses.[83] The two struggle to go to sleep, "burning with joy" (*inflammati gaudio*) and aflame with excitement for the goals of the *professio*.[84] In *Conference* 2 their enthusiastic spirit and zeal are further sparked as the young companions are "inflamed with such a burning desire" (*tanto desiderii ardore flammatos*) to learn about discernment as the cornerstone of monastic life.[85] Abba Moses both extols this "fervor of yours" (*uestrum ... feruorem*) and warns against tepidity of spirit. One must be inflamed by burning desire and fervor for the ascetic way of life, unlike the lukewarm old monk whose story opened this chapter.[86]

The initial emotions of awe and wonder establish the orientation of the young Cassian and Germanus toward the exceptional *abbas* and their glorious ways of life. Cassian sets up his first lesson for his own readers: to learn the ascetic *professio*, one must first approach *abbas* with sincere awe and wonder at the ascetic way of life, oriented fully toward their emulation and submitting to their wisdom. One must be open to being affected in the appropriate way. Cassian accordingly highlights the awestruck yearning of the young John and Germanus. *Conferences* 7 and 8 close with descriptions of the friends' enthusiasm, which is so great that Abba Serenus forces the two to rest their bodies in sleep.[87] *Conference* 9, like *Conference* 7, closes with Abba Isaac forcing the young companions to sleep despite their extreme rejoicing: "Amazed by these words of the holy Isaac rather than satisfied by them, we rested our limbs in sleep for a short while after the evening synaxis had been celebrated."[88] Closing *Conference* 16, on friendship, Cassian reflects on how Abba Joseph inspired the young Cassian and Germanus "all the more ardently to make enduring the love of our companionship."[89] Abba Piamun, in *Conference* 18, likewise "inflamed more ardently our desire" (*desiderium nostrum ... ardentius inflammauit*) to investigate the anchorite's life in more depth by continuing deeper into Egyptian asceticism.[90]

The disposition to emulate the *abbas* is transmitted from Cassian, the author, to his reader. Just like the young Cassian and Germanus in the desert, one must read the text in front of one with the intensity and openness required to hear the *abbas'* words. One must learn to take in the affective power over the discursive knowledge alone. Cassian and Germanus's sleepless anticipation operates like a cliffhanger, propelling one forward in the text. The two burn with joy, in great excitement for the proximate and ultimate goals of the ascetic *professio*. So, too, must the reader of Cassian's *Conferences* hang upon the words of the *abbas* to experience the fullness of their instruction.[91] Affective desire opens the possibility of learning to cultivate the appropriate *affectus*.

Stress in Progress

As when reading any good cliffhanger, readers find themselves, at this point, not rescued but thrust deeper into the ascetic crisis. Enthusiasm is fitting for those who hear about the monastic life and truly desire its wisdom. It is a different story as one progresses in one's practice. As the companions gradually apprehend the contours of the monastic life in theory and practice, so, too, do they recognize its challenges. While awe and joy are the appropriate responses to the wondrous wisdom the desert elders impart, the second set of emotions highlights the anxiety and sadness that come as one struggles to advance in the monastic *professio*.

Having learned enough from esteemed *abbas* to know their own ignorance, the young Cassian and Germanus frankly express the dejection that comes when awe wanes, replaced by the stark difficulties of overcoming long-standing habits of behavior and belief. *Conference* 12 closes, for example, with Abba Chaeremon urging sleep for the young Cassian and Germanus, who are "stupefied and anxious" (*stupentibus atque anxiis*) concerning their own chastity.[92] Cassian and Germanus start to lose hope that they themselves could attain the blessed states the *abbas* discuss, especially outside of Egypt. *Conference* 13 presents another response to doctrinal views on chastity and perfection, with young Cassian and Germanus "bewildered" (*mouebatur*) about the relevance of human effort to foster "the highest desire for an as yet untried chastity" (*summum desiderium incognitae nobis castitatis*).[93] In *Conference* 14, young Cassian identifies one of the primary roadblocks to the pursuit of chastity as education in pagan literature, whose images continue to populate his mind's eye, even when he prays. "Upon hearing these things I was at first very moved by a hidden compunction," he declares, tying his compunction to his desire to advance in chastity against this impediment.[94]

In *Conference* 17 (*De definiendo*), on promises, Cassian writes of the young friends: "We bore witness by groans alone to the distress of our most difficult situation."[95] Before they set out for the Egyptian desert, the two companions had promised to return to their monastic community in Bethlehem, yet they find themselves in a "wretched condition" (*miserabili condicione*), knowing that their spiritual progress relies on remaining in Egypt.[96] Germanus ultimately uses fear of Gospel command to justify staying in Egypt and for the two to postpone their return to Bethlehem.[97] "Cast down in desperation, then," Cassian says in *Conference* 20, "and showing by our very looks the profound bitterness of our thoughts, we hastened back to the blessed old man in a very anxious state."[98] Abba Pinufius, unlike the old man suffering from vainglory, gives the consolation needed, both stating the difficulty of this way of life and stressing practical strategies to advance forward, inclining "to true humility and contrition of heart" (*ad humilitatem ueram et contritionem cordis*).[99] This consolation puts the spirits of sadness and *acedia* in check. Moved to compunction and humility, the friends recognize the realities of struggle and the necessity of confronting difficult aspects of being human.

Conference 3 closes with Cassian's reflection on the three renunciations, "not so much cheerful as moved with compunction in our hearts" (*non tam alacres quam conpunctos corde*).[100] Knowing the good end of chastity and not being able to get there, in *Conference* 6 Cassian returns us to the "melancholy mood" of the young Cassian and Germanus, "touched with sadness" at the slaughter of monks in Palestine, which yet turns to a "joy of soul" produced through the "boundless delight" Abba Theodore effects through his instruction.[101] Cassian closes the conference stressing how the friends' eventual joy even exceeds the sadness that preceded it, suggesting the ascetic utility of sadness in its ability to lead to reflection that contributes to the affirmation of ascetic orientation.[102] *Conference* 10 sees the two shaken by the Christological controversies that put desert figures like Abba Serapion at risk for his doctrinal error.[103] "For we are struck with no little sense of despair," since despite the *abba*'s "great labors" (*labores tantos*) he runs the risk of "everlasting death" (*perpetuae mortis*).[104] The companions' fear also stresses the real repercussions of challenging doctrinal orthodoxy in the face of ecclesial powers.

Fortifying the *Professio*

The third stage of emotional experience moves beyond awestruck enthusiasm and realistic anxiety, where the young friends recommit to the ascetic *professio* through expectation and hope. Here joy and zeal recommit them to the ascetic *professio* through the orientation toward *puritas cordis* as the proximate goal of the monastic life and the kingdom of God as its ultimate end. Tempering the friends' joy with frank accounts of real ascetic challenges, the *abbas* nevertheless give them the hope and means of advancing in this *professio*.

The companions evince the required emotional motivations and commitments where, in *Conference* 21, Abba Theonas commends them for their "zealous desire to attain to the way of perfection, not merely for a while but fully and perfectly."[105] In *Conference* 22, Abba Theonas similarly applauds the friends for "your ardent zeal" (*ardentissimum studium uestrum*), "your ardor" (*uester ardor*), and "your anxiety" (*uestra sollicitudo*).[106] *Conference* 24, finally, sees the two companions put into practice the strategies discussed in the preceding conferences by Pinufius and Theonas, not allowing themselves to be dispirited but working even more ardently to maintain their orientation.[107] Confession of such challenges means that embarrassment does not silence them, as Cassian states: "And so, in an anxious confession, we laid before this Abraham the struggle of our thoughts," including their struggle to overcome their devotion and love for their families.[108]

Enacting the relationship in such confession, *Conference* 7 features the awe and admiration for Abba Serenus that fuels their discussion: "When we have returned after the synaxis we shall discuss with redoubled joy the things that the Lord will have given for our common instruction in accordance with your desire."[109] Fostering their spiritual ardor and their thirst for continued accomplishment as humans battling the hierarchy of demons and even angels, *Conference* 8 stresses how inflamed the companions become: "The words of the conference so inflamed us that, leaving the old man's cell with greater spiritual ardor than when we arrived, we thirsted for the accomplishment of his teaching."[110] The words of Abba Isaac amaze the two further by teaching them how to pray the Lord's Prayer as the daily achievement of monastic life.[111] The two rejoice that they possess the teachings they set out to pursue. They themselves model *discretio*, the critical capacity of ascetic discernment needed for moderation, tending toward neither blind awe nor paralyzing dejection.

Such amazement in *Conference* 9 reaches its apex in *Conference* 10, where the despair the friends felt at the prospect of losing such eternal life through doctrinal error requires that they earnestly and fervently adopt the ascetic disciplines.[112] *Conference* 10 includes a complicated set of emotions, where (1) amazement at the beauty of the perfection Abba Isaac paints in *Conference* 9 is coupled with (2) despair that such perfection is unreachable for them, which is yet met with (3) greater desire to behold such sublime blessedness.[113] The means of acquiring such discipline and practice unfolds in Abba Isaac's treatment of fiery prayer, which strikes the companions with a renewed and fervent desire to practice the discipline "in our wonderment" (*adtonitis nobis*).[114] Finishing where we began, the emotions do not reduce to a straightforward and fixed progression in the *Conferences*. One does not leave behind joy and awe, just as one does not rest in despair and sadness, but intensely cultivates them with zeal.

The emotions of the young Cassian and Germanus illuminate a crucial ethical intersection between Cassian's prescriptions for ascetic formation and his descriptions of the young friends' experiences. Methodologically, analyzing the intersection between theory and practice helps us analyze the potential of the emotions as a distinct historical category.[115] Cassian's *Conferences* affect the reader by both stating the emotions needed (prescription) and enacting them (description) through his dramatized experience, providing a view of what the cultivation of *affectus* looks like and inspiring the reader to take on this arduous ascetic path.

In a contrasting reading, Boniface Ramsey reduces the behavior of young Cassian and Germanus to "a certain pallid characterization" since they "hardly give the impression" of existing on their own outside of the texts.[116] Of the narrative role of the young Cassian and Germanus, Ramsey states: "The periods of time preceding and following the conferences are given over entirely, on the part of the two friends, to anticipatory emotions and to feelings of wonder, gratitude, sadness, or compunction, based on whatever they may have heard."[117] Ramsey suggests that this reduces the young Cassian and Germanus to merely passive figures who are affected by the *abbas* but have no vitality or capacity for formation of their own. Cassian and Germanus are characterized primarily passively, shaped by the affects transmitted by the stories that inspire them to seek out the *abbas*.

What Ramsey notes as a negative feature of the text, however, I read as essential to Cassian's narrative strategy—a strategy central to his program of ascetic formation, in both direct prescription and indirect description. Young Cassian and Germanus present a lively portrayal of desert asceticism through their approach to the *abbas* and their negotiation of complex emotions without relying on their biographical specifics. Cassian represents himself and Germanus not in historical depth but as ethically vital textual figures who dramatize how readers might be affected by their stories in turn.

TRANSFORMATION THROUGH AFFECTIVE CULTIVATION

How might we understand the ethical force of these affective practices where one is not just affected but also self-shaping? Cassian's texts suggest how ascetic formation features the cultivation of an *affectus* through bodily practices of consumption and labor and especially through his practices of reading and recitation. As Hollywood points out, such practices enable the "acquisition of proper dispositions through habit."[118] We can see the multivalence of *affectus*: a term that includes its English cognate affect as well as emotion, state of mind, and disposition.

Ascetic *Affectus*

Cassian describes this *affectus* as "a disposition for the good itself and a love of virtue" (*affectus boni ipsius amorque uirtutum*).[119] Such an *affectus*—"a good disposition and a pious will" (*bono affectui et piae uoluntati*)—leads to "the reward of an eternal legacy."[120] Cassian uses *affectus* to designate a disposition to action that an ascetic can cultivate, orienting bodily, affective, and reflective forms of attention together. Purity of heart (*puritas cordis*) and the disposition of belief (*affectus fidei*) toward God render affect and emotion central to Cassian's asceticism.[121]

To return to the three domains of affective reading practices, the goal of *meditatio*—notably when engaged as a form of constant prayer—is to shape the disposition or *affectus* in "our heart" with each scriptural passage and psalm as it is recited, so fully that one becomes "like its author."[122] As the Psalms bear all human dispositions within them and engage the range of human emotions, Cassian frames the scriptural encounter as a way to learn appropriate responses to given situations. Still one cannot forget that every scenario will be different and therefore will require *discretio* in one's reflective adaptation.[123] Through this training, one learns to anticipate emotions when reading the scriptural stories so much that one experiences a textual figure's affects as one's own in one's own context. Affected like the psalmist, they come to affect their communities in turn.[124]

Meditatio engages emotional meditation, bodily recitation, and reflective adaptation. We can see recitation and laborious memorization of scriptural practices as a practical skill with a host of assistant strategies.[125] As a reading practice, Cassian's learning "by heart" requires that one engage in rote repetition, on the one hand, and in focused reflection, on the other. Meditating on Scripture provides an exemplary way of occupying the "mind's attention" (*mentis intentio*) so that the mind cannot simultaneously be distracted by "harmful thoughts" (*noxiarum cogitationum*).[126] Recall Cassian's imagery of the mind analogized to a high ship in a tempest: If one engages activities that focus on David and on fighting adversaries, one can fight to right the ship.[127] "Continual meditation" (meditationis iugitas) depends on affective motivation to sustain this process.[128]

Such affectus-shaping practices involve two different elements beyond mere repetition. First is the process of recognizing how scriptural figures' experiences resonate with one's own experiences. This process requires not just the mimicking of scriptural figures' actions. Reciting passages, one imaginatively takes the place of the scriptural figure, accessing one's corollary experiences as analogues. One recognizes, engages, and cultivates emotions in one's own historically and geographically removed context. One contributes to one's own constitution via these practices. Derek Krueger ties such dynamics to the formation of Christian ascetic identity: "Texts played a crucial role in the promulgation of ascetic beliefs and practices. Oral traditions and written texts often served as road maps toward this new identity. Fittingly, the perfected self conformed to models embedded in writings. Exegetes drew ascetic lessons from scripture reading patriarchs, prophets, and apostles as models of moral rectitude and self-control."[129] With "the face of Scripture" changing with the reader, comprehension correlates with progress. Only "the one who is singing the psalm, who is moving forward in the undefiled way with the stride of a pure heart, will understand what is sung."[130]

The relationship between recitation and affective experience contributes to our understanding of the relation between praktike and theoretike in Cassian. Contemplative knowledge requires not just excellence in the practical skills of memorization and reflective understanding but putting such reflection into action and allowing this understanding to shape one's way of life. Such contemplative knowledge as a reflective form of understanding requires the mastery of associated practical skills and comes only as one transforms oneself through this process. As Burton-Christie argues: "Here is a hermeneutic firmly embedded within the practical challenges presented by the ascetical life the monks had taken up in the Egyptian desert: a hermeneutic that demands, ultimately, that the meaning of a text be expressed in a life."[131] Contemplative knowledge and practical knowledge meet here in a tutoring of the emotions that form monastic selves through scriptural understanding that contributes to all of one's daily practices. "For," as Cassian claims, "it is impossible for the soul which is even slightly taken up with worldly distractions to deserve the gift of knowledge or to beget spiritual understanding or to remember the sacred readings."[132]

Genre and Transmission

Illuminating the interplay between the emotions, ascetic formation, and affect-transmitting literary strategies is necessary to grasp the transmissive power of Cassian's work. These features enable Cassian's new monastic audience of elite males in Gaul to recognize the prestige of Cassian's literary program. Despite the prestige, however, two roadblocks remain: (1) the ongoing challenges of the ascetic life and (2) the fact that different locales and contexts mean different adaptations and accommodations. Direct prescription cannot work and still be flexible and affectively resonant with different needs and challenges. Cassian thus recommends recognizing various challenges, contexts, and aptitudes in his flexible approach to detailing the ascetic life. Refusing to dogmatically produce a rule of life, he presents exemplars to follow and adopt, critically adapting practices to one's own context. Cassian addresses these issues by stressing the affective and embodied challenges of the ascetic life, giving a sense of its lure as well as the ups and downs involved. He also assists in his affective modeling of ascetic formation through himself and Germanus, as they were affected by and emulated *abbas* in the Egyptian desert. Cassian's Gallic readers are then able to adopt and adapt these models.

These features speak to the historical challenges Cassian faced in his translation of Egyptian desert wisdom to Gallic monasticism. Cassian takes great pains to affirm the necessity of experience in the teacher and the priority given to experience over abstract knowledge. Indeed, his focus on experience and practice as the markers for ascetic authority affirms both his own authorial legitimacy in propagating monasticism in Gaul and the legitimacy of his readers who engage his exemplary yet challenging asceticism. Forging a tradition of affective exemplarity, connecting new communities and monastics to authoritative practices and models to adopt and adapt, Cassian transmits to Gallic monastics of his time examples of how one can shape one's dispositions through the cultivation of emotions that together facilitate the production of an ascetic *affectus*.

CASSIAN'S TEXTS PERFORM the affective relationship between text and reader using the engagement between the young Cassian and Germanus and the *abbas* as a model for how Cassian's own reader can engage his texts, the *abbas*, and the reading practices they model. Through both direct prescriptions in the mouths of his *abbas* and indirect literary characterizations of his central figures, Cassian's textual examples enact how *meditatio* transmits affects, tutors the emotions, and shapes ascetic selves. Reading Cassian's texts has effects analogous to reading scriptural texts; by analyzing Cassian's texts, we glean the mechanisms of affective *meditatio* and their centrality to shaping ascetic subjectivities.

Grasping the multivalence of *affectus* as immediate affect, emotional engagement, and cultivated disposition, we can understand Cassian's asceticism without imputing a stress on interiority or belief as too narrowly defining ascetic subjectivity. Cassian's complex figuration of affective practices—culled from both the Egyptian desert and his own writings—brings an account of ethical agency to life. The emotions help to constitute and fortify ascetic dispositions oriented toward a *scopos* and *telos* through the integration of embodied, affective, and reflective attention. Part literary strategy, part ethical necessity, Cassian presents the emotions in the *Conferences* (and, to another extent, in the *Institutes*) as integral to the formation of ascetic subjectivities and the transmission of ascetic *professio*. The "seething emotions" experienced by the old man cast him out of lukewarm complacency into the violent struggle with *fornicatio*, exposing his subjection to vainglory, which perilously allows the disjunction between one's observable behaviors and one's way of life. The counter to such potent affects requires the cultivation of an ascetic *affectus* by imitating laudable emotions and inculcating desirable affects, forming a life that integrates observable behavior with reflective integrity inflamed by *exempla* in this challenging *professio*.

CHAPTER 6

Communal Practices

The "most savage beast" (*saeuissima . . . bestia*), as Cassian describes the apex of the eight struggles, is the spirit of pride (*spiritum super-biae*).[1] One can hope to conquer this spirit "fiercer than all those previously mentioned" (*superioribus cunctis inmanior*) only once the first seven have been vanquished.[2] Attacking "those who are nearly established in the perfection of virtue," this spirit is also the oldest vice, belonging to the Adversary who contested the authority of God and "believed that he had acquired the splendor of his wisdom and the beauty of his virtue . . . by the power of his own nature (*naturae suae potentia*)."[3] Instead of recognizing God as the source of his power, this light-bearer "relied on the power of his free will" (*liberi scilicet arbitrii facultate confisus*), thinking himself the source of his own virtue.[4]

Once banished from his seat among the angels, the Adversary set out to forge his own kingdom, tempting Adam and Eve into insubordination. Cassian links the struggles of being human to this original dance with the Adversary, who "crept into the first man and produced the weaknesses and the wherewithal of all the vices."[5] Pride subjects all creatures to its "yoke of servitude" and, "like a most savage tyrant," divests them of the very freedom they believe they exercise. When one acts from pride one attains a delusory, not actual, sense of empowerment.[6] By thinking oneself superior and self-determining, one becomes a threat to the order that Cassian works to develop, for "all of this makes a person no longer content to bear the yoke of the monastery or to be instructed by the teaching of any elder."[7]

Genuine spiritual excellence is perversely the greatest temptation to pride. It preys on the most advanced ascetics, who have progressed so far that they begin to think themselves more angelic than human. Recall old man Heron, who in his extreme asceticism refused himself any laxity for Easter; in addition to upsetting the community's celebration through his excessive fasting, he thought himself immune from physical harm and, attempting to fly like an angel, plummeted to the bottom of a well.[8] Pride also plagues beginners in the ascetic life who do not yet know how to submit to the goods of the community and instead think themselves exceptional. A man was convinced by the spirit of pride to be as glorious as Abraham and sacrifice his own son; luckily the son proved wiser than Isaac and ran away after spotting his father carefully sharpening the blade.[9] Both types of pride, according to Cassian, stem from "a harmful self-exaltation" (*noxia inflet elatio*).[10] Their referent differs: beginners exalt themselves over other humans; advanced ascetics exalt themselves next to divinity.

Communal formation is both the primary antidote to pride's delusory self-exaltation and the lens through which the work of this vice is most clearly visible. Such pride noxiously not only poisons the individual but extends to the broader community. We see the prideful monk refusing to "so much as cock his ear when there is instruction in perfection."[11] Instead of listening with rapt attention to an *abba*'s words, he allows his attention to be as errant as his eyes, which move aimlessly around the room:

> Instead of producing salutary sighs he will clear his dry throat and incessantly bring up phlegm; he will play with his fingers, fiddling with them and tracing with them as if he were writing; and all the members of his body will be so agitated for as long as the spiritual conference continues that he will give the impression of being utterly at the mercy of swarming worms or sharp thorns. Whatever may be said in a simple conference for the benefit of its hearers he will think is being said for his discomfort. The whole

time that the spiritual life is being examined and discussed he will
be busy with his own suspicious thoughts and will not be on the
watch for what he should take in for his well-being; instead, he
will anxiously look for reasons as to why such and such a thing
was said, and in silence he will go over in his heart what objections
he could raise against it.[12]

Whereas the solitary monk suffering from *acedia* contends with listlessness and lack of meaning, the prideful monk is in a community
without being of it: "And so, having become unreceptive to salutary
advice, he relies on his own judgment in every respect rather than
on that of the elders."[13] A masterful example of self-centered reason,
he refuses to listen to the conference for its salutary messages. When
he finally engages, "his voice will be raised, his speech defensive, his
replies harsh and agitated, his behavior high-handed and capricious."[14]

As a counter to the threat of individualism and the pride that
amplifies it, the ascetic's humility and receptivity to the formation and
judgment of others are necessary. To read social relationality as only
obedience and submission to authority—as Foucault tends to read
Cassian—obscures the practicality of such communal shaping. Cassian's texts foreground the fact that no ascetics are shaped in isolation
and that monasticism requires social relations as the condition of their
constitution. Where the bodily and affective practices of chapters 4
and 5 depict particular mechanisms of formation, these practices occur
within a matrix of relations with other people, places, and traditions.

Cassian foregrounds the communal body forged in a common *professio*. He also recognizes the plurality of adaptations of the ascetic way
of life and the irreducibly particular ways in which one can stylize one's
life in concert with others. In this chapter I focus on three social relations centrally constitutive of the ascetic *professio* and its possibilities
for ethical formation. First, friendship as an intimate relation is central
both to Cassian's theoretical musings and to his narrative relationship
with Germanus. Second, practices of directorship and *discretio* (discernment) between an advanced elder and a younger ascetic constitute
the glue of community. Third, liturgical practices shape both particular
subjectivities and corporate traditions through Cassian's texts. These

interrelational sites of the ascetic self come into focus through contemporary framings of sociality that are both intimate and structural.

SOCIAL CONSTITUTION AND INTIMATE RELATIONS

Attention to intimate relationships builds from the day-to-day level of social analysis as these relationships shift and develop. Such analysis assumes and operates in tandem with the social production of religious subjects, constellating power, materiality, and discursive processes as Talal Asad influentially analyzes in disciplinary forms of Christian monasticism.[15] Rejecting the perpetuation of "an individualist notion of the religious subject," Constance Furey calls for a more robust and interrelational understanding of the religious subject.[16] She argues that theoretical attempts to understand subjectivity in terms of the body have recapitulated problems with viewing the subject in isolation and autonomous abstraction. While scholars have made the necessary move to study "bodies" in relation to the social forces that shape them, Furey argues, "the religious subject stands alone in a crowd, participating in communal rituals, subject to religious authorities and disciplinary practices, but oddly detached from intimate relationships."[17] Focusing on communal bodies can isolate and flatten analysis of the religious subject, emphasizing rituals and subjection without recognizing the intensity of intimate relations and their role in constituting religious subjectivities.

Intimate relations are both constitutive of religious subjects and dramatized in ascetic formation. Brenna Moore argues for the category of friendship as salient "for scholars interested in the inner life, subject formation, and even religious experience."[18] We can also learn from late ancient scholars and their articulation of communal and particular subjectivities as shaped through liturgical practices and ritual forms. At this intersection, Mary Carruthers notes: "The constant balance of individual and communal, *ethos* and *pathos*, is adjusted and engineered with the tools of rhetoric: images and figures, topics and schemes."[19] Within Byzantine liturgical settings, Derek Krueger writes that "a program for the formation of subjectivity worked, in part, through the words of prayers and the singing of hymns, through the adoption of subjectivating speech as one's own, that is, as a coherent description of the self."[20] Susan Harvey illuminates the continuity between liturgical ritual contexts and sensory experience "at the most mundane level in their daily habits," writing that the formation of subjectivity occurs at the intersection of religious identity, epistemology, and soteriology.[21] In the constitution of communities, the interdependence of particular subjectivities — to each other and to the community — communicates contingency, reliance, and intimacy.

I opened this chapter with an interrogation of the question of pride because in Cassian's construction of asceticism, the spirit of pride becomes a lens for understanding the vital role community and intimate personal relations play in processes of subjective formation. Judith Butler's account of vulnerability resonates with my reading of Cassian's stress on social constitution in its temporal, social, and cultural alterity as contributing to "a new kind of scholarship that seeks to bring theory to bear on the analysis of social and political life, in particular, to the temporality of social and political life."[22] In relation to the force of discursive social formations (Asad) and intimate social relations (Furey), the conditions for the constitution and transformation of subjectivity are nuanced. Cassian's texts are shaped by the cultural conditions of their emergence and shape their cultural formations in turn, extolling the training of ascetics and the transmission of desert asceticism to others in a matrix of social and intimate relations. Cassian's communities operate as corporate bodies shaping traditions primary to particular subjectivities. Recognizing relational dependence better contextualizes Cassian's accounts of ascetic formation and *liberum arbitrium* in immediate and extended communities. I therefore close this book with an account of ethical agency that recognizes the social production of subjects without assuming their formation through blind obedience to authority or uncritical adoption of mores.

FRIENDSHIP, DIRECTORSHIP, AND CORPORATE BODIES: THREE INTERRELATIONAL PRACTICES

Cassian's texts encode intimate social relations as foundational to the ascetic traditions in which he trained and those he transmitted to western monasticism. The *erotapokriseis* structure of the *Conferences* situates Germanus as the primary interlocutor who poses questions, seeks clarification, and occasionally protests *abbas'* views. Recall *Conference* 13, where Germanus protests that Abba Chaeremon's position on divine grace negates human agency. The young Cassian is present but remains mostly silent, both because Germanus is more senior and because Cassian models deference to the wisdom of others. Yet the relationship between Cassian and Germanus is the backbone of the whole text, as Cassian declares it was instrumental to their spiritual journey, sharing and vocalizing their concerns as they progressed together. Cassian's *Conferences* provides an intimate view into the concerns they boldly voice to each other. Intimate relations include friendship and two other notable forms in Cassian's texts: directorship, in which elders guide novices, and liturgical communities, which forge corporate bodies.

Friendship as Relations of Care

The friendship of Cassian and Germanus features so centrally that Cassian begins the *Conferences* with his relationship with "the holy Abba Germanus" (*sancto abbate Germano*), "with whom I was so closely befriended from the very time of our basic training and the beginnings of our spiritual soldiery, both in the cenobium and in the desert, that everyone used to say, by way of pointing out the identity of our companionship and our chosen orientation, that we were one mind and soul inhabiting two bodies."[23] Expanding the Aristotelian formula, theirs is a friendship notable for both its longevity and its consistency since the beginning of their ascetic training.[24] Their friendship spans geographical locations and ascetic communities, "both in the cenobium and in the desert" (*in coenobio quam in heremo*).

In Cassian's words, the *abbas* testify to the friendship's chastity and profundity based on "the identity of our companionship and our chosen orientation" (*sodalitatis ac propositi nostri parilitatem*). Their friendship is declared fueled not by homoerotic attachments but by a unified desire to pursue the spiritual life as coparticipants. They are akin to soldiers preparing for battle in *tirocinium*—as the soldiers' first training—and *militiae spiritalis*—as the practice of spiritual soldiery. Such insistence on a united discipleship ties to regulations of one's domicile, as monastic cells were "allowed to be inhabited by only one or two persons whom a common task or instruction in discipleship and discipline has joined or whom at least a likeness of virtue has made equal."[25] Companions of similar aptitude do not distract from individual progress and instead support each other through inevitable struggles. This embrace of friendship contrasts with the suspicion of intimate relations as a danger to *philia* extended to the broader community, as well as distracting and detrimental to the monastic ethos as such.[26]

Theorizing friendship in *Conference* 16 (*De amicitia*), Abba Joseph is an ascetic fluent in Coptic and Greek from a distinguished family in Thmuis.[27] Classically trained in both Greek language and philosophy, Joseph is the perfect interlocutor for this conference on a typology of friendship similar to that of Aristotle's *Nicomachean Ethics* and perhaps influenced by Cicero.[28] Noting the close bond between the young companions, Joseph asks if they are blood relations. With Cassian declaring their friendship "joined not by a fleshly but by a spiritual brotherhood," Joseph celebrates their unique friendship.[29]

Such true friendship is the uncommon yet celebrated apex in the typology of friendships. As Claudia Rapp notes, this type of brotherhood was not the norm, yet there is ample precedent of pairs of friends living together or a disciple living with his elder.[30] Abba Joseph goes on to discuss "many kinds of friendship and companionship which, in different ways, bind the human race by the fellowship of love."[31] In addition to the terminology of *sodalitatis* (companionship) and *dilectionis societate* (fellowship of love), David Konstan notes that Cassian frames the beginning and end of *Conference* 16 with the Latin *amicitia*, shifting to the less classical language of *caritas* for the majority of the conference.[32] Konstan argues that Cassian frames the conference with classical terminology to attract elite monastics who share classical training, but employs the Christianized language with which he is more comfortable throughout the text.

The first form of friendship indicates relations of social engagement and care more broadly. For these relations, Abba Joseph notes the importance of social reputation or, in its absence, a contractual agreement: "For a good reputation is sufficient for some people to enter upon a relationship of acquaintance first and afterward of friendship as well. In the case of others, a contract or agreement about something given and received forges a bond of love."[33] A relationship "of acquaintance" (*notitiae*) sometimes deepens to become that "of friendship" (*amicitiae*), and a social agreement can become formalized in a "bond of love" (*depectio caritatis*) in which *caritas* includes esteem or affection. Cassian's terminology suggests a reciprocation of regard.

Abba Joseph describes the second type of friendship as "founded on a natural instinct and on the law of kinship."[34] The love (*dilectio*) extended to members of one's family or tribe characterizes a lasting relation of care, with preferential treatment corresponding "naturally" (*naturaliter*) to one's blood relations in humans and "every winged creature and animal" alike.[35] All creatures have a "natural disposition" (*naturali affectu*) to care for their kin, and Cassian describes how even "basilisks and unicorns and griffins," known for their "unbearable ferocity and deadly poison," tend to their own with great care.[36]

In the first and second types of friendship, relations of care can be shared between good and bad people and are common to humans and animals alike. Only the third kind of true friendship is based on "likeness of virtue alone" (*sola similitudo uirtutum*).[37] Whereas the first two types rely on "various relationships of gain or lust or kinship or different needs," true friendship relies solely on the shared pursuit of virtue and "grows by the combined perfection and virtue of the friends."[38] Carolinne White argues that in Cassian's view "it is only the soul which has been purified by ascetic training in the monastic life that can experience genuine friendships."[39] Such true friendship exists only between ascetics who have sufficiently advanced in the ascetic *professio* and who are therefore capable of a "properly ordered love" (*uere caritas ordinata*) oriented toward the *scopos* and *telos* of ascetic life.

General care for neighbor and family is the precondition for the intimacy of true friendship. In addition to the "particular affection" (*peculiari affectione*) common to love of kin, Cassian promotes the extension of care to everyone as a function of Christian love, which "loves everyone in a general way" (*generaliter diligat cunctos*).[40] One is to love everyone (*diligio* here, although Cassian varies his terminology), while still having particular affection (*affectio*) for those who share similar pursuits, the love of virtue, and admirable "good qualities" (*meriti*).

Discernment and Directorship as a Social Practice

While true friendship is an intimate relationship predicated on similarity of virtue and ascetic progress, the most typically formative relation in the ascetic *professio* is between a novice and an elder. In addition to a shared orientation (*propositum*) and mutual relations of care (*amicitia*), the mentoring relationship between an elder and novice binds ascetic communities. Under such spiritual direction, young ascetics are not to adjudicate their own thoughts and feelings in this process. Instead, all thoughts are to be revealed to the elder for examination. Novices are "taught never, through a hurtful scheme, to hide any of the wanton thoughts in their hearts but to reveal them to their elder as soon as they surface, nor to judge them in accordance with their own discretion but to credit them with badness or goodness as the elder's examination discloses and makes clear."[41] By discerning the source of the novice's thoughts, the elder differentiates those roused by demons from those from the novice or from God. Such discernment is part of the diagnostic assessment of the spiritual progress of the novice.

Absolute transparency is central to the relationship at this stage, and Cassian urges ascetics not to hide thoughts out of embarrassment or fear; he and Germanus themselves model this in discussing nocturnal emissions in *Conference* 22. The more the novice submits his own thoughts to the elder for evaluation, the less fearful or embarrassed the novice is of the thoughts themselves and the more they become destigmatized. Cassian develops the common relationship of obedience of the novice to the elder that also features in texts like Basil's *Rule*.[42] Each and every ascetic must undergo this training in humility, "for the superstructure of the virtues will never be able to rise in our soul if the foundations of true humility have not first been laid in our heart."[43] As Abba Pinufius's flight away from his community reflects, humility must be constantly cultivated in order to curb pride. Ascetics remain bound to and dependent on others in the communal body, and the novice monk relates to an advanced elder in a way similar to that of a pupil and a teacher.

The confessional relation works because the *abbas* exercise both authority and discernment that comes from experience-based wisdom. They build from their own experience as novices submitting to an elder earlier.[44] While each ascetic "is subject at every moment to their elder," "only obedience could hold in check so powerfully charged a network of relationships," and this is part of the transmission of tradition over time in which novices can become elders who shape novices in turn.[45] Cassian stresses the discretion at the heart of elders' support for novices, the classical roots of which Ramsey notes: "Already in classical thought, under the name *phronesis* or *prudentia*, discretion was seen as the governing virtue, distinguishing good from bad, and Cassian in one respect does no more than repeat that insight."[46] Cassian's adaptation of φρόνησις as *discretio* involves a technical relation between *discretio*, the capacity for distinguishing correlating with διάκρισις, and *iudicium*, referring to judgment, notably with legal connotations.[47] The practice of *discretio* involves the *abba*'s *iudicium* in the ability to judge a younger ascetic's motivations. On the basis of this assessment, the *abba* prescribes a personalized course of action to help the novice overcome his difficulties.

In *Conference 2* (*De discretione*), Abba Moses narrates an account of discretion by the most authoritative of desert elders, Antony the Great (*beatus Antonius*).[48] Hearing Antony speak to "some elders" soliciting his advice, Abba Moses notes the heart of *discretio* in instruction:

> Nor can another reason be found for their fall, except that they were less well instructed by the elders and were utterly unable to grasp the meaning of discretion, which avoids excess of any kind and teaches the monk always to proceed along the royal road and does not let him be inflated by virtues on the right hand—that is, in an excess of fervor to exceed the measure of a justifiable moderation by a foolish presumption—nor let him wander off to the vices on the left hand because of a weakness for pleasure—that is, under the pretext of controlling the body, to grow soft because of a contrary lukewarmness of spirit.[49]

Antony describes discretion as the cultivated ability to avoid excess, following instead the *uia regia monachum*. He advocates neither excessive asceticism nor pursuit of pleasure, for the ascetic becomes prey to the spirit of pride (*superbia*) in the former case and to that of gluttony (*gastrimargia*) in the latter. Inflamed by neither solely spirit nor flesh, the middle way shows how excessive asceticism and pleasure-seeking are comparably problematic.

To advance in the ascetic life, then, one needs to cultivate the skill of discernment, forging a soundness of mind and an equilibrium to curb against excess. Not all ascetics prove capable of such discernment, and age does not necessarily entail growth in this virtue. At times a youth's discernment catches a gray-haired ascetic off guard for his superior ability. So vital is discretion that Abba Moses notes the role that divine grace plays in its development. "The gift of discretion is no earthly or paltry matter but a very great bestowal of the divine grace."[50] While discretion marks the presence of divine grace, human effort is also required, as Moses continues: "Unless a monk has sought this grace with utter attentiveness and, with sure judgment, possesses discretion concerning the spirits that enter into him, it is inevitable that, like a person wandering in the dark of night and in deep shadows, he not only will fall into dangerous ditches and down steep slopes but will even frequently go astray on level and straight ways."[51] It is necessary that the ascetic "has sought this grace with utter attentiveness" (*omni intentione fuerit adsecutus*), devoting his attention to cultivating discretion. One learns to differentiate between these spirits in order to embrace positive thoughts and spirits and to reject negative ones "with sure judgment" (*certa ratione*). On the one hand, the goal is to cultivate one's own discernment through a moderation that encourages beneficial thoughts and proscribes negative ones. On the other hand, one cannot hope to cultivate one's own discernment without first benefiting from the guidance of an elder. Discernment is therefore twofold: It involves an ascetic distinguishing between the sources of different thoughts in order to commit to more salubrious courses of action and, relationally, it is the means by which the elder reads and diagnoses the spiritual state of the novice. *Discretio*, while seemingly a solitary achievement, requires intimate relationships with others in community as one learns from one's elder's exercise of judgment. One cannot "grasp the meaning of discretion" (*rationem discretionis adipisci*) or develop the capacity for discernment without first having proper instruction from elders. What later becomes sacramentalized as "confession" begins as the therapeutic relation between a young ascetic and an elder—yet not in the absolute and never-ending state of obedience that Foucault reads in Cassian.

Liturgy as Communal Practice

These examples of friends, fellow ascetics, and novices/directors show the centrality of intimate relations in shaping ascetic subjectivities every day. Framing such relations are the liturgical practices through which subjects are shaped, which Cassian distinctively contributes to western monasticism.[52] Amplified in cenobitic communities, yet common to anchoritic ones as well, ascetic subjectivities are forged in community and shape it in turn. This renders prideful musings of grumbling ascetics a danger not only to themselves but to the community as a whole.

The forms of liturgical offices framing everyday life illuminate the dynamics of corporate formation. *Institute 2, The Canonical Method of the Nighttime Prayers and Psalms (De canonico nocturnarum orationum et psalmorum modo)*, describes the liturgical services celebrated by Egyptian ascetics and prescribes for future readers the correct number of offices and their features.[53] In "services, which they call *synaxes*" (*sollemnitates, quas illi synaxis uocant*), including *uespertinis* (evening) and *nocturnis* (night) services, all ascetics in the community come together in an evening gathering (around 6:00 p.m.) and the night vigil (at midnight).[54] Cassian stresses the sanctity of these practices in Egypt and the Thebaid that "remain through a succession of elders and their traditions even to the present day and are founded to stay."[55]

Cassian describes these offices down to their temporal regulation, with the monastic in charge of waking the community for "the daily vigils" (*cotidianas uigilias*), watching the stars in order to ensure the correct ritual hours for these night offices, which conclude "after cockcrow and before dawn" (*ante gallorum cantum consurgere*).[56] One may neither oversleep nor rush the timing of the service in order to return quickly to sleep. Cassian constructs the traditional way of performing the liturgy, responding to a lack of standardized liturgical practices for monastics in Gaul. His influence on Gallic monasticism largely stems from the combination of his regulated practices and his figuration of those practices as continuous with the Egyptian desert tradition. He appeals to "when the perfection of the primitive Church remained inviolate and was still fresh in the memory of succeeding generations" as the foundation for "what form daily worship should take throughout the whole body of the brotherhood."[57]

With *meditatio* central to Cassian's program, the psalms remain at the heart of services even as their precise practice lacks agreement. To advocate for the "traditional" practice of singing twelve psalms with interposing prayers, Cassian tells the story of an angel joining a community of ascetics, singing twelve psalms, and immediately disappearing from the gathering. Cassian's description includes several components of a *synaxis*: "And when all were seated, as is still the custom throughout Egypt, and had fixed the full attention of their hearts upon the cantor's words, he sang eleven psalms that were separated by the interposition of prayers, all the verses being pronounced in the same tone of voice. Having finished the twelfth with an Alleluia as a response, he suddenly withdrew from the eyes of all, thus concluding both the discussion and the ceremony."[58]

Community members are seated and devote their attention to the cantor, who alone stands and sings the psalms. Regarding the attitude essential to liturgy in the fourth century, Denis Crouan notes: "During this time the assembly remained mute, so to speak: its 'active participation' consisted first and foremost in keeping themselves in the presence of God and in listening to his Word."[59] The community members are not passive, because each actively reflects on the words of the psalms as the cantor sings them. Susan Harvey's description of the homily in liturgical celebrations with laypeople resonates as well with these Egyptian ascetics: "Thus listening required attention, discernment, and a conjoining of purpose to that of the homilist, so that both preaching and listening should become one and the same act of offering thanksgiving to God."[60]

Cassian frames the story of the angel as establishing "a universal rule" (*generalem canonem*) to set twelve psalms as the absolute divinely issued standard for "both the evening and the morning assemblies" (*in uespertinis quam in nocturnis conuenticulis*).[61] Two readings from "Holy Scripture" (*diuinarum scripturarum*) then follow the singing of the psalms in order to best enable scriptural *meditatio*.[62] During the weekdays, these readings are drawn "one from the Old and another from the New Testament" (*unam ueteris et aliam noui testamenti*), but on Saturday and Sunday both readings come from the New Testament, "one from the Apostle or the Acts of the Apostles and another from the Gospels" (*unam de apostolo uel actibus apostolorum et aliam de euangeliis*).[63] Cassian does not mandate any additional content for the liturgy, requiring neither specific homilies nor particular psalms.[64]

Regulating the transmission of psalmody, Cassian further specifies that a psalm is not sung in its entirety but is broken up "into small and separate parts, in two or three sections, interspersed with prayers, in accordance with the number of the verses."[65] With the "interposition of prayers" the monastic sings the psalms with a different number of arrangements. A longer psalm is broken up into more sections, providing more opportunities for prayer. The twelve psalms sung in each service are divided up among participants in the *synaxis*, with up to four brothers singing. Cassian notes that "if there are two brothers they sing six each; if three, four; and if four, three. . . . Never more than four brothers sing during the *synaxis*."[66]

Cassian gives a sense of how small these gatherings could be in the Egyptian desert, where even two ascetics constitute a corporate body of worship. The brother singing takes great care to communicate the meaning and significance of the psalm, and Cassian chastens ascetics against sloppy and half-hearted performances.[67] The listening ascetics must be really silent, both to cultivate their own attention and to avoid distracting others.[68] Once the *synaxis* concludes and the psalms are finished, the ascetics immediately go back to their cells and their work, and "none of them dares to linger or to chat for a while with anyone else."[69]

Despite such regulation of liturgical practice, Cassian stresses adaptations and accommodations for different geographies and times—just as he does with individual ascetic formation. Common to Egyptian, Palestinian, and Mesopotamian contexts is the celebration of public services on Saturday and Sunday, where people "gather at the third hour for Holy Communion" (*in quibus hora tertia sacrae communionis obtentu conueniunt*).[70] Communities celebrate the Eucharist at Terce on Saturday and Sunday. Yet Cassian explains a special adaptation for Egyptian ascetics, whose physical exhaustion from constant bodily labor and fasting induces them to sit down: "When celebrating these same services in their gatherings according to custom, all settle down on very low seats, apart from the one who has gotten up in their midst to sing the psalms, and they give their heart's undivided attention to the cantor's voice. For they are so worn out from fasting and from working the whole day and night that, if they were standing and were not helped by this kind of rest, they would in fact be unable to get through the number in question."[71] Egyptian ascetics require bodily respite during these liturgies, because bodily rest better enables the heart's attention to remain undivided and focused on the psalms. Ascetics, in turn, "acquire a loftier insight into spiritual contemplation with a pure mind the more intently and zealously they focus on work and toil."[72]

Owen Chadwick observes that liturgical practices emerged in response to practical needs, as opposed to purely theoretical or doctrinal concerns.[73] The objective is not to blindly follow rules but to advance in ascetic formation. Therefore dedicated attention to the liturgy is paramount. The integrity of the community relies on the focus and discipline each ascetic cultivates. The quality and pacing of liturgical observance help focus attention of body, heart, and mind in each ascetic in turn. Attention is inimical to haste, as Cassian writes of Egyptian ascetic practice: "They begin and end the aforementioned prayers, then, such that once the psalm is finished they do not immediately rush to kneel down, as some of us do in this region who hasten to go down for prayer when the psalm is not yet completely over and hurry to get to the conclusion as quickly as possible."[74]

A collectively unified attention involves bodily, affective, and reflective foci brought together, individually and corporately. With the end of the night vigil concluding with Psalms 148, 149, and 150, after cockcrow and before dawn, the collective of particular ascetics unifies in such orientation.[75] The beginnings of each psalm express exultant praise for God as creator. Psalm 150 develops the expressive practices by which one praises God: "Praise him with trumpet sound; praise him with lute and harp! Praise him with tambourine and dance; praise him with strings and pipe! Praise him with clanging cymbals; praise him with loud clashing cymbals!"[76] As Harvey notes of the importance of sound for Jacob of Sarug, the sonic focus of these psalms fosters jubilant affective moods within the celebratory *synaxis*.[77] Praise intensifies in the cycle of three psalms, culminating in collective exuberance.

Sung as the daylight breaks, Cassian suggests that this psalmody best shapes ascetics together, "so that when daylight breaks it finds them more fervent and careful, maintaining them in readiness for the conflict and, thanks to the practice of the nighttime vigil and spiritual meditation, fortified in the face of the daytime struggle with the devil."[78] As the ascetics praise God with a fervent spirit that shapes them throughout the day, these psalms shape ascetic subjectivities not just during their expression but also in and through their cultivated disposition. With collective fortitude, all ascetics fortify their resolve and ability to take on the daily challenges of the *professio*. Shaped through the imaginative accompaniment of cymbals, tambourines, and dancing, each ascetic's fervent spirit enthusiastically participates.

While night practices are common to anchoritic and cenobitic communities, Cassian differentiates "the perfection of the Egyptians and the inimitable rigor of their discipline" (*perfectionem Aegyptiorum et inimitabilem disciplinae rigorem*) from communities in Palestine and Mesopotamia with daytime services.[79] Egyptian ascetics do not require set offices during the day because they aim to shape their lives as constant prayer.[80] These daytime services still importantly develop communal liturgical subjectivities against a soteriological backdrop: "In the monasteries of Palestine and Mesopotamia and the entire Orient," three weekday daytime gatherings include the "services at the aforesaid hours" (*horarum sollemnitates trinis psalmis*).[81] Cassian correlates these three times and their three psalms with the soteriological background of the *uita Christi*, "since in them was accomplished the fulfillment of the promises and the whole of our salvation."[82] The third hour, Terce (roughly 9:00 a.m.), is the hour of Pentecost in which the Holy Spirit "came down for the first time upon the apostles as they were gathered for prayer."[83] The sixth hour, Sext (noon), is the crux of salvation history, in which the crucifixion of Christ "freed all of us who were subject to and burdened by the record of our unpayable debt."[84] At the ninth hour, None (3:00 p.m.), Christ descended into hell.[85]

Cassian's scriptural and Christological justifications are notable for how they shape communal subjectivities. Cassian exhorts ascetics to foster the appropriate dispositions that reflect the cosmic significance of each gathering. Their community participates in a communal body extending across time and space. Like the apostles who received the Holy Spirit at Pentecost and spoke the truth of Christ to the unbelieving, ascetics are exhorted at Terce to imitate the apostles and cultivate an attitude of openness to the presence of God through the support of their ascetic community. At Sext, the suffering and death of Christ crucified calls each ascetic to recognize the dissolution of his debt and to follow the Gospel message as "divinely revealed to Peter" at this very hour.[86] At None, Christ broke the doors of Hell, effecting freedom from death for all humans, and ascetics are to come to this service with a sense of gratitude for their liberation together as a Christian body.

COLLECTIVE AGENCY IN ASCETIC EXPERIENCE

Cassian influences the development of cenobitic monasticism in Gaul through forms of life refusing to isolate cenobitic from anchoritic asceticism.[87] Foregrounding the work of community via intimate relations and the communal constitution of everyday life, Cassian indicates the conditions for the formation of ascetic subjectivities. Through the bonds of friendship, relationships of spiritual direction, and liturgical communities, Cassian stresses the social constitution of ascetic subjectivities, recursively forging individual and communal ways of life. Each intimate relation is enabled by the communal body and shapes it in turn. I conclude by analyzing how ethical agency is predicated on communal relations, shaping both their practices and the intimate relations that shape and transmit the *professio*.

Collective Friendship

Despite *Conference* 16's attention to friendship (*amicitia*), most of the conference focuses on forging the communal body of the monastery. Living in community quickly reveals tensions between different temperaments and characters, and Abba Joseph admonishes ascetics to refrain from anger, prescribing a host of attitudes needed for a community to function. Joseph hilariously chastises monastics who sing the psalms really loudly in order to show up their brethren in virtue and to ignore those with whom they are annoyed.[88] He also chastens ascetics who perform virtuous works such as fasting not out of virtue but out of anger and spite. These ascetics employ an array of creative strategies that abrogate the spirit of these communal practices while maintaining their observable letter.

Maintaining communal cohesion requires individuals to integrate their deeds and intentions as they cultivate ascetic dispositions. This involves fostering virtues and mitigating community-fracturing vices, including the imperative to forge a singular disposition: "As we said a short while ago, it is not merely the thing itself which is done but also the character of the mind and the intention of the doer that must be looked at."[89] The "character of the mind" (*qualitas mentis*) and the "intention of the doer" (*propositum facientis*) must be considered in relation to the action, where thought, emotion, and action need to spring from the same disposition. As community members test their resolve with irritants, one cannot hide a discordant disposition.

Being shaped in relation to the broader community is useful to check one's own conceits. The devil likes to stir up adversity, prompting ascetics to become angry or irritated with each other. Each is challenged by impulses toward anger (*ira*, the fourth dangerous spirit) and other destructive vices that trouble communal living. To live in community requires the cultivation of discernment, as one judges one's desires against the health of the community and evaluates the particularity of one's wants in relation to the goods of the communal body.

To address this concern, Cassian urges the monastic "to trust not so much his own decision as his brother's judgment, in accordance with his will."[90] Trusting others' judgments enables concord in the community and checks the threat of pride.

It is tempting to read this attention to others' judgments in terms of obedience and blind submission. Certain passages in Cassian might indeed suggest an overly obedient view of asceticism in which one renounces one's desires for the sake of others. In *Conference* 16, Abba Joseph starkly claims, "You must first strive, after having expelled your vices, to put to death your own will" (*Festinandum est uobis, ut expulsis primitus uitiis mortificetis proprias uoluntates*).[91] Yet scriptural context shows how this "death" involves not mere submission to the *abba* but a fortification of one's commitment to the ascetic *professio*. Ramsey rejects the abject reading of ascetic submission in Cassian because "the act of submission, however highly recommended it may have been, still presupposed the exercise of free choice on the part of those seeking counsel."[92] One's "own will" (*proprias uoluntates*) is not put to death, for one does not renounce one's self as such.[93] Recall that Cassian sees the will as occupying an intermediary place between the flesh and the spirit, neither fully autonomous nor fully determined.

Cassian does not flatten interrelational dynamics to mere oppositions. He expects that trusting the judgments of others becomes constitutive of one's own capacity for judgment and progress in virtue. The ideal monastic scenario characterized by "a stable and unbroken love" (*caritas stabilis atque indisrupta*) involves a community of ascetics who, following Cassian's description of true friends, are "men of the same virtue and chosen orientation" (*uiros eiusdem uirtutis atque propositi*).[94] Ideally, the monastic community will be constituted by people of like virtue (*uirtus*) and orientation (*propositum*), as one's discernment grows in relation to the broader community. The communal body then promotes greater discernment as a whole, as individual ascetics progress in the practice. One's own judgments conflict only when they are out of sync with those of the community.

Autonomy is never the goal, as the spirit of pride reflects darkly. Interdependence and interrelationality remain basic to the formation of subjectivity and the ascetic *professio* alike. "A link was thus forged," Philip Rousseau notes, "between authority and community. Cassian reminds his readers that they must submit themselves to the 'definitions' of their fellows."[95] Even the elder responsible for the community does not have the authority to self-determine and is "not his own master and has no power over himself" (*ne sui quidem ipsius esse se dominum uel potestatem habere*), nor does this render the elder completely abject.[96] All members are shaped through community, and the conceit of self-mastery is a form of autonomy neither desirable nor possible in this context: "For they declare that to rule well and to be ruled well is typical of the wise person, and they insist that this is a most lofty gift and a grace of the Holy Spirit" (*bene enim regere uel regi sapientis esse pronuntiant summumque donum et gratiam sancti spiritus esse definiunt*).[97] To rule requires being ruled, to shape requires being shaped, to guide requires being guided.

Discernment as Literary Topos

Discernment comes from being guided and shaped by elders who came before. It comes in the form of the critical judgment required for the exercise of ethical agency. Contextualized in monastic community, the intimate relationship between spiritual director and advisee is needed for such subjects to develop. It also provides the means by which communities transmit traditions constructed as "orthodox." Cassian dramatizes this social practice of discernment through literary framings, bringing the form of seeking and giving guidance to life. Analyzing these encounters helps better clarify the role of ethical agency.

Abba Moses speaks directly about discernment in *Conference* 2, yet each of the twenty-four conferences sees the young Cassian and Germanus benefit from the virtue of discretion as they approach the *abbas* with specific questions, seek direction, and work out issues of real importance to them.[98] Consider *Conference* 17, where they ask Abba Joseph to weigh in on promise-keeping, with the two friends expressing anxiety over breaking their promise to return to the Bethlehem monastery. In his response Abba Joseph not only describes how the spirit should be embraced over the letter of the law but also directly advises the young Cassian and Germanus, who decide to stay in Egypt and leave "strengthened as by a divine oracle."[99]

In *Conference* 6, the young Cassian and Germanus express their sadness and bafflement over the killing of ascetics in Palestine. Instead of hiding their struggle, they bring their sadness and questions to the *abba* in order to gain direction. "When this was over we took such boundless delight in our spiritual repast that we were filled with more joy of soul from this conference than we had been touched with sadness before because of the death of the holy ones."[100] The young friends even bring embarrassing questions—like those related to nocturnal emissions—to Abba Theonas because they want guidance on how to read their own bodies.[101] In *Conference* 22, Theonas models discernment, counseling them to quell their anxieties by contextualizing their dangers and urging therapeutic means of combat.

As in Cassian's self-description as Hiram, the *abbas* are architects of concrete courses of action.[102] The elder provides spiritual direction to the novice based on the power of discernment cultivated at the feet of his own elder. Should the elder truly have discernment, he models a life of moderation, becoming an exemplar for the novice. As Cassian counsels: "You should seek out, while you live in the community, examples of a perfect life that are worthy of imitation . . . that a person is more carefully schooled and formed for the perfection of this chosen orientation (namely, the cenobitic life) by the example of one."[103]

One should seek out elders as exemplars worthy of imitation—behaviorally, affectively, and reflectively. This dual relationship between the novice monk and elder—that of discernment and of exemplarity—is central to understanding interrelationality as the precondition for ascetic formation and the transmission of the ascetic *professio*. *Conference* 2 dramatizes discretion in the mouth of Abba Moses, who directly receives guidance from Antony. Cassian's use of Antony—an unquestioned authority—as interlocutor confirms Cassian's own claim to direct training by illustrious elders. Cassian presents the elders and his own literary self and companion as exemplars to be followed in action, affection, and critical discernment.[104] He stresses forms of proximate and distal exemplarity while also authorizing the transmission of his asceticism.

Liturgizing Everyday Life

Cassian prescribes liturgical and communal practices directly yet also uses these practices as framing devices. Using mechanisms similar to those discussed in chapter 5, where the reader can participate in the affective exemplarity of the young Cassian and Germanus, Cassian frames his *Conferences* with embodied liturgical and communal ritual observances constitutive of the ascetic *professio*. Despite geographical and temporal distance, Cassian's readers can learn the shape of every-day ascetic life, including bodily practices, affective responses, and reflective orientations.

Part I of the *Conferences*, *Conferences* 1–10, features seven different *abbas* receiving the young Cassian and Germanus into their ascetic communities. *Conference* 1 opens with the introduction of the esteemed Abba Moses and closes with the young Cassian and Germanus going to bed after the *abba*'s illuminating discourse on the goal and end of the monastic life.[105] The next conference begins with their small community waking at the first light of dawn after only a "very short time of rest" due to the friends' joyful anticipation and attendant restlessness, where Moses delivers his promised discourse on *discretio*.[106] *Conference* 3 begins after the *synaxis* observed on Saturday morning with Abba Paphnutius and concludes just before midnight.[107] Abba Serenus, the host of *Conferences* 7 and 8, engages the friends in conversation until nearly dawn, eventually urging them to take a short sleep in order to be rested for *synaxis* on Sunday.[108] After *synaxis* on Sunday closes around the ninth hour, Serenus presents the friends with the feast noted in chapter 4, followed by conversation into the evening "by lamplight."[109] *Conference* 9 closes earlier in the evening, with Abba Isaac sending the friends to bed after they celebrate the evening *synaxis*, with the intention of beginning conversation again early in the morning, after the night vigil.[110]

Part II, *Conferences* 11–17, moves temporally to the first stage of young Cassian and Germanus's visit in Egypt. *Conference* 11 ends with Abba Chaeremon coaxing the friends to eat "so that after eating the attention of our mind may be given over to what you desire to investigate more carefully."[111] *Conference* 12 begins with all three taking their meal, although Cassian declares that he wished it were the sustenance of teaching instead of literal food.[112] This conference on chastity relates closely to fasting, reinforcing the importance of food, and warns against excessive abstinence. To close, Chaeremon urges the friends to remember the necessities of the body and to take the "natural food of sleep, since the greater part of the night had already slipped by and it had gradually become more quiet."[113] Waking after a short sleep, they celebrate the morning *synaxis* in *Conference* 13, completing it an hour before cockcrow.[114] *Conference* 15 starts after evening *synaxis*, with Cassian describing how they sat down on their mats for the conference.[115] At the close of *Conference* 16 and the beginning of *Conference* 17, Abba Joseph brings the young Cassian and Germanus to their cell to rest. However, the young friends are so energized that they speak through the night, expressing their angst over not keeping their promise to return to their cenobium in Bethlehem.[116] Joseph assuages the friends' anxieties during the full conference the following day.

Part III, *Conferences* 18–24, takes place after Part II temporally and discusses conferences in both anchoritic and cenobitic communities. The close of *Conference* 18 has Abba Piamun discussing the rudiments of solitary living.[117] *Conference* 21 discusses the mores around the observance of Pentecost, moving on to standards surrounding fasting as well as broader issues of conversion and purification. The young friends raise the uncomfortable question of why nocturnal emissions occur, and Abba Theonas defers the conversation until after the three take a rest. This rest ends up lasting seven days during which Pentecost is celebrated. After the evening *synaxis*, in *Conference* 22 Theonas discusses nocturnal emissions with the young friends in his cell until he urges them to sleep so that they might start again the following day.[118] As it becomes light, Abba Theonas begins *Conference* 23 discussing the need for "frequent examination" of one's spiritual status. *Conference* 24 closes the *Conferences* with the young Cassian and Germanus confessing their thoughts to Abba Abraham, who explains their thoughts as would a good medical doctor in terms of sicknesses of the soul, diagnosing the two friends, and reaffirming their joyful embrace of the ascetic *professio*.[119]

The framing of each conference gives an experiential sense of how the friends interacted with these esteemed elders in their dynamic communities and how the reader might participate in turn. Intimate relations shape not only particular ascetics but the communal body of the ascetic community in the shared practices and liturgical observations of daily life. From narrative frames to exemplars' practices, readers can see how ascetic communities are the precondition for the exercise of ethical agency as ascetics rely on each other to engage bodily practices, affective cultivation, and reflective attention. Cassian depicts ascetics as subjects in desert communities and, by modeling liturgical practices, performs the means of transmitting the technologies of the ascetic self that they develop.

CO-OPERATING AGENCIES IN GALLIC COMMUNITIES

Recognizing the force of intimate relations can help clarify how agencies cooperate, synergistically at times, within the fold of communal and individual formation. Rebecca Weaver's distinction between the operation of grace in Cassian versus that in Augustine amplifies this centrality: "[Cassian's] instruction presupposed that the properly regulated communal life of a monastery provided a context propitious to the operation of grace. In contrast, the congregational setting with which Augustine had to deal lacked just such pervasive regulation. Accordingly, he identified a different arena for the operation of grace. The benefits of grace that Cassian could locate in the regulated community Augustine located in the outworking of the divine decrees on the human heart."[120] Divine grace works synergistically both with the ascetic and with the communal body, especially when they work to become well-regulated. The coimbrication of individual and communal provides the precondition for the operation of such grace. Ascetic communities shape subjects who, in turn, reshape communities.

Cassian's monasticism self-consciously forms itself in relation to spiritual referents, including the apostolic ministry in the book of Acts and the early church observances of the Jerusalem community. Peter Brown discusses this focus on community in relation to

Cassian's treatment of sexuality, notably in the conferences of Abba Chaeremon, who discusses chastity "with a reference to the state of the first Christians of the Jerusalem community after the coming of the Holy Ghost: holding *all things in common* there was among them *one heart and one soul*."[121] The ascetic is to shed the external markers of "the world," including material wealth, ties to civil society, and disordered personal desires. Obsession with external values is traded for those internal to the ascetic *professio*.

Recognizing ethical agency in daily practices involves recognizing the agency of particular ascetics shaped by the conditions of community as well as the intimate relations therein. Yet cultivating an ascetic *affectus* integrates the external and the internal, the self and the community. The external appearance is nothing without the internal intention and the *affectus* requiring their integration. David Brakke argues that Cassian's attention to community relies on a particular construction of the ascetic self: "Thus his program attempts to form a self that coheres with communal life: that is, an increasingly transparent self, a self that seeks to be completely accessible to the sight of one's self, of others, and of God."[122] There is no "self" that precedes communal life; the integration of internal and external stems from communal life as its precondition. Cassian stresses integration and relationality over what Brakke calls transparency, where it is not accessibility of sight but the recognition of dependence and interconnection that is vital. Ascetics contribute proximately to the communities in which they participate and distally to the traditions forged.

Sites of liturgical practice become vital for thinking through this community, bound together through Christian *caritas*. Communal practice shapes the subjectivities of the ascetics involved and the traditions Cassian translates from Egypt and forges for western monasticism. Daytime services help constitute ascetic communities liturgically and as Susan Harvey writes of Christian lay communities, the drama of salvation can be seen played out in these services.[123] Participating in liturgical services that unify them in bodily ritual, affective experience, and mental discretion, ascetics constitute a communal body. Through liturgy, individual ascetics can experience their most virtuous and loving selves against a soteriological background—even as they are tested by social irritants and pedestrian challenges. Carolinne White's reading of friendship demonstrates the integration and parity of participants "because it provides a foretaste of the equality which is to exist among men in the world to come."[124] For Cassian, the bonds of true friendship help constitute the body of Christ in both communal living—as individuals advance in virtue together—and liturgical performance—as a concentrated enactment of the unity anticipated in the eschaton.

Communal practices forge an identification and Christian identity constituted through harmoniously ordered parts. When joined in communal praxis, ascetics together adopt the dispositions of the Psalter and affectively experience meditative reflection and bodily focus together. John Alford describes such dynamics of individual and communal formation: "They tended to see themselves less as individuals than as individual manifestations of well-known and codified forms of behavior."[125] Not autonomous individuals but tradition-informed subjectivities enable group ritual identification and subject formation.

Cassian's liturgical technologies of communal subjectivities would, in Foucault's language, translate as the "techniques that human beings use to understand themselves."[126] In *Institute* 3, Cassian suggests that Christian monastic subjectivities are shaped through both the practices one engages in and how a community comes together.[127] Nathan Mitchell describes such technologies in a way resonant of Cassian's texts: "But if self-care is personal, it is also, for Christians, inherently and decisively social. Technologies of the self include both the 'rites' practiced by individuals and the 'ritual construction' of the whole social order."[128] Cassian recognizes the necessity of both rites *and* ritual construction for regulating monasticism in Gaul and for shaping subjectivities through intimate relations of friendship, discretion, and liturgical practice.

CONSIDERING THESE MANY elements of social formation together, Cassian offers a distinctive view of how monasticism might be shaped in Gaul. George Demacopoulos argues regarding Cassian's innovation for ascetical direction in the west: "No longer was ascetic perfection found in the monk who lived alone in the desert. Cassian admonished his readers to take responsibility for others, and he elaborated the pastoral mechanisms through which that could be achieved (e.g., discernment, interiorization, and the saintly exemplar)."[129] Ascetic progress involves social elements as the necessary medium in which ascetics realize spiritual excellence. How much Cassian's asceticism was to extend beyond the monastery remains an open question, but as Demacopoulos notes, "Cassian displayed an increasing concern for the monk's responsibility to his neighbor, and he emphasized that many of the Egyptian elders were themselves clerics."[130] Self and society—with their political, social, economic, cultural, and ecological registers—are coconstituitive.

Through friendship, spiritual direction, and liturgical communities, intimate relations are also the precondition for ascetic formation. Such relations of care not only establish the conditions of possibility for ascetic formation; they also enable the exercise of ethical agency. Tying together the foci of the prior chapters, Cassian's recognition of the synergism of agencies (chapter 3), as well as the constitutive necessity of bodily (chapter 4) and affective (chapter 5) practices alongside reflective social ones (chapter 6), together contribute to a view of ethical agency as embedded socially and enacted in daily practices that enable the stabilization of dispositions to action, emotion, and thought. They also together elucidate Cassian's formation of the ascetic *traditio* enacted and transmitted through his exemplary figures. Rebecca Weaver stresses divine grace in community, Marcia Colish articulates the synergism of agencies together, and we can understand Cassian's view of community as a complex synergism of multiple agencies involved in ethical formation that enables individuals to cultivate desired dispositions and advance in a way of life.[131]

Even memory, which we tend to think of as an individual faculty from Book 11 of Augustine's *Confessions*, becomes communal in this context and is, as Mary Carruthers argues, "a truly civic activity."[132] In the *Institutes*, Cassian urges forgetting memories of one's past life, because they hinder progress in the monastic life. This harsh rejection of one's former social identity and familial lineage supplants one's individual memories with those of the Christian community, both social and scriptural.[133] What was once a feature of the individual becomes inextricable from the communal. Cassian, then, constructs a collective memory with a common repertoire of rituals, stories, and historical figures through which individual and communal identification are forged.

Pride is the great threat to community, luring advanced ascetics into considering themselves the source of their own excellence without recognizing their contingency upon other agencies, both human and divine. These communal practices reflect just how contingent individuals are on others, from proximate relationships of mentoring and training to broader social formations that produce the possibility of adopting such practices and ways of life. Cassian affirms his account of intimate relations and social practices by referring to their continuity with tradition, which gives shape to forms of western monasticism in turn.

Cassian speaks to the particularities of ascetic formation while recognizing that all ascetics are already shaped as subjects and, in turn, help shape traditions. His texts are fascinating not only for what they illuminate about his own practices and historical situatedness but for the way they come to influence the monastic tradition in the west. Cassian writes to other monastics in southern Gaul in order to share his expertise of desert asceticism and the relations that shape, support, and enable extreme feats of self-transformation and social transmission alike. His writings and influence both construct the desert tradition as authoritative for Gaul and help construct the monasticism in Gaul.[134] Cassian repeatedly emphasizes how one must "learn by experience," and now we can evaluate this claim on two fronts. To change the world, one must also change oneself. And changing oneself helps to constitute a changed world.

Conclusion

FLOWERS IN THE DESERT

For Cassian, the desert valley of Scetis was where "the most experienced fathers of the monks and every perfection dwelled."[1] In this field of "splendid flowers" (*egregios flores*) Abba Moses blossomed supreme.[2] The host of the first two *Conferences*, this outstanding *abba* nourishes the young Cassian and Germanus with his teaching on "the reasoning behind renunciation and the goal and end of our chosen orientation."[3] With the contours of the ascetic life presented, it is Moses's "grace and virtue of discretion" (*discretionis gratiam atque uirtutem*) that open the young friends' eyes to the clarity of the ascetic path.[4]

It might be surprising, then, to learn about Abba Moses's sordid past. Moses, as Abba Paphnutius relays in *Conference* 3, came to his monastery as a refugee from Calamus in the Egyptian desert. Of Moses—this great ascetic of whom "nothing was lacking for him to be rewarded with perfect blessedness"—we learn that he was avoiding charges of murder.[5] Other desert literature describes an Abba Moses as a former robber, perhaps even murderer, fleeing a death sentence.[6] Cassian's account demurs on these details, stressing instead the transformation wrought by this individual. Once in the monastery, Moses "so seized upon his need to be converted that with a virtuously ready spirit he turned it into a voluntary act and arrived at the highest summit of perfection" (*ita necessitatem conuersionis adripuit, ut eam in uoluntatem prompta animi uirtute conuertens ad perfectionis fastigia summa peruenerit*).[7]

Abba Moses, who moves from great sinner to earthly saint, testifies to Cassian's affirmation of the potential to change one's way of life through the maximization of human effort. "With a virtuously ready spirit" (*animi uirtute*) he converts his whole way of life "into a voluntary act" (*in uoluntatem prompta*). Other monastics have had less controversial beginnings, but Abba Paphnutius warns that many "slipped away into a harmful lukewarmness" and failed to progress in the ascetic life "due to subsequent laziness and hardness of heart" (*cordis ignauia ac duritia subsequente*).[8] Engaging just the bodily practices with a lukewarm spirit, having a prideful spirit with decimated flesh, or allowing one's heart to become hardened through vicious thoughts—any one of these precludes ascetic transformation. By contrast, Moses recognizes his need to change, so inflames his whole life with struggle and intensity. He exhibits the force of the ascetic *professio* by forging *puritas cordis* and orienting himself toward the kingdom of God, perhaps even inaugurating its eschatological promise.

ANXIETIES ACROSS THE MEDITERRANEAN

To understand Cassian's emphasis on what humans can do to shape their lives and the kind of labor, intensity, and community required, it has been necessary to read his texts in historical context and through theoretical lenses together. Studying Cassian's texts with an eye to the contexts of their production involves appreciating the political, social, cultural, doctrinal, and rhetorical milieus shaping his own late ancient attention. Along with the "magnifying focus on the physical body" noted by Averil Cameron, Cassian's asceticism includes attention to the emotions, affects, and reflection together.[9] Reading constructions of ethics alongside power in Cassian's asceticism recognizes the dialectical constitution of social structuring and subjective shaping. Cassian is an ascetic living around the Mediterranean as shifts in imperial institutions, invading forces, social formations, and the production of normative Christian doctrine and ecclesial hierarchy are all unfolding simultaneously and unpredictably. As a linguistic and cultural translator, Cassian moves amphibiously between different geographies, societies, cultures, and political orders. He navigates contexts as disparate as ascetic settlements in the Egyptian desert, urban ecclesial politics in Constantinople and Rome, and bourgeoning monastic communities in southern Gaul.

Cassian's stress on the possibilities of human effort can be understood better in relation to this backdrop of social and political concerns than to doctrinal ones alone. Cassian has theoretical and practical stakes in the construction of monasticism and the traditions of Christianity. He receives his training in prestigious contexts, he was commissioned and authorized by various ecclesial figures, and he expresses aching fidelity to the desert traditions and figures whose guidance helped him forge his own way of life even as his filiation to unorthodox views put him at risk. He saw the ramifications of theological and doctrinal contentions over questions of human effort and divine grace, over human anthropology and Christology, and over desert asceticism and coenobitic monasticism. Cassian focuses on what is practicable and pragmatic in response. Associated during his lifetime with a diversity of Christianities and in propinquity to multiple heresies—Anthropomorphitism, Origenism, Pelagianism, and Nestorianism—Cassian walks a fine line to affirm bourgeoning orthodoxy, especially on the centrality of divine grace. And his legacy suffered for his insistence on human effort.

Cassian's disciplinary background in Egyptian communities and the ascetic *professio* affirms the work of human effort through practical attention to everyday life. Cassian's concern for the psychological and physiological challenges that human beings experience in the ascetic *professio* comes to life in the contexts of their production. He writes to address real anxieties and difficulties faced by people forging ways of living amid the birth pangs of institutionalized Christianity as a political, economic, and social force across the Mediterranean. And to do so, he addresses not just the idealized excellences of ascetic living but also the challenges and ongoing failures of human nerve.

Cassian writes on the basis of his own experience, empathetically foregrounding the sweat of struggle and the difficulty of staying committed to the arduous task of producing new forms of life. He therefore strikes a remarkable balance between social concern for affirming tradition, forging regulative practices, and shaping the institutional identity of Gallic monasticism, on the one hand, and existential concerns for speaking to the vulnerabilities of human beings, their contingency on myriad agencies, and the necessity of accommodation and self-shaping in asceticism, on the other.

From traditions to practices, Cassian theorizes the role of human effort neither from an idealist position nor from an assumption of holism. Instead he starts with attention to fragmentary selves, fraught politics, and interconnected agencies. He writes, as he says, as a foreigner to foreign lands, but he writes because he knows the stakes and the struggle. His works stand as a profound and historically significant analysis of the difficulties of learning how to forge new ways of living in the face of uncertainty. And his texts stress how crucial it is to commit to forging a way of life in and through contingency, vulnerability, and suffering, even against competing political and cultural norms that marginalize such options. Instead of asceticism as predicated on abstinence, restriction, or vitiation as productive for economies that exploit ascetic labor in the service of others' gain, Cassian's asceticism opens up a way of considering discernment as part of everyday life, critical of demonic, self-delusional, and dogmatic normalizing mechanisms alike. He recognizes challenges as part and parcel of human lived experience; they are even occasions to imaginatively and critically forge different ways of life.

A Genealogy of Ethical Agency

Foregrounding the critical possibilities that emerge in the encounter between difference and repetition, we see Cassian's construction of ascetic subjectivity as focused neither on an impossible autonomy nor on interiority alone. The subject is not the same thing as the agent, following Asad's distinction, and yet subjectivities can still be constituted partially through the exercise of ethical agency.[10] In ascetic worlds, they even need to. This takes us further than Mary Keller's location of "instrumental agency" as inhering "in the inter-relationships of bodies with systems of power . . . and religious systems with the regimes of discipline."[11] Agency does "not reside in individual subjectivities," as Keller stresses, but in interrelationships that include not just discursive and intimate social relations but also the relationship of self to self.[12]

When read in relation to contemporary critical discourses of embodiment, affects, and interrelationality, Cassian helps us think through subjectivity as continuously constituted at different sites — embodied, affective, and reflective — while always already imbricated within systems of power and knowledge in Foucauldian terms. By analyzing the practices that foreground different sites in different ways, he opens up nuanced and everyday ways of articulating a pragmatics of transformation and the mechanisms by which ethical formation takes place. The "self" is not singular and static, nor is human effort located in a discrete faculty of "the will"; instead, subjectivities are fragmentary and dynamic. Cassian does not abrogate human agency understood as cultivated effort. Ascetic subjects are culturally shaped and discursively produced, in our modern theoretical language, yet their actions are not fully determined. There are, instead, countless options for critically adopting, adapting, and accommodating practices to oneself and for attending to such shaping with degrees of intensity (as does Moses) that open new possibilities for individual transformation. For Cassian, cultivating the ascetic *professio* is not simply about coercion and submission but about cultivation and transformation through the influence of Moses and other exemplars.

I analyze Cassian's texts not only as a comparative foil for rethinking contemporary concerns for subjectivity, ethics, and agency — though I see such comparisons as instructive in themselves. I engage Cassian, among all historical figures, because of how he is positioned within particular constructions of asceticism. Reading Cassian in historical context is necessary to critique modern readings of his texts and to nuance approaches to asceticism that assume the normative use of categories like interiority and renunciation. Cassian is linked, historically and theoretically, to contemporary mores, but an obsession with interiority and renunciation of the self does not define his broader legacy. Reading Cassian helps us consider possibilities for subject formation historically removed from, yet genealogically connected to, the "autonomous subject of modernity." And his texts enable reflection on how to think beyond (and before) this fictional subject in a way similar to the way Jeremy Biles and Kent Brintnall have recently argued of Georges Bataille yet from a historically anterior perspective.[13]

Cassian's focus on practice, experience, and struggle has remained part of the monastic current since the fifth century, notably through Benedictine and Benedictine-influenced monasticism, as well as eastern Byzantine and Orthodox Christian spiritualities. By focusing on lived experience and dramatizing everyday challenges to motivation, Cassian's texts help us think through forms of embodied, affective, and reflective self-shaping. This ethical project resonates with Foucault's investment in Greek and Roman antiquity and the ascetic potentials in the early Christian period. Cassian's texts open space for conceiving subjectivity without the binaries of autonomy and determinism that inflect modern discourses by negotiating the complex interplay between human effort and a host of social, environmental, and spirited agencies.

Cassian can therefore help us to pose important questions to contemporary ethical predicaments, inviting reflexive engagement with our own categories, especially in their articulation of the importance and the means of forming a way of life in and through these daily challenges. He helps us answer the call that Hollywood hears in Bataille, which echoes the call of Hadot and others to "begin to think about what it might mean to live well," notably in the face of suffering and loss.[14] And he does so by giving an account of practice motivated not by the moralizing fears of death but by an orienting hope that helps motivate transformations possible each day in the ascetic life. Human effort, though not autonomous and fully determining, is a precondition for critically shaping one's own life—in body, heart, and mind—and for reshaping the social conditions of their emergence.

BRINGING THE DESERT TO GAUL

Like Hiram, the humble architect of the temple of Solomon, Cassian claims himself a foreigner describing a tradition, not inventing it. Yet through his narration and his texts' broad circulation, he propagates the traditions of Egyptian desert asceticism on the southern shores of Gaul and constructs the mythos of his desert exemplars and a detailed practical asceticism. Cassian's stories of extreme asceticism and transformative religious experience help to foster both the awe of other Christians and their motivation to commit to the ascetic life in their Gallic monastic context. In addition to his ideal exemplars, Cassian provides his readers with relatable exemplars in his younger self and Germanus. As novice monks training with the *abbas*, they confront asceticism's daily emotional, behavioral, and reflective challenges.

To present asceticism in its challenges and possibilities, Cassian returns his reader to his beloved Egyptian desert. Established in flight from urban centers, anachoretic asceticism made "the desert . . . a city," in Athanasius's famous words, a city populated with peoples, behaviors, and values eschewing the social norms of a dying empire.[15] These ascetics commit themselves to disciplines characterized by deprivation and austerity. Two prunes do not constitute a fourth of a feast by any medical metric. Living in constant prayer is a fantastic goal, yet such equanimity and integrated attention is an aspirational yet not typically achievable good. Nevertheless, deprivation and austerity—especially when critically contesting or adapting conventional norms—reintegrate around new forms of life. These ascetics do not renounce their selves but rather stylize their lives.

Bringing Egyptian desert asceticism to bourgeoning monasticism in Gaul, Cassian urges the imitation of desert *exempla*. These larger-than-life figures show what achievement in particular virtues looks like by emphasizing the ways of life they forged, eschewing convention and transforming themselves and their communities.[16] Such transformation occurs not "in" the individual, but through the complex, sometimes intimate, relationships of multiple agencies, divine and demonic, environmental and social. Importantly, there is no moral formula or *regula* assumed as fixed, binding, and totalizing to which one must be obedient as Foucault's attention to *regula* over *forma* in Cassian assumes. Cassian does not moralize vices as damnable, nor does he see them as solely destructive. His exemplars all struggle with the spirits of anger, sadness, and *acedia*, among others, and their presence in the ascetic life can signal progress (not just regress) if used properly. Cassian is concerned not with deadly sins but with how to negotiate dangerous spirits who cajole ascetics away from formation. These demons never fully conquer the ascetic, nor are they ever fully conquered. Their conquering involves not a simple renunciation of desire, much less of "the self," but a conative cultivation of subjectivities through a matrix of behaviors, emotions, and beliefs.

Far from the renunciation of self, such adoption of the ascetic life and adaptation to one's particular strengths require the effort and agency we see in Abba Moses. Self-transformation goes hand in hand with the recognition that one *can* change one's life, along with the laborious work of forging the path to do so. It is fitting that Moses declares to the young Cassian and Germanus the effectiveness of human effort: "Otherwise, there would be no free will in a person, nor would the effort expended in our own correction be of any help to us."[17] While myriad agencies must come together to shape necessary conditions, one's effort must also be engaged in order to effect ethical formation.

Integrating, not Interiorizing, Selves

From an ethical perspective, Cassian most vitally contributes this emphasis on human effort, the possibilities for transformation through everyday practices, and the practices constituting ascetic subjectivities as a way of life. Analyzing the mechanisms of transformation, he convinces his readers that change is possible and shows them how to effect it. We stand to benefit from this integration of a theory of human agency with the practical considerations of ethical formation. Cassian's texts urge not conformity to preexisting codes but the exercise of critical *discretio* as one lives the ascetic *professio*.

Through his emphasis on lived experience, Cassian shows how the moving, breathing, sleeping, reading subject is shaped through particular practices. Interiority is neither "mind" nor the seat of the self; exteriority is neither "body" nor that to be renounced. Rather, integrating sites of embodiment, affectivity, and reflection contribute to the constitution of stable but dynamic subjectivities. And it is because these sites are not static but dynamic that one can change through daily practices. Vulnerability to change also bears the potential for transformation. Cassian thus helps us consider the question: How do we think about self-formation when there is no fixed and unitary self? And this relies on a terminological difference. Cassian does not assume that there is a discrete "self" or identity that awaits shaping or molding. Subjects are shaped through cultural, political, social, geographical, and economic particulars as well as intimate relations folded therein. Each configuration of particulars constitutes an assemblage, a Deleuzean potentiality of contingent affects and forces, rhizomatically constituted in an ongoing transformation of structure and subjectivity. Such constitution, however, does not preclude activities of self-shaping. It precludes only any view of "the self" as autonomous and not subject to any determinants beyond itself. Analyzing the ethics of daily practices involves the articulation of different sites of subjectivity, considering how they are shaped when integrated and intensified through unifying orientations, both proximate and distal.

Cassian also helps us think about how ascetic formation is possible when living a flourishing life, or even living at all, seems improbable due to forms of violence or psychological challenges. He gives us a way to break down how to live when one's will is insufficient to live a coherent and stable life and when one is at odds with prevailing norms—in our contemporary terms, when a subject position is undermined by regimes of truth and forms of power so often aligned with racist, misogynist, classist, ablist, and heteroexclusive structures. Cassian's texts provide a way of thinking through how to live by focusing on the mundane daily practices that one *can* slowly start to engage in over time, and in that engagement partially constitute one's subjectivity. He helps us understand how important it is to have orienting goals that keep one motivated to pursue everyday practices even before one has cultivated the bodily habits, the affective drive, or the reflective insight that sustain asceticism as a practice of self-cultivation. Cassian shows how self-formation is basic to social formation. He shows us how we can negotiate mental struggle, conflicting desires, bodily exhaustion, and social precarity. And he shows us how the devastating effects of these challenges can be provisionally navigated by training with oneself and others each and every day. I therefore see Cassian's texts as opening space for thinking about an agency that is circumscribed yet vital for thinking about living when one cannot conceive of living well, and for thinking about constituting one's self as an ongoing process.

IMPLICATIONS FOR AGENCY AND ETHICS

While my argument about ethical formation in Cassian's asceticism is historically particular, broader critical questions can be proposed. Considering the construction of ethics in Cassian's texts can help us glean particularly modern limitations when it comes to dealing with the possibilities for understanding ethical formation and agency. Reading Cassian against an overly renunciatory reading of asceticism helps illuminate three domains of subject formation that invite more nuanced engagement. When applied to Cassian's texts, contemporary theoretical lenses can help us to frame the force of daily practices in chapters 4, 5, and 6—in chapter 4, the role of the body via transformation over renunciation; In chapter 5 the role of the emotions and affects via the subject of action over the subject of knowledge; and in chapter 6 the role of reflective social relations as intimate and not just hierarchical. Cassian's ascetic ethics illustrates how these three domains are not only relevant separately but are best understood in dynamic interrelationship. Cassian's ascetic ethics can, by extension and implication, contribute in three main ways to contemporary thinking about human agency and ethical formation that are central to the study of religion today.

First, the sites of subjectivity I have parsed in Cassian's texts suggest one way to analyze subjectivity without the binary logic that dichotomizes an "interior" and autonomous will over the "exterior" and passive body. Cassian draws pronounced attention to the body, heart, and mind as together enabling ethical practices. So, while he conceives of the human as necessarily capable of engaging in ethical formation, he does not suffer from the romantic notion of a unified or holist "self" needing to be uncovered. With a focus on challenging processes of formation and the effort required to dynamically relate embodiment, affectivity, and reflection, ethical agency does not rely on an already achieved "self" but is enacted in the processes of formation, shaping ascetic subjectivities (in Cassian's case) through action, feeling, and thinking in conjunction with various agencies and other conditions.

Second, Cassian gives us insight into the pragmatics of transformation, breaking down the mechanisms of ethical formation through embodied, affective, and reflective practices. Describing daily practices constituting the ascetic *professio*—manual work, dietary practices, reading, and prayer practices alike—he describes the means by which one cultivates desired dispositions and forges an integrated way of life. One needs both the motivation to engage the practices and the openness to being affected and shaped through narrative and ritual practices. Ascetics transform themselves and their ways of life with some degree of intentionality and critical reflection if and only if the affective motivations are inflamed and embodied aptitudes support their realization. Cassian's account of ethical practices invites analysis of the way the body, emotions, and mind are engaged and the necessary ways in which they support and become trained together through the support of intimate relations and transmission of affects.

Third, Cassian operates in contexts where the communal dimension of subject formation is basic to lived experience. He starts not with the "I" but with the "we." And he describes the necessary work of community and intimate social relations alike. From the "one mind and soul inhabiting two bodies" intimacy of Cassian and Germanus to the communal body of anchoritic and cenobitic communities to the Christian body temporally and geographically spread across cultures through Cassian's translation of monasticism, subjectivities are always forged in relation to and through communities.[18] Cassian's texts do not isolate the individual ascetic. Instead, ascetics—like all human beings—are culturally embedded, constituted in communities, and subject to the vicissitudes of various agencies—weather, politics, people, power, and one's own physiology and psychology. Communal practices produce subjectivities without assuming an individual, autonomous subject. In Cassian's pre-Cartesian milieu, the subject is not a subject of knowledge who can rely on his *cogito* in isolation. Instead, continuing the project Foucault inaugurates with the ancients, the subject is a subject of action among other agencies, and only within the folds of social relations can one shape oneself and participate in social development.

CASSIAN AND THE STUDY OF RELIGION

Reading Cassian thus offers a nuanced way of analyzing the intersection of ethics, philosophy, and the study of religion today. This rereading of Cassian from a historical and theoretical perspective opens a broader critique of any construction of asceticism that assumes vitiation, renunciation, and economic ideology as definitional. I write about Cassian because he offers a view of human effort and ethical agency in relation to religious practices in cultures not determined by modern western categories. And yet the direct historical and theoretical links between Cassian and contemporary discourses also render him an ideal focal point for critical analysis. I have established the necessity of looking within the western tradition to reconsider the Nietzschean narrative of modern interiority because a careful historical-critical reading within western traditions illuminates ethical possibilities that otherwise seem out of reach.

Reading Cassian helps us understand how philosophical, hermeneutic, and historical lenses are needed to analyze his own texts. Illustrating the power of theoretical approaches to ethics and agency when constellating the philosophy of religion, religious ethics, and feminist, gender, and queer theories, I showed how his texts yield powerful insights when read according to theoretical analysis of structure and of agency alongside historically contextualized accounts of lived experience. Aware of the structural limitations on human agency, my analysis recognized the complex social, cultural, and environmental features that shape the possibilities of self-stylization available and articulates an account of everyday ethical agency produced through, but not fully reducible to, structural determinants. Reading Cassian in relation to modern assumptions helps us reflect on the limitations of our own categories by posing alternatives to binaries of autonomy and agency.

Readings of asceticism can contribute to the line of analysis that, following Foucault, Butler, Mahmood, and Hollywood, address the critical need for theories of subject formation that give robust accounts of human agency. Theorizing asceticism in Cassian via cultivation contributes to a robust account of ethical agency. I think that this fifth-century ascetic, when read through contemporary theoretical lenses, has something to teach us about analyzing ethics and religion today. Notably, through a dual historical-theoretical reading of his texts, we can draw out the very dimensions of ascetic analysis that Foucault enables—and that Nietzsche and Weber cannot see—but does not accept when he reads Cassian and, by extension, monastic Christianity as proleptic of modern dysfunction. Cassian's theory of the ascetic life is inseparable from his methods of practicing it.

Cassian's relationship with difficult issues in historical context also invites reflection on him among other figures more traditionally central to the history of Christianity, including Augustine, Evagrius, Chrysostom, and Leo, not to mention the curio cabinet of desert *abbas*, ecclesial authorities in southern Gaul, and detractors like Prosper. As the translator between eastern and western Christianities, Cassian not only moved between worlds but also bridged worlds, cultures, and experiences to help constitute a continuous tradition drawing upon the optimisms of eastern anthropologies and the realities of vulnerable western frontiers. Despite his doctrinal marginalization, the heart of monastic life would beat on with Cassian's texts. Reading Cassian helps us reconsider his role in the history of western Christianities and the complex relations between practical monasticisms and theoretical doctrinalisms.[19]

Turning to Cassian to consider issues of religion today proves beneficial from historical, critical, and constructive perspectives.[20] Cassian addresses so many of the themes and questions central to the academic study of religion today, including ritual, body, culture, performance, person, tradition, experience, and transformation. But he does so from a perspective that does not assume a rigorous divide between description and prescription. He describes in order to suggest new ways of thinking through traditional practices and how to adapt them to one's own ends, where one does not merely blindly submit and obey. Instead, every act of translation is a paraphrase open to the sensibilities and strengths of the person. Rereading this old ascetic through contemporary historical, theoretical, and practical frameworks helps us to both see his texts anew and to critically reflect on methodological issues central to religious studies.

Agency at the End of Empire

Cassian can help us think through how ethical formation involves self-shaping practices. This is not a simple and mindless inculcation of disciplinary subjectivity where subjects might follow the letter of the law but are "lukewarm," for they simply mimic and perform practices without making the way of life their own. Each individual must struggle to adapt discrete disciplines in complex matrices of agencies and determinants. It is the attention Cassian gives to human effort while also recognizing the personal and social challenges to living well that might speak to us most. His is neither a hyperelitist and exclusionary ancient ethics nor a neoliberal contemporary consumerist aesthetic considering human flourishing from the perspective of considerable resources and the aspiration toward productivity-enhancing optimal health and vigor. This is an ethics that can also address broken people in broken times.

Cassian refuses to pathologize psychological struggle, and he opens ways of thinking about how to address and cope with such challenges instead of moralizing their presence. He addresses the challenges of *acedia* (one of the best descriptions of something akin to modern massive depressive disorder) by refocusing attention on what one can do: When one's thoughts turn enduringly listless or despondent, one should keep one's hands busy and use one's body to hone attention. Cassian addresses the perils of vainglory as the disjunction between one's observable behaviors and one's whole way of life; is one merely performing the role of a perfect ascetic, he questions, when one goes without sleep or food? Transformation must occur through work at all sites of subjectivity, so bodily actions with discordant affective motivation must be addressed through the fostering of emotions that are consonant with one's chosen *professio*. And Cassian's account of pride is a reminder that not only is unconstrained autonomy impossible, but aspiring toward it preempts ethical formation that necessarily occurs in relation to other agencies, be it as friend, teacher, or adversary.

Cassian breaks down the seemingly impossible task of living well into discrete practices that one can learn to make one's own, even as we should adulate not his practices or society but his ethos. One cannot change one's way of life through a momentary conversion; one can only participate in the transformation of one's life through everyday practices that are affectively transmitted and engaged. And such transformation is possible only by supporting all of one's activities with embodied, affective, and reflective attention together. As Cassian says, it is to make one's entire life a prayer. It is to participate in the forging of one's life through the forging of stable dispositions and cultivating one's chosen orientation. From an ethical perspective, we can learn from his emphasis on imbuing one's entire life with the intensity and overarching sensibilities that transform it. I therefore foreground in Cassian what I see as an ethics for fractured selves in shifting worlds. Both his psychological acumen concerning mental operations and his social acumen concerning interrelations illuminate how necessary ethical formation is for navigating challenging contexts in precarious times. Critique takes a central role in how one shapes one's way of life, stylizing it to meet one's own strengths and aptitudes and changing social forms and practices accordingly. One need actively consider and curtail the claims that tradition and its practices make upon the subjects it produces.

What is the end of such self-shaping, then? I deliberately reject the neoliberal reading—particularly uncharitable when applied to Foucault—in which individuals "take responsibility" for themselves and shape a way of life that makes them strong and immune to the social networks in which they live. Shaping one's way of life and keeping these forms of ethical agency open to all involves contesting the norms and values that police social contexts. Forging asceticism as a way of life encodes the ability to contest forms of social, cultural, and economic power that naturalize their own consumptive values. This is the political dimension that Cassian's ethics opens up and remains to be theorized in more depth. I am committed to analyzing his texts because they help us reflect on how nonnormative subjects can shape themselves and their societies in and through that very struggle. Cassian helps us think through an ethics for the nonunitary subject, for subjectivities marginalized or occluded by the masculinist, rationalist, intellectualist logics that do not value the importance of the body, the emotions, and interrelationality.

Human agency can take on a particular ethical form in which people can work to transform their own lives in their own ways while subjected to and in dynamic interrelationship with myriad other factors. It can call for us to recognize that we can each make a choice about how we are to live and what it is to live well, constrained as we are within social, cultural, political, and economic contexts that make such choices more or less available. Yet, as we change through our own formations, we can fight to change these in tandem. Social violence against people unjustly maligned for their race or religion, political marginalization for those deemed perverse for their sexuality or gender identities, psychological instability in those suffering from mental illness — all these markers of identity need to be fought against by castigating the normative operations of power intent on dehumanization. Clearing the space for the flourishing of all people by critiquing institutional injustice and bias is necessary to consider as we forge political identities moving forward.

Subjectivities are shaped at sites — embodied, affective, and reflective in a relational space — that have been politically or philosophically marginalized in favor of rationality as dominant. How can forms of subjectivity like embodiment and affectivity be recognized when such sites were occluded as part of human subjectivity in favor of an individualized interiority? And how do we humanize subjects — women, people of color, those differently abled, and children—whose association with (and reduction to) embodiment and affectivity occlude their own humanity and social force? Indeed, this is why Foucault's shift toward ethics is so powerful to my mind. The great theorist of how subjects are constituted through regimes of truth and power dramatically moves to shore up sites of self-relation and care for the self. The recognition that technologies of domination require an appreciation for technologies of the self as forms of resistance at last galvanized Foucault's own theoretical shift to ethics.[21]

Cassian stands at the end of empire, forging new possibilities for social community and for individual formation at the same time. He constructs the monastic *traditio* to authorize his view of asceticism and to provide a bedrock for monastics seeking his advice to adapt themselves. Cassian's construction of human effort and ethics cannot apply to us in its particularities, but it is also incredibly flexible in ethos and so serves as a welcome starting point for considering such questions today. Take this way of life, he says, and make it your own. Adapt it to the needs of your weather, climate, personality, society, and strengths. Cassian shows sensitivity both to the stabilizing force of tradition and to the galvanizing force of human agency. In this view, we can engage in practices of ethical formation that enable the transformation of subjectivities while also staying cognizant of our interrelational dependence. Self-shaping depends on and develops broader communities in turn.

Ethical agency is an ascetic practice for Cassian, not a faculty or a merely structural effect. Human effort should not aspire toward full conformity with the *nomos*. Instead, Cassian suggests, cultivate for yourself the ascetic spirit, recognize you can change your life, take up the practices that help you to do so, and hone your critical capacity to consider how changes in your life can lead to changes in the lives of others through the transvaluation of norms. Through human effort we together change lives and societal conditions. And sometimes these shifts prove radical, as the ascetic selves of Abba Moses and Cassian exemplify.

Introduction

1. Concerning Cassian's origins, see Chadwick, *John Cassian*; Coman, "Les 'Scythes' Jean Cassien et Denys le Petit," 27–46; Goodrich, *Contextualizing Cassian*; Harmless, *Desert Christians*; Marrou, "Jean Cassien à Marseille," 1–17, and "La patrie de Jean Cassien," 588–96; Stewart, *Cassian the Monk*; and Rousseau, *Ascetics, Authority, and the Church*.

2. Cassian, *Conferences* (*Conf.*) 11.5. I cite Boniface Ramsey's translation throughout. Cassian is said to have gone to Palestine around 380, and there he settled in Bethlehem, near the Cave of the Nativity of Jesus, perhaps for reasons of both pilgrimage and monasticism (Stewart, *Cassian the Monk*, 6). Stewart's *Cassian the Monk* remains the exemplary account of Cassian's historical theology.

3. His contemporaries called him "Cassianus," but Cassian refers to himself twice as "Iohannes" ("John") (*Institutes* [*Inst.*] 5.35; *Conf.* 14.9.4). Cassian is younger than Germanus (14.9.4.) and yet, through the voice of Abba Moses, he describes the two as "one heart and soul in two bodies" (*Conf.* 1.1).

4. *Inst.* 4.24–26.

5. *Inst.* 4.27–28. Patermutus would even be chosen by his elder as his successor to head the monastery because of his devotion.

6. *Inst.* 4.29.

7. *Inst.* 4.30.2–5; *Conf.* 20.1. Cassian describes the cenobium as "not far from the city of Panephysis" (*Inst.* 4.30.2), more thoroughly in *Conf.* 7.26 and 11.3. Stewart notes that Panephysis is located at or north of modern al-Manzalah, Egypt (*Cassian the Monk*, 145fn57).

8. *Conf.* 20.1.5; Harmless, *Desert Christians*, 375.

9. *Conf.* 20.1.5. To contextualize this improbability, Brouria Bitton-Ashkelony argues for "the infrequency of pilgrimage to Palestine among Egyptian monks" (*Encountering the Sacred*, 158).

10. *Conference* 20 opens with this biographical narrative of Abba Pinufius and transitions to the young friends coming upon his cenobium near Panephysis as the context for the conference. Abba Pinufius also gives the most comprehensive speech concerning the monastic life in *Institutes* 4.33–43; formally, the speech is reminiscent of Antony's discourse in Athanasius's *Vita Antonii*, which was perhaps included in order to construct its own authoritative status.

11. Iohannes Cassianus, *Conlationes XXIIII*. Young Cassian and Germanus seek instruction from *abbas* to whose authority Cassian "subsumes his teaching" according to Rebecca Krawiec ("Monastic Literacy in John Cassian," 774).

12. For the use of *erotapokriseis* in late antique and Byzantine Christian literature, see Papadogiannakis, "Instruction by Question and Answer," and "'Encyclopedism' in the Byzantine Question-and-Answer Literature." I stage preliminary responses to questions raised by Papadogiannakis in "Instruction by Question and Answer," 100–101.

13. On the fourth-century "golden age of the expansion of Egyptian monasticism," see Burton-Christie, *The Word in the Desert*, 36, and the classic account of desert monasticism in Derwas James Chitty, *The Desert a City*. On Cassian's promotion of exemplars for training purposes, see Kelly, *Cassian's Conferences*.

Conf. 10.2.1–2 refers to Theophilus's written attack on Anthropomorphism dated to 399, but Cassian does not include how Theophilus would then turn against the Origenists, with whom he was allied during the Anthropomorphite fight. The Origenist purge of the Egyptian desert followed from Theophilus's condemnation of Origenism and his success in promoting an anti-Origenist cause. See Clark, *The Origenist Controversy*, 105–120.

14. For *exempla* see *Conf.* 2.13.3, 3.7.7, and 17.21.1.

15. Mahmood, *Politics of Piety*, x. Mahmood's account of how feminist scholarship since the 1970s "has focused on the operations of human agency within structures of subordination" and her vital account of agency as a cultivation of dispositions are also touchstones in my work (ibid., 6); the phrase "ethical agency" appears once in this work (ibid., 35).

16. Markus, *The End of Ancient Christianity*, 19.

17. *Inst.* Pref. 8. *propositum siquidem mihi est non de mirabilibus dei, sed de correctione morum nostrorum et consummatione uitae perfectae secundum ea, quae a senioribus nostris accepimus, pauca disserere.* I cite Boniface Ramsey's translation thoughout.

18. Kelly, *Cassian's Conferences*, 9.

19. Stewart, *Cassian the Monk*, 17. In this, Cassian follows his teacher Evagrius, "the great theoretician of monastic Origenism," whose questionable orthodoxy made it imprudent for Cassian to name him directly (ibid., 11).

20. *Conf.* 15.

21. For *paraenesis* as a genre of ethical instruction and exhortation, see Rubenson, "Wisdom, Paraenesis, and the Roots of Monasticism," 521–534, and Fiore, "Parenesis and Protreptic," 162–165.

22. These emphases correlate with Richard Valantasis's three components of ascetic discipline: subjectivity as deviating from the culturally normative unmasking of "the material and performative aspects of power," the "restructuring of social relations," and constructions of symbolic economies, all understood as practices of power (Valantasis, "Constructions of Power in Asceticism," 795–796).

23. *Conf.* 1.2.3 refers to "our occupation" (*nostra professio*) and *Inst.* 2.5.2 to "the arduous profession of their way of life" (*ardua conuersationis eorum professio*).

24. *Inst.* Pref. 5. *Totum namque in sola experientia usuque consistit, et quemadmodum tradi nisi ab experto non queunt, ita ne percipi quidem uel intellegi nisi ab eo, qui ea pari studio ac sudore adprehendere elaborauerit, possunt.*

25. Ibid. *Studio ac sudore* might be rendered in a variety of ways. I follow Ramsey's translation but read *studium* as involving application, inclination, zeal, and study, while *sudor* is more accurately rendered as sweat, perspiration, or moisture: "sūdor, ōris, m. (sudo). I. Lit., sweat, perspiration; II. Trop. (cf. sudo, I. B.), *sweat*, i.e., *toil, severe labor, weariness, fatigue* (class.; syn.: labor, contentio)." See Lewis and Short, eds., *A Latin Dictionary.*

26. In his significant work on ethics, Michel Foucault comes to articulate "techniques" or "technologies of the self" as a necessary counter to "technologies of production," "technologies of sign systems," and "technologies of power." For the published version of this account from his 1982 lectures at the University of Vermont, see Martin, Gutman, and Hutton, eds., *Technologies of the Self: A Seminar with Michel Foucault*, 18. In my research in the Michel Foucault archives at the Bibliothèque nationale de France, however, I found an early draft of Foucault's October 1980 Berkeley Howison lectures dated "*septembre 1980*" in which he composes this account of technologies that he will return to two years later (Paris, Bibliothèque nationale de France, NAF 28730, dossier XL, *Berkeley et New York University 1980*, chemise 1, feuillet 1, "Berkeley: Première conférence"). Foucault's 1982 lectures at the Collège de France make explicit his focus on the "ethics of the subject defined

by the relationship of self to self" (Foucault, *The Hermeneutics of the Subject*, 252). I thank Laurence Le Bras and Philippe Chevallier for their exceptional support in navigating the archives of Foucault, as well as the estate of Michel Foucault for their generous access.

27. *Conf.* 19.7. Frank, "John Cassian on John Cassian," 431.

28. Stephen Driver, *John Cassian*, 67.

29. Krawiec, "Monastic Literacy," 776.

30. Consider *Conference* 10, which opens with a tearful Serapion no longer knowing how to envision Christ while he prays, since Anthropomorhite tendencies are rejected (*Conf.* 10.3).

31. Shaw, *Burden of the Flesh*, 112–128.

32. For subjectivity as "not a substance" but "a 'form' which has a history and a future" and "a form which is constituted through practices that are always specific to particular social and historical contexts," see O'Leary, *Foucault and the Art of Ethics*, 111. For "the problem of an ethics as a form to be given to one's behavior and life," see Foucault, "The Concern for Truth," 263.

33. Foucault articulates these foci in his 1974 *Discipline and Punish*, 137. As he develops his reading of Christianity throughout his last decade, Foucault comes to a positive estimation of ascetic possibilities and their potential for resistance to power. For example, Foucault's reading of Gregory of Nyssa on virginity as an art of life and a form of care of the self counters readings of asceticism in terms of renunciation of self. *Les Aveux de la chair* (2018) confirms Elizabeth Castelli's stress on Foucauldian "askesis as renunciation" as also encoding the "transformative work on the self" (*Martyrdom and Memory*, 75, 235).

With the publication of Foucault's lectures at the Collège de France and abroad, as well as the 2018 release of his archival draft of *Les Aveux de la chair*, we can more fully appreciate his growing nuance in textual and conceptual analysis of both ancient texts and the ethical possibilities of ascetic formation. This is most clear in Foucault's exquisite note-taking practices, which are evident in the Foucault archives at the Bibliothèque nationale de France, NAF 28730; his engagement with primary sources in antiquity, from Plato to Augustine, becomes remarkably detailed and rigorous. See particularly Bibliothèque nationale de France, NAF 28730, dossier no. XXI, "Notes de lecture"; dossier no. XXII, "Pères de l'Église"; dossier no. XXIII, "Notes de la fin de sa vie pour ses dernières livres"; dossier no. XXIV, "Seminaire 'Dire vrai sur soi-même'"; and dossier no. XXVIII, "Ultimes papiers."

Even as Foucault carefully works through ethical possibilities in other early Christian texts (including those of Clement of Alexandria, Tertullian,

Methodius of Olympus, Gregory of Nyssa, John Chrysostom, and Augustine), he insists on his framing of Cassian in terms of obedience, submission, and self-renunciation, negatively viewing chastity as a condition of knowledge of scripture and self, unlike positive constructions of virginity as an art of living (Foucault, *Les Aveux de la chair*, 117–145 and 216–245). My next monograph in process, *Foucault the Confessor*, analyzes Foucault's engagement with Christianity in relation to ethics and antiquity over his last decade to glean his own changing views in both published and archival materials.

34. Clark, *Reading Renunciation*, 17 and Harvey, *Scenting Salvation*, 130. Harvey vitally decouples asceticism and sexuality in favor of attention to subjectivity and other forms of sensory embodiment (ibid., 5).

35. *Conf.* 21.14.7.

36. *Conf.* 4.12.1–6.

37. Kathy Eden similarly stresses how Martin Luther claims Scripture must be "brought home (*zu haus*), that is experienced (*experiatur*)." See Eden, *Hermeneutics and the Rhetorical Tradition*, 4.

38. Nietzsche, *Genealogy of Morals*, § II.22: 93.

39. Ibid., § II.16: 84.

40. Ibid., § III: 97–162.

41. Weber, *The Protestant Ethic and the Spirit of Capitalism*, 132.

42. Ibid., xiv.

43. Ibid., 140.

44. Ibid., 181.

45. Harpham, *The Ascetic Imperative in Culture and Criticism*, xvi. Dana Logan performs an excellent analysis of this dynamic in Gwyneth Paltrow's lifestyle brand *goop* as a modern form of asceticism in which evacuation is correlated with increased status/capital, which is, in turn, correlated with moral/spiritual worth. See Logan, "The Lean Closet," 600–628, and Clements, "Asceticism and Self-Cultivation."

46. Hadot, *Philosophy as a Way of Life*, 128.

47. Ibid.

48. Ibid.

49. Foucault's emphasis on how discursive regimes shape subjects stages his inquiry; on the construct of sexuality in relation to "modern hermeneutics of the self," see Boyarin and Castelli, "Introduction: Foucault's *The History of Sexuality*," 357–374.

50. Foucault, *The Hermeneutics of the Subject*, 424 and 439. Although the publications of Foucault's texts transliterate the Greek, I note that the archives show how Foucault engages Greek texts with admirable sophistication

in his last few years and does not transliterate. See particularly Bibliothèque nationale de France, NAF 28730, dossiers XXI, XXII, XXIII, XXIV, and XXVIII.

51. Foucault, *The History of Sexuality*, Vol. 2: *The Use of Pleasure*, 9; Foucault, *L'Usage des plaisirs*, 14–15. "*au lieu de légitimer ce qu'on sait déjà, à entreprendre de savoir comment et jusqu'où il serait possible de penser autrement.*" Foucault, *The History of Sexuality*, Vol. 3: *Care of the Self*; Foucault, *Le souci de soi*.

52. Foucault, *Security, Territory, Population*, 205.

53. Ibid., 208. Such forms of counter-conduct are invoked yet not developed in the language of *resistance* in *Discipline and Punish* (1975) and *the History of Sexuality*, Vol. 1 (1976).

54. Ibid., 208. Foucault, *Security, Territory, Population*, 208. For the implications of Foucault's reading of Christian asceticism in terms of "the self" and self-mastery, see Wills, "Ascetic Theology before Asceticism?," 902–925.

55. Foucault, *The Hermeneutics of the Subject*, 416–417.

56. Mark Jordan, *Convulsing Bodies: Religion and Resistance in Foucault*, 10.

57. Foucault, *The Hermeneutics of the Subject*, 424. As I will argue, Cassian's asceticism exhibits a shared concern with utilizing sets of exercises to achieve spiritual objectives by cultivating a form of life rather than merely obeying a rule, correlating with Foucault's late (yet provisional) articulation of "spirituality" in 1984 as "that which precisely refers to a subject acceding to a certain mode of being and to the transformations which the subject must make of himself in order to accede to this mode of being." See Foucault, "Ethics as the Care of the Self as a Practice of Freedom," 14.

Ludwig Wittgenstein's formulation of "form of life" (*eine Lebensform*) also opens ways of considering ethics in relation to the epistemic norms of daily life. See Wittgenstein, *On Certainty*, 89–90. I am also interested in how Giorgio Agamben connects monastic *regulae* and forms of life through medieval monasticism, aiming "to construct a form-of-life, that is to say, a life that is linked so closely to its form that it proves to be inseparable from it" and "the apparatus through which the monks attempted to realize their ideal of a communal form of life." See Agamben, *The Highest Poverty*, xi–xii. See also Agamben's *The Use of Bodies*, 195–262.

58. Foucault, *On the Government of the Living*, 193–222. Foucault refers to Tertullian's *De baptismo, De paenitentia,* and *De pudicitia* in his redescription: "You see that this problem of subjectivity-truth relations was entirely re-elaborated, reorganized, and renewed, I believe, around the third

century, around a very simple problem: [not] the problem of the individual's identity, [but] rather [that] of conversion" (ibid., 159).

59. Foucault, *Les Aveux de la chair*, 106–145, 177–205, and 247–361. As Foucault frames early Christian sexual ethics in *Aveux*, "The *flesh* is understood as a mode of experience, that is to say, a mode of knowledge and transformation of the self by the self" (ibid., 50–51). The "prière d'insérer" of 1984 notes: "*Les Aveux de la chair* traitent enfin de l'expérience de la chair aux premiers siècles du christianisme, et du rôle qu'y jouent l'hermé- neutique et le déchiffrement purificateur du désir." See Foucault, *Les Aveux de la chair*, ed. Gros, III. I find it notable that hermeneutics and the purifying decipherment of desire barely figure into *Les Aveux* as published.

Peter Brown and Michel Foucault met on October 21, 1980 at the Uni- versity of California–Berkeley, where Foucault solicited Brown's feedback on Cassian "for over two hours in the Bear's Lair pub" after Foucault's public talk. A few days later, Foucault attended Brown's meeting with the Philoso- phy Department to discuss Augustine. I cite and thank Peter Brown for his generous direct communication on this matter, dated August 12, 2019. The influence of Brown on Foucault can be felt in Foucault's increased public engagement with Augustine, which becomes central to both (1) his Novem- ber 1980 lectures at New York University, where he directly cites Brown (see Foucault and Sennett, "Sexuality and Solitude") and (2) his extended reading of Augustine in *Les Aveux de la chair*. In the one excerpt from *Les Aveux* published in Foucault's lifetime—"The Battle for Chastity," on Cassian— Foucault also cites Brown in its conclusion. See Michel Foucault, "Le com- bat de la chasteté," and "The Battle for Chastity." Daniel Defert's annotation on an archival folder also shows that Foucault had a lecture by Peter Brown, "Augustine and Sexuality," ready at hand for his revisions to *Les Aveux*. See Dossier no. LXXXIV, *Les Aveux de la chair*, chemise 11, "Ms de Aveux? Chemise trouvée sur *le table de Michel*."

60. Foucault, *The Courage of Truth*, 316.

61. Ibid., 317–318. For the methodological double movement rec- ognizing the role of religion in French philosophy and the retrieval of early Christian writings, see Jones, *A Genealogy of Marion's Philosophy of Religion*.

62. Foucault, *On the Government of the Living*, 288–289.

63. Foucault also argues here that these dynamics "will also entail, for Western subjectivity, a relation to discourse and a relation to confession (*aveu*) that is absolutely characteristic of our civilization" (ibid., 211).

64. Foucault, *The Hermeneutics of the Subject*, 301. Sergey Horujy argues that Foucault's limitations stem from reading Cassian vis-à-vis the

"'juridical' character of the Western Christian consciousness in contrast to the 'personalistic,' 'existential' character of the Russian and Orthodox Christian consciousness" (Horujy, *Practices of the Self and Spiritual Practices*, 123).

65. Among other issues, Foucault's stress on three primary metaphors (the mill, the moneychanger, and the officer) and his selection of particular stories of obedience without broader context (those of Abba John, Abba Patermutus, and Abba Pinufius, featured in this introduction) occlude the practical foci I trace in this book on the basis of my and other scholars' historical and theoretical work on Cassian.

66. Part of what is at stake is Foucault's effect on how we read Cassian. Judith Butler reiterates Foucault's reading of Cassian on the renunciation of self through the performative force of confession, Virginia Burrus understands Cassian's confession as a technology for transformation generative of both the psychological reality of such thoughts and the obsessive return to them, and David Brakke reads Cassian as internalizing the cosmic struggle between monks and demons, muting the impact of demonic forces and emphasizing the locus of struggle as within the individual monk (Butler, *Undoing Gender*, 161–173; Burrus, *The Sex Lives of Saints*, 165fn15; and David Brakke, *Demons and the Making of the Monk*, 240–248).

However, just as Brakke critiques Foucault for reading Evagrius as invested in a split between interior and exterior, I extend Brakke's reading of Evagrius in my reading of Cassian, critiquing the imposition of critical categories of analysis (including "interiority") that reinforce a dualism that does not apply. See Brakke, "Making Public the Monastic Life," 222–233.

67. Dale Martin and Patricia Cox Miller, eds., *The Cultural Turn in Late Ancient Studies*, 8.

68. Behr, *Asceticism and Anthropology in Irenaeus and Clement*, 7.

69. On the education of the senses in the production of subjectivity from the mid-fourth century, see Harvey, "Locating the Sensing Body," 140–162; Frank, "Dialogue and Deliberation," 163–182. See also Frank, *The Memory of the Eyes* and Chidester, *Word and Light*.

70. Valantasis, "Constructions of Power in Asceticism," 797.

71. Harvey, "Asceticism," 317.

72. Demacopoulos, *Five Models of Spiritual Direction in the Early Church*, 109.

73. Elm, *Virgins of God*, 1.

74. Clark, *Reading Renunciation*, 17.

75. Ibid., 15.

76. Wimbush and Valantasis, eds. *Asceticism*. I follow Clark's attention to issues of how "the body is inscribed with cultural value; the constitution of the 'self'; how praxis both creates and challenges theory." See Clark, *The Origenist Controversy*, 3.

77. Elizabeth Clark maps out the vital transition from "patristics" to "early Christian studies" as scholars move away from "'ecclesiasticism, maleness, and 'orthodoxy.'" See Clark, "From Patristics to Early Christian Studies," 7–41 and 14. On asceticism as an exercise of power, see Peter Brown, "The Rise and Function of the Holy Man in Late Antiquity," 80–101, and on techniques of power in Christian discourse in late antiquity, see Averil Cameron, "Redrawing the Map," 266–271.

78. Miller, "Desert Asceticism and 'The Body from Nowhere,'" 137, and "Shifting Selves in Late Antiquity," 28.

79. Brakke, "The Lady Appears," 390–391.

80. Burrus, *Saving Shame*, 151.

81. Brakke, Satlow, and Weitzman, eds., *Religion and the Self in Late Antiquity*, 1. See also pp. 27–28 and 150. For continuities with Byzantine subjectivities, see Krueger, *Liturgical Subjects*, 16–17.

82. There are, for example, only three brief references to cultivation (as opposed to renunciation) in asceticism in the massive and foundational volume by Vincent L. Wimbush and Richard Valantasis, eds., *Asceticism*, 116, 165, and 202. Michael Satlow urges us to "cease to use valuable analytic terms, like 'myth' or 'asceticism', with no definitional comment" (Satlow, "Disappearing Categories," 295).

83. Foucault, *Les Aveux de la chair*, 243. My translation.

84. I think we can read Foucault's attention to sexual ethics in parallel across Volumes 2, 3, and 4 of his *History of Sexuality*. *The Use of Pleasure* (Vol. 2) treats *the body* in Part II: Dietetics, *marriage* in Part III: Economics, and *young males* in Part IV: Erotics; *Care of the Self* (Vol. 3) includes Part IV: The Body, Part V: The Wife, and Part VI: Boys; and *Aveux de la chair* (*Confessions of the Flesh*, Vol. 4) treats *the flesh* in Part I: The Formation of a New Experience, the status of *marriage* in Part II: Being a Virgin, and the status of *erotics* in Part III: Being Married.

85. Foucault, "An Aesthetics of Existence," 49.

86. Valantasis, "Constructions of Power in Asceticism," 800. This attention accommodates Valantasis's claim that asceticism can have "contradictory meanings" as well (ibid., 794).

87. I follow arbĭtrĭum "A.1. *The judgment, decision of an arbitrator*; 2. Transf. from the sphere of judic. proceedings, *judgment, opinion, decision*;

B. *Mastery, dominion, authority, power, will, free-will*" (Lewis and Short, eds., *A Latin Dictionary*).

88. Hwang, Matz, and Casiday, eds., *Grace for Grace*, xxix; Lamberigts, "Pelagius and Pelagians," 258–278.

89. *Conf.* 13. Boniface Ramsey, "John Cassian and Augustine," 114–115. Ramsey notes that Cassian positively references Hilary, Ambrose, Jerome, Rufinus, Gregory Nazianzen, Athanasius, and John Chrysostom— and "Augustine alone is referred to without any encomium" (ibid., 115).

90. "*affectus* (adf-), ūs, m. afficio. I. A state of body, and esp. of mind produced in one by some influence (cf. affectio, I.), a state or disposition of mind, affection, mood: *adfectuum duae sunt species: alteram Graeci* πάθος *vocant, alteram* ἦθος" (Lewis and Short, *A Latin Dictionary*).

91. In the difference of a macron, we move from "ἦθος, εος, τό (cf. ἔθος), A. *an accustomed place*; II. *custom, usage*: in pl., *manners, customs*, 2. *disposition, character*" to "ἔθος, εος, τό, A. *custom, habit*," with ἔθει (noun sg neut dat epic ionic) indicating "by habit, habitually." See Liddell and Scott, eds., *A Greek-English Lexicon*.

Ethical virtue, ἠθική, comes primarily from habit, ἔθους, as opposed to nature or teaching. Consider, for example, how Aristotle differentiates these three sources: "γίνεσθαι δ' ἀγαθοὺς οἴονται οἳ μὲν φύσει οἳ δ' ἔθει οἳ δὲ διδαχῇ" ("Now some thinkers hold that virtue is a gift of nature; others think we become good by habit, others that we can be taught to be good"). See Aristotle, *Nicomachean Ethics*, 1179b.

92. Consider Gilbert Ryle's distinction between declarative knowledge and procedural knowledge, where "know-how" requires training and habituation in the particulars of the practices. See Ryle, "Knowing How and Knowing That," 25–61.

93. Hollywood, *Acute Melancholia and Other Essays*, 63.

94. Hollywood, *Sensible Ecstasy*, 278.

95. Hollywood, "Song, Experience, and the Book," 68.

96. Cassian is often read in terms of "interiority," not just in Foucault, but in twentieth-century French scholarship contemporary to his own work. Terrence Kardong notes in a poignant footnote: "The insight that all of Cassian's works are part of a drive toward interiorization is from Adalbert de Vogüé. I was fortunate enough to sit in his classes on Cassian in Rome (1975–76), and the notes from those lectures form the backbone of this article." See Kardong, "John Cassian's Evaluation of Monastic Practices," 82–105.

97. Malina, "Pain, Power, and Personhood," 164.

98. Martin, *The Corinthian Body*, 21.

99. Castelli, "Mortifying the Body, Curing the Soul," 136.

100. Paul Dilley similarly stresses how strict Cartesian divisions between mental and physical processes do not apply to contexts like that of late antique monasticism, focusing instead on how "cognitive disciplines trained *embodied* minds, through 'heart-work' on thoughts and emotions that was closely integrated with vigils, labor, fasting, corporal discipline, and other forms of physical exertion." See Dilley, *Monasteries and the Care of Souls*, 15.

101. Clark, "Foucault, the Fathers, and Sex," 619–41, esp. 622.

102. Foucault redescribes his intellectual work over decades: "Connecting together modes of veridiction, techniques of governmentality, and practices of the self is basically what I have always been trying to do." See Foucault, *The Courage of Truth*, 8.

103. Khawaja, *The Religion of Existence*, 60, 61.

104. Martin, Gutman, and Hutton, eds., *Technologies of the Self*, 19. See note 26 above for the archival material from "*septembre 1980*" as the earlier iteration of this work by Foucault in "Berkeley et New York University, 1980."

105. A particularly radical form of *parresia* is rooted in Cynicism, notably in "the themes of scandal, of indifference to the opinion of other and to the structures of power." See Foucault, *The Courage of Truth*, 318 and *Le Courage de la vérité, Le Gouvernement de soi et des autres II*. Foucault describes how certain forms of Christianity radicalize Cynicism.

106. Furey, "Body, Society, and Subjectivity in Religious Studies," 13.

107. Miller draws the distinction between "life" (βιός) and "way of life" (πολιτεία) in the *Vita Antonii* and the *Historia monachorum*, the latter of which uses "individual biographical sketches as metaphors for the form of human subjectivity to which the text as a whole is devoted." See Miller, "Strategies of Representation in Collective Biography," 231.

Chapter 1   Forms of Agency and Ways of Life

1. *Inst.* 4.24.2. *ut scilicet diurnis umoribus radicatum atque in antiquam arborem reuiuiscens diffusis ramis amoenitatem oculis atque umbraculum in aestu feruenti subter residentibus exhiberet.*

2. *Inst.* 4.24.4. *sedulitatem tacitus senex latenter diebus singulis exploraret uideretque eum simplici cordis affectu mandatum suum uelut diuinitus emissum sine ulla permutatione uultus uel rationis discussione seruare.*

3. Ibid. Note the centrality of the sense of smell to the construction of Abba John's sanctity. For more on smell in late ancient Christianity, see Susan Ashbrook Harvey's *Scenting Salvation*. For the senses as part of a broader turn to materiality in the fourth through the seventh centuries, see Patricia Cox Miller's *The Corporeal Imagination*.

4. Ward, trans., *Sayings of the Desert Fathers*, 73. "It was said of Abba John the Dwarf that he withdrew and lived in the desert at Scetis with an old man of Thebes. His Abba, taking a piece of dry wood, planted it and said to him, 'Water it every day with a bottle of water, until it bears fruit.' Now the water was so far away that he had to leave in the evening and return the following morning. At the end of three years the wood came to life and bore fruit. Then the old man took some of the fruit and carried it to the church, saying to the brethren, 'Take and eat the fruit of obedience.'"

Διηγήσαντο περὶ τοῦ ἀββᾶ Ἰωάννου τοῦ κολοβοῦ, ὅτι ἀναχωρήσας πρὸς Θηβαῖον γέροντα εἰς Σκῆτιν, ἐκάθητο ἐν τῇ ἐρήμῳ. Λαβὼν δὲ ὁ ἀββᾶς αὐτοῦ ξύλον ξηρὸν, ἐφύτευσε καὶ εἶπεν αὐτῷ· Καθ' ἡμέραν πότιζε τοῦτο λαγύνιον ὕδατος, ἕως καρπὸν ποιήσει. Ἦν δὲ μακρὰν ἀπ' αὐτῶν τὸ ὕδωρ, ὡς ἀπὸ ὀψὲ ἀπελθεῖν καὶ ἐλθεῖν πρωΐ. Μετὰ δὲ τρία ἔτη, ἔζησε καὶ καρπὸν ἐποίησε·καὶ λαβὼν ὁ γέρων τὸν καρ πὸν αὐτοῦ, ἤνεγκεν εἰς τὴν ἐκκλησίαν, λέγων τοῖς ἀδελφοῖς·Λάβετε, φάγετε καρπὸν ὑπακοῆς. See Migne, *Patrologiae cursus completus*, vol. 65.

5. Ibid.

6. Williams, *Ethics and the Limits of Philosophy*, 4. For more on ancient ethics and philosophy as a way of life, see Hadot, *Philosophy as a Way of Life*, and Cooper, *Pursuits of Wisdom*.

7. Williams, *Ethics and the Limits of Philosophy*, vii.

8. Bernard Williams would turn his inquiry to tragedy in *Shame and Necessity*.

9. Nussbaum, *The Fragility of Goodness*, 12. Nussbaum opens up a range of ethical questions in ancient literature in *The Fragility of Goodness* and *Upheavals of Thought*.

10. Hadot, *Philosophy as a Way of Life*, 264.

11. Ibid., 102. Hadot, *Exercices spirituels et philosophie antique*, 20.

12. Ibid., 57.

13. Taylor, *Sources of the Self*, 3.

14. Ibid.

15. Wyschogrod, *Saints and Postmodernism*, xiii.

16. Roberts, *Encountering Religion*, 18.

17. Schilbrack, *Philosophy and the Study of Religions*, 3, 25.

18. Bush, *Visions of Religion*, 17.

19. Lewis, *Why Philosophy Matters to the Study of Religion*, 29–42, 52–53.

20. Hollywood, *Acute Melancholia and Other Essays*, 238.

21. Lewis, "Ethnography, Anthropology, and Comparative Religious Ethics," 398, and Lewis, Schofer, Stalnaker, and Berkson, "Anthropos and Ethics," 177. Lee Yearley establishes an influential approach to ethics and religious studies in *Mencius and Aquinas*.

22. Bucar, *Creative Conformity*, 3.

23. Stalnaker, "Virtue as Mastery in Early Confucianism," 407; "Comparative Religious Ethics and the Problem of 'Human Nature,'" 187–224; and *Overcoming Our Evil*.

24. Schofer, "Embodiment and Virtue in a Comparative Perspective," 715–728, and "Self, Subject, and Chosen Subjection," 255–91.

25. Lewis, "Ethical Formation and Ordinary Life"; "Frames of Comparison," 225–253; and *Freedom and Tradition in Hegel*.

26. "Autonomy of the will is the property of the will by which it is a law to itself." See Immanuel Kant, *Groundwork of the Metaphysics of Morals*, 89. This view is similar to Augustine's view of the will as singular for its self-determining capacity, as we will see in Chapter 3. See Augustine, *On the Free Choice of the Will . . . , and Other Writings*.

27. Bourdieu, *The Logic of Practice*, 56–59, 68, and Bourdieu, *Outline of a Theory of Practice*.

28. Mauss, "Les techniques du corps." Asad points out that Bourdieu does not credit Mauss's use of *habitus* and gives an excellent account of how "Mauss was attempting to define an anthropology of practical reason—not in the Kantian sense of universalizable ethical rules, but in that of historically constituted practical knowledge, which articulates an individual's learned capacities." See Asad, *Genealogies of Religion*, 75–76.

29. Butler, *Gender Trouble*, 195.

30. Ibid., 175–193. See also Butler, *Excitable Speech*, 134–163.

31. Butler, *Bodies That Matter*, 15. See also Butler, *The Psychic Life of Power*, 83–86.

32. Butler, *Excitable Speech*, 152.

33. Butler, *Bodies That Matter*, ix, 83–84.

34. Butler, *Precarious Life*, 26.

35. Hollywood, "Performativity, Citationality, Ritualization," 95.

36. Ibid., 96.

37. Common to these accounts is Talal Asad's basic differentiation of agent from subject, where the former need not have conscious recognition in order to have effects. See Asad, *Genealogies of Religion*, 16.

38. Young, *On Female Body Experience*, 8–26.

39. Ibid., 7. Young's critical stance toward existential phenomenology allows her ethics to sidestep a popular warning given by scholars of religion, such as Gavin Flood, that "adopting phenomenology, the science of religion carries with it the idea of the detached observer or epistemic subject who understands the presentations to consciousness from a privileged distance." See Flood, *Beyond Phenomenology*, 117.

The peril for the study of religion, Manuel Vasquez explains, is that "this distancing allows the phenomenologist to ignore the body and claim that s/he can retrieve the unchanging essence of religion through successive reduction." See Vasquez, *More Than Belief*, 107–108.

40. Young, *On Female Body Experience*, 6.

41. Burrus, "*Begotten, Not Made*," 5.

42. Hollywood, *Acute Melancholia and Other Essays*, 60.

43. *Inst.* 11.16.

44. *Inst.* 11.18.

45. *Inst.* 6.13.1; *Inst.* 5.38; *Inst.* 9.6. Citing Basil of Caesarea, Cassian notes that "incorruption of the flesh" comes not from abstinence as such but from *puritas cordis* (*Inst.* 6.19).

46. *Conf.* 7.26.3. For the virtue of the monk who does not even see the face of his mother, see *Inst.* 5.38.

47. Passing references to women (sometimes generically referred to with men) include: *Inst.* Pref. 1; *Inst.* 1.8; *Inst.* 4.16; *Inst.* 10.2; *Inst.* 10.6; *Inst.* 10.21; *Conf.* 1.20; and *Conf.* 19.16. For references to women in connection with avarice, see *Inst.* 7.11, and, with lust, *Conf.* 24.17. *Inst.* 6.12 includes a reference to Matthew 5:28 in which even looking at a woman with lust involves adultery. Eve, of course, is present in *Conf.* 8.11.

48. Caesarius of Arles, *The Rule for Nuns of St. Caesarius of Arles.*

49. Foucault, *The History of Sexuality*, Vol. 1: *Introduction*, 86.

50. Foucault, *The History of Sexuality*, Vol. 2: *The Use of Pleasure*, 9.

51. On the need to critique modernity's limited construction of agency, Thomas Pfau argues for an account of agency vis-à-vis concepts of the human will and the human person, foregrounding the western thirteenth-century synthesis of Augustine and Aristotle. See Pfau, *Minding the Modern*, 14.

52. See Theodore Schatzki, *The Site of the Social*, 45–46, 191, 206, and *The Timespace of Human Activity*, 204.

53. Cassian's texts counter Foucault's reading of him at these three points.

54. *Inst.* Pref. 5: "For the whole of [the monastic life] consists in experience and practice alone." *Totum namque in sola experientia usu que consistit.*

Chapter 2   CASSIAN THE ETHICIST

1. *Conf.* 6.1.1–2.

2. *Conf.* 6.1.2.

3. *Conf.* 6.1.3.

4. Aurelii Augustini, *De civitate Dei*, Liber XI.IX, 40–41; Marcus Dods, trans., *City of God*, 11.9. *mali enim nulla natura est; sed amissio boni mali nomen accepit.*

5. *Conf.* 6.1.2. *dominus passus fuerit erga suos famulos facinus perpetrari.*

6. *Conf.* 6.16.3. *qui bonitatem non industriae studio, sed naturaliter possidens.*

7. Sulpicius Severus, "Life of Martin of Tours," and Harper, "John Cassian and Sulpicius Severus."

8. *Inst.* Pref. 8. *non de mirabilibus dei, sed de correctione morum nostrorum et consummatione uitae perfectae secundum ea, quae a senioribus nostris accepimus.*

9. For more on Cassian's origins and biography, see Chadwick, *John Cassian*; Coman, "Les 'Scythes' Jean Cassien et Denys le Petit"; Theodor Damian, "Some Critical Considerations and New Arguments"; Goodrich, *Contextualizing Cassian*; Harmless, *Desert Christians*; Marrou, "Jean Cassien à Marseille," and "La patrie de Jean Cassien"; Rousseau, *Ascetics, Authority, and the Church*; Shepherd Jr., "John Cassian by Owen Chadwick"; and Stewart, *Cassian the Monk*.

10. Stewart notes that Castor is Bishop of Apta Julia from 419, making it the earliest time for the composition of the *Institutes*; the first set of *Conferences* (1–10) were then composed in the "early to middle 420s" (Stewart, *Cassian the Monk*, 16).

11. For general treatments of Cassian, see Fernand Cabrol, "Cassien"; Cappuyns, "Cassien"; Cristiani, *Jean Cassien*; Dunn, "Asceticism and

Monasticism, Vol. 2: Western"; Godet, "Jean Cassien"; and Michel Olphe-Galliard, "Jean Cassien."

12. The paucity of Cassian's autobiographical details versus the richness of Augustine's, for example, is notable, yet, as I will argue in chapter 3, can be read as having ethical objectives. Panayiotis Tzamalikos has argued that John Cassian is a historical fiction and the writings attributed to him were actually penned by a sixth-century Greek author, Cassian the Sabaite. I find Tzamalikos's textual analysis and interpretive claims interesting, but I rely on the accrued historical evidence for the fifth-century John Cassian and remain skeptical of his erasure. Columba Stewart's review deftly addresses (and dismantles) Tzamalikos's argument in "Another Cassian?" See Tzamalikos, *A Newly Discovered Greek Father*, and *The Real Cassian Revisited*.

13. Cassian refers to his family's land as wooden (*Conf.* 24.1.3), with cold weather (*Conf.* 24.8.5) and not many monks in the area (*Conf.* 24.18). Cassian had at least one sister, to whom he refers in his *Institutes* (*Inst.* 11.18); he learned literature and was well educated (*Conf.* 14.12). Marrou argues for how Cassian describes his homeland in *Conference* 24.8.5 (Marrou, "La patrie de Jean Cassien"). However, Karl Suso Frank thinks *Conference* 24 presents an ideal, not real, landscape (Frank, "John Cassian on John Cassian," 424). See also Tracy Keefer Seiler's, "Gennadius of Marseille's *De Viris Inlustribus* and John Cassian."

14. On Cassian's bilingualism and education, see Chadwick, *John Cassian*, 9–10; Harmless, *Desert Christians*, 374–75; and Stewart, *Cassian the Monk*, 5.

15. *Conf.* 11.5.

16. Cassian is younger than Germanus (*Conf.* 14.9.4), and, in the words of Abba Moses, describes them as "one heart and soul in two bodies" (*Conf.* 1.1), clearly reminiscent of Aristotle's view of true friendship (Aristotle, *Nicomachean Ethics*, Books VIII–IX).

17. Stewart, *Cassian the Monk*, 7.

18. Stewart notes that Macarius was probably still alive when Cassian and Germanus were in Scetis, but Cassian does not mention meeting him (ibid., 10). See also Devos, "Saint Jean Cassien et Saint Moïse l'Éthiopien." For the influence of Evagrius on Cassian, see also Dysinger, *Psalmody and Prayer in the Writings of Evagrius Ponticus*, and Demacopoulos, *Five Models of Spiritual Direction in the Early Church*.

19. Kalvesmaki and Young, eds., *Evagrius and His Legacy*, 11. Direct resonance with Evagrian thought includes precise overlap of theme and formulation between Evagrius's *Praktikos* and Cassian's *Institutes* (*Inst.* 1

further elaborates the symbolism of the monastic habit for Evagrius, and *Inst.* 5–12 address the spirits and their remedies in a consolidated way). In *Conf.* 2–3, Cassian transmits Evagrius's attention to discernment and three renunciations (*Thoughts* 26; *Kephalaia Gnostica* 1.78–80). See Evagrius Ponticus, *Evagrius of Pontus*, 171–172. Other examples include (to name just a few) how Evagrius's attention to the concupiscent and irascible parts of the soul in *Thoughts* 27 corresponds to Cassian's treatment in *Conf.* 24; Evagrius's warning against excessive asceticism in *Thoughts* 35 corresponds to Cassian's ethos throughout the *Conferences*; and Evagrius's account of the dangerous demons permeates Cassian's work, notably in *Inst.* 5–12 and *Conf.* 5. Evagrius's *Chapters on Prayer* inform Cassian's work in their address of (A) The Practical Life, (B) True Prayer, and (C) Concluding Miscellany (as translator Robert E. Sinkewicz lays out the schema of the treatise)—with *Conf.* 9–10 centrally engaging questions of psalmody and imageless prayer.

   20. *Conf.* 1.1.

   21. *Conf.* 18.15.2–7. Harmless, *Desert Christians*, 376. Abba Paphnutius was the leader of the Origenist minority in Scetis when Theophilus of Alexandria turned against the Origenists, having defeated the Anthropomorphites. Other mention is made of Macarius the Great in *Conf.* 19.9.1.

   22. Stewart, *Cassian the Monk*, 12.

   23. Elizabeth Clark notes Cassian's claim to be present in 399 at Epiphany when Theophilus's letter against the Anthropomorphites arrived with the declaration that, of the four heads of congregations at Scetis, only Paphnutius (heading Cassian's own congregation) accepted Theophilus's position on the incorporeality of God (Clark, *The Origenist Controversy*, 50–51). We can recall Cassian's lament concerning the pitiful Serapion with his attachment to his physical friend, Christ; Cassian rhetorically affirms his own orthodoxy.

   24. Of the Anthropomorphite controversy and Cassian's depiction of Sarapion, Terrence Kardong views "a symbol of a general theme that runs throughout the work of Cassian, namely, the need to continually internalize and spiritualize the piety and practices of religion." See Kardong, "John Cassian's Evaluation of Monastic Practices," 82–105.

   I resist this stress on internalization and spiritualization with reference to the materialism of embodiment, affectivity, and community in Cassian's texts. I draw from Miller's argument concerning "'the material turn' in the fourth century, in which the religious significance of the material world was revalued. The phrase 'material turn' indicates a shift in the late ancient Christian sensibility regarding the signifying potential of the material world (including especially the human body), a shift that reconfigured the relation between materiality and meaning in a positive direction." See Miller, *The Corporeal Imagination*, 3.

25. Harmless, *Desert Christians*, 374. Theophilus's condemnation of Origenism and success with promoting an anti-Origenist cause made it imprudent for Cassian to connect himself to Evagrius, even though his teacher's views permeate his asceticism, instead "changing controversial terminology (e.g., *apatheia* becomes 'purity of heart')." See Stewart, *Cassian the Monk*, 12.

26. Lawrence J. Johnson, *Worship in the Early Church*, 159.

27. Stewart, *Cassian the Monk*, 14. A singularly reliable date in Cassian's biography is 404, when he was in Rome. See Dunn, "Cassian in Syria?"

28. Dunn, "Cassian in Syria?," 14. For those claiming that Cassian went to Antioch as an envoy for Alexander, see Driver, *John Cassian and the Reading of Egyptian Monastic Culture*; Griffe, "Cassien a-t-il été prêtre d'Antioche?," and *La Gaule chrétienne à l'époque romaine*, 342; Marrou, "Jean Cassien à Marseille"; and Rousseau, *Ascetics, Authority, and the Church*. Griffe notes: "Comme on le voit, aussi bien dans ce court billet que dans la lettre officielle, Cassien fait figure de chef de la délégation. Il est tout naturel de croire qu'une fois sa mission remplie, il soit réparti pour Antioche pour apporter la réponse du pape." See Griffe, "Cassien a-t-il été prêtre d'Antioche?," 244.

29. Johnson, *Worship in the Early Church*, 159. Massilia was a city with sea trade and Greek roots; the city was held against the Visigoths in 413 and remained "siege-proof" through the sixth century through "an effective, defensible wall-circuit throughout late antiquity." See Loseby, "Marseille," 168.

Its bishop during Cassian's time there was the renowned Proclus. This fact has made Richard Goodrich hypothesize that Cassian did not live in Massilia at all and was actually writing from Apta Iulia, for why would he neglect to honor his own bishop, Proclus, in his prefaces if he were indeed Massilian (Goodrich, *Contextualizing Cassian*, 225–227)? The scholarly consensus I follow, however, assumes that Cassian lived out his last years in Massilia.

30. When Arles would be under siege around 507/508, accounts have Caesarius sending his sister Caesaria and her fellow sisters to Cassian's monastery for women until 512. See Klingshirn, *Caesarius of Arles*, 107. After training in Cassian's female monastery, Caesaria went on to become abbess of Saint Jean of Arles. See McNamara and Halborg with Whatley, ed. and

trans., *Sainted Women of the Dark Ages*, 112–113. As Alexander Hwang notes, the tradition associating Cassian with the Abbey of St. Victor goes back only to the eleventh century. See Hwang, "Manifold Grace in John Cassian and Prosper of Aquitaine," 95.

31. For a later dating of the *Institutes* (c. 425), *Conferences* Part I (c. 426), Part II (c. 427), Part III (c. 428), see Cameron, "The Transmission of Cassian," 361–365, and Demacopoulos, *Five Models of Spiritual Direction*, 108.

32. Stewart, *Cassian the Monk*, 21–22, and Wessel, *Leo the Great and the Spiritual Rebuilding of a Universal Rome*, 235. See also Cassiani, *De incarnatione Domini contra Nestorium Libri VII*, and Cassien, *Traité de l'Incarnation*.

33. Humphries Jr., *Ascetic Pneumatology from John Cassian to Gregory the Great*, 3.

34. Weaver, "Introduction," xi. Eugene Teselle outlines two doctrinal questions motivating the controversy: one, on the transmission of "'original sin', and two, on the return to God vis-à-vis will and grace" (Eugene Teselle, "The Background: Augustine and the Pelagian Controversy," 1).

35. Susan Wessel notes that "Valentinian's decree in 425 to remove the Pelagian bishops from Gaul had resulted in only limited success." See Wessel, *Leo the Great and the Spiritual Rebuilding of a Universal Rome*, 84fn105.

36. Weaver, "Introduction," xii. See also Humphries Jr., "Prosper's Pneumatology," 103.

37. A.M.C. Casiday also calls for further consideration of Augustine's influence on Gallic contemporaries. See Casiday, "Grace and the Humanity of Christ."

38. "Prosper recognizes a problem of agency posed by the categories grace and will, at least enough to state explicitly that being led by the Spirit is not necessarily to be deprived of freedom." See Humphries, "Prosper's Pneumatology," 107.

39. Ibid., 101.

40. Stewart, *Cassian the Monk*, 19.

41. For the variety of Augustinianisms, see Humphries, *Ascetic Pneumatology*, 201–204.

42. Casiday, *Tradition and Theology in St. John Cassian*, 36–39.

43. Terrence Kardong, "John Cassian's Teaching on Perfect Chastity," 261, and "John Cassian's Evaluation of Monastic Practices," 103.

44. Weaver, *Divine Grace and Human Agency*, 198.

45. Stewart is careful to point out how polemics might have resulted in skewed views not practically lived: "In terms of the practice of the Christian

life, Augustine and Cassian may scarcely have differed: Augustine, after all, was a monastic founder himself. But in theological reflection on experience (and in controversy) Augustine and the monks of Gaul moved in opposite directions." See Stewart, *Cassian the Monk*, 19.

By contrast, Peter Brown points out how diametrically opposed the two authors were: "It is seldom that two Latin writers, each as gifted in their differing ways with such powers of introspection and each capable of such magnetic literary expression as Augustine and John Cassian, have reached such diametrically opposite conclusions as to what precisely they had seen in their own hearts." See Brown, *The Body and Society*, 423. Foucault's own embrace of Augustine over Cassian in *Les Aveux de la chair* suggests that he follows Brown's logic (Foucault, *Les Aveux de la chair*).

46. Demacopoulos, *Five Models of Spiritual Direction*, 110.

47. Harmless, *Desert Christians*, 403.

48. Kelly, *Cassian's Conferences*, 9. See also Stewart, *Cassian the Monk*, 5, 25. For more on Cassian's influence, see the last chapter of Chadwick, *John Cassian*, 148–162, and Saak, "Ex vita patrum formatur vita fratrum," 191–228.

49. Kelly, *Cassian's Conferences*, 7.

50. Chadwick, *John Cassian*, 148–162; Fiske, "Cassian and Monastic Friendship," 190; Stephen Lake, "Knowledge of the Writings of John Cassian in Early Anglo-Saxon England," 27–41; Lake, "Usage of the Writings of John Cassian," 95–121; Ramsey, *Conferences*, 7; and Stewart, *Cassian the Monk*, 24–25.

51. Caeserius of Arles pens the *Rule for Nuns* (*Regula virginum*) in 512 (Caeserius, *The Rule for Nuns of St. Caesarius of Arles*). For Cassian's influence on the Master, see Hagan, "The Master's Rearrangement of John Cassian's Signs of Humility."

52. For Cassian's reception by Benedict see *Regula Benedicti*, Caput 42 and 73 and de Vogüé, "Les mentions des oeuvres de Cassien chez Benoît et ses contemporains."

53. Stewart, *Cassian the Monk*, 156.

54. Ramsey, *Conferences*, 459.

55. Rapp, "Desert, City, and Countryside," 110.

56. In his classic "study of social and cultural change," Peter Brown notes: "After 240, the sprawling empire had to face barbarian invasion and political instability on a scale for which it was totally unprepared." See Brown, *The World of Late Antiquity*, 22.

57. Castelli, *Martyrdom and Memory*, 37.

58. "The ease with which Christianity gained control of the upper classes of the Roman empire in the fourth century" is notable for Brown (*The World of Late Antiquity*, 26–28).

59. Wendt, *At the Temple Gates*, 40–73. Of the way that Christian discourse addressed political and cultural aspects of "the new social order," see Cameron, *Christianity and the Rhetoric of Empire*, 43. For the role of gnostic practices, see DeConick, Shaw, and Turner, eds., *Practicing Gnosis*.

60. Berzon, *Classifying Christians*, notably 4–27. Berzon argues: "As the heresiologists investigated the diversity of Christian sectarianism across the Mediterranean, they produced a textual world and worldview driven by the comparison of theologies and dispositions" (ibid., 9).

61. For an account of competition between cultic groups ("a conflict not between Christian and non-Christian, nor between Nicene and non-Nicene, but between Nicene and Nicene") and communal ritual action in the civic community of Constantinople, see Rebecca Stephens Falcasantos, *Constantinople*.

62. Paul M. Blowers succinctly notes the connection between themes of creation, evil, and suffering and "the collapse of the Roman regime, the cultural shifts attending barbarian occupation, and a series of natural disasters." See Blowers, "Doctrine of Creation," 919.

63. Susanna Elm describes the climate and the geographical, social, and political conditions of the Egyptian centers (*Virgins of God*, 21–22). While the characterization of people fleeing debt requires nuance, this picture gives a sense of the deterioration of social order. For more on the social upheaval of the late fourth and early fifth centuries, see Markus, *The End of Ancient Christianity* and, for its impact on how life as a Christian was to be understood, see Phelan Jr., "The Long Shadow of Augustine."

64. Goodrich argues for the influence of such upheaval on the work of Cassian (*Contextualizing Cassian*, 9). For changes in Gaul, see Cameron, *The Mediterranean World in Late Antiquity*, notably 1–10, 33–56.

65. Harmless, *Desert Christians*, 379. Demacopoulos, in *Five Models of Spiritual Direction*, 108–109, makes a similar point.

66. *Inst.* Pref. 3; Claudia Rapp analyzes this threefold force "as a geographical setting," as a "state of mind," and as a "typological landscape" ("Desert, City, and Countryside," 111).

67. Guy, "Jean Cassien, Historien du Monachisme Egyptien?," 363–372.

68. *Inst.* Pref. 1–2.

69. *Conf.* Pref. 1.2–3; *Conf.* 9.1.

70. *Conf.* Pref. 2.1–2. Honoratus founded the monastery between 400 and 410, yet by the time of Cassian's visit around 427, he claims it boasts "a large cenobium of brothers" (*Conf.* Pref. 2.1). See Klingshirn, *Caesarius of Arles*, 23.

71. Stewart, *Cassian the Monk*, 18.

72. Demacopoulos, *Five Models of Spiritual Direction*, 109.

73. Ibid., 13.

74. Casiday, "Tradition as a Governing Theme in the Writings of John Cassian," 194–195.

75. *Inst.* 2.3.4–5, 4.16.3; *Inst.* 2.1–3.1.

76. Harmless, *Desert Christians*, 379.

77. Chadwick, *John Cassian*, 42. Chadwick notes that this was an independent document probably codified by a monk in the eighth century.

78. Ramsey, trans., *Institutes*, 4.

79. *Inst.* 5–12.

80. Krueger, *Writing and Holiness*, 102.

81. Cassian's texts function similarly to how Derek Krueger describes Leontius, whose "text functions in the stead of a living saint, much as pilgrim narratives function for those unable to travel. Moreover he substitutes this narrative for his own body as a place from which to illustrate virtuous deeds." See Krueger, *Writing and Holiness*, 219–220.

82. Harmless, *Desert Christians*, 386. See also Papadogiannakis, "Instruction by Question and Answer," and "Encyclopedism." This choice of style by Cassian deserves further exploration because of the dearth of scholarship on it: "'*Erotapokriseis*'-literature has thus far been neglected by most scholars." See Volgers and Zamagni, eds., *Erotapokriseis*.

On the "moral exhortation" central to *paraenesis* in Cassian and other early monastic literature, see Rubenson, "Wisdom, Paraenesis, and the Roots of Monasticism," 521. Rubenson reflects modern assumptions concerning ethics as a domain of moral judgment by claiming that paraenesis is not ethical and provides "no theory from which to derive specific admonitions" (ibid.).

Stanley Stowers helps expand the understanding of *paraenesis* as including "not only precepts but also such things as advice, supporting argumentation, various modes of encouragement and dissuasion, the use of examples, modes of conduct and so on." See Stowers, *Letter Writing in Greco-Roman Antiquity*, 23.

83. Kelly, *Cassian's Conferences*, 7.

84. Michel Olphe-Galliard, classically, separates the two ways of life. Of the active life in comparison to the contemplative life, he says: "La 'voie'

de la vie 'active' est moins ambitieuse. Parfaite, elle resetera inférieure à la Contemplation parfait. Mais plus facile, plus humble, et partant moins exposée à la ruine, elle a pour elle plus d'un sérieux avantage. S'il est rare qu'elle procure la jouissance de la prière perpétuelle, image du Bonheur eternal et perfection propre à la vie contemplative, elle n'est point dépourvue de ces faveurs plus fugitives que Dieu accorde, quand bon lui semble, à ceux qui s'y consacrent." See Olphe-Galliard, "Vie Contemplative et Vie Active d'après Cassien," 288.

85. *Inst.* 2.5.2; *Conf.* 1.1.1. *propositi nostri.*

86. *Conf.* 1.2.1. *Omnes, inquit, artes ac disciplinae scopon quondam, id est destinationem, et telos, hoc est finem proprium habent: ad quem respiciens uniuscuiusque artis industrius adpetitor, cunctos labores et pericula dispendiaque universa aequanimiter libenterque sustentat.*

87. See also *Conf.* 1.4.1; *Conf.* 1.4.4.

88. *Conf.* 1.2.1–3.

89. *Conf.* 1.2.3. *Habet ergo et nostra professio scopon proprium ac finem suum, pro quo labores cunctos non solum infatigabiliter, uerum etiam gratanter inpendimus, ob quem nos ieiuniorum inedia non fatigat, uigiliarum lassitudo delectat, lectio ac meditatio scripturarum continuata non satiat, labor etiam incessabilis nuditasque et omnium rerum priuatio, horror quoque huius uastissimae solitudinis non deterret. ob quem uos ipsi procul dubio parentum spreuistis affectum et patrium solum ac delicias mundi tot pertransitis regionibus despexistis, ut ad nos homines rusticos et idiotas atque in hoc heremi squalore degentes peruenire possetis.*

90. *Inst.* 4.39.3.

91. I engage Cassian in a way similar to Mark Jordan's use of Thomas Aquinas to unfold an "exhortation to rereading" the *Summa* with attention to how "moral formation ultimately depends on these scenes of embodied instruction." See Jordan, *Teaching Bodies*, 15–16.

92. The influence of Evagrius of Pontus on Cassian has been well documented since Salvatore Marsili wrote *Giovanni Cassiano ed Evagrio Pontico*, and included his constructions of prayer, scripture, and demonology. More proximately, see Columba Stewart's "Evagrius beyond Byzantium."

93. *Conf.* 14; *Conf.* 1.3. Consider, for example, Aristotle's *Nicomachean Ethics*, Book 6, where development of practical knowledge (a coupling of *techne* and *phronesis*) and theoretical knowledge (*episteme*) alone leads to wisdom (*sophia*) when coupled with intellect (*nous*). Ramsey notes that the *praktike/theoretike* divide appears most influentially in Aristotle's *Metaphysics*, 2.1, and that Cassian likely inherited it from Evagrius. See Ramsey,

Conferences, 499. This resonates with Luke Dysinger's account of Evagrius, for whom "spiritual progress occurs in simultaneous rhythms of ascetical practice (*praktike*) and contemplation (*theoria*)." See Dysinger, "Evagrius Ponticus, Exegete of the Soul," 74–75.

Paul Devos notes: "C'est-à-dire ce qui caractérise, d'une part, l'anachorète parfait et, d'autre part, le cénobite consommé; en termes evagriens, qui avaient cours sur place: la praktike et la theoretike." See Devos, "Saint Jean Cassien et Saine Moise l'Ethiopien," 69. See also Olphe-Galliard, "Vie Contemplative et Vie Active d'apres Cassien," 253, and Stewart, "Writing about John Cassian in the 1990s," 346.

94. Dysinger, *Psalmody and Prayer in the Writings of Evagrius Ponticus*, 27. Evagrius, *Praktikos* 50, 79, and 83. Evagrius futher differentiates between πρακτική as ascetical practice and understanding of the self and θεωρητική as contemplative knowledge in the form of both contemplation of the scriptures and contemplation of creation (φυσική), as well as knowledge of God (θεολογική) (ibid., 29).

95. Kardong, "John Cassian's Evaluation of Monastic Practices," 89. See Cassian Folsom on the monastic conversation: "That goal is two-fold: a life of virtue and a life of prayer. (These correspond to the active and contemplative aspects of life in the earliest understanding of those terms)." See Folsom, "Anger, Dejection, and Acedia in the Writings of John Cassian," 219.

96. *Conf.* Pref. 5. *Proinde ab exteriore ac uisibili monachorum cultu, quem prioribus digessimus libris, ad inuisibilem interioris hominis habitum transeamus, et de canonicarum orationum modo ad illius quam apostolus praecipit orationis perpetuae iugitatem ascendat eloquium.*

97. Chadwick's influence is certainly felt in Foucault's reading of Cassian—and Foucault's archives at the Bibliothèque Nationale de France include copious notes on Chadwick's *John Cassian* as well as the work listed on bibliographies. See particularly Bibliothèque Nationale de France, NAF 28730, Dossier No. XXII, "Pères de l'Église" and Dossier no. XXIV, "Seminaire 'Dire vrai sur soi-même.'"

Passages on inner versus outer include: "These books are designed more for the observance of the outer man, and the formation of cenobites" (*Inst.* 2.9); "Those following will relate more to inner discipline, the perfection of the heart, and the life and teaching of anchorites" (*Inst.* 2.9); and "Thus, if your outer right cheek has received a blow from the striker, the inner man should offer his right cheek to be struck as well in humble accord, suffering along with the outer man and as it were submitting and subjecting its own body to the injustice of the striker, so that the inner man may not be disturbed even silently within itself at the blow dealt the outer man." *Per hoc omnem penitus iracundiae fomitem de profundis cupiens animae penetralibus extirpare, id est, ut si exterior dextera tua inpetum ferientis exceperit, interior quoque homo per humilitatis adsensum dexteram suam praebeat uerberandam, conpatiens exterioris hominis passioni et quodammodo succumbens atque subiciens suum corpus ferientis iniuriae, ne exterioris hominis caede uel tacitus intra se moueatur interior (Conf.* 16.22.2).

98. Harmless, *Desert Christians*, 401.

99. Ibid., 402.

100. Rousseau, *Ascetics, Authority, and the Church*, 182.

101. Ibid., 178.

102. *Conf.* 22.3.4. *omnem perfectionis et castimoniae summam in sola credat exterioris hominis castigatione consistere . . . disciplinis interioris hominis instituta.*

103. Stewart, *Cassian the Monk*, 54.

104. Alexander Golitizin, "A Testimony to Christianity as Transfiguration," 131.

105. Humphries, *Ascetic Pneumatology*, 29.

106. See Niki Kasumi Clements, "The Asceticism of Interpretation."

107. Brun, *Hermeneutics Ancient and Modern*.

108. Torjesen, *Hermeneutical Procedure and Theological Structure in Origen's Exegesis*, notably 138–147, and de Lubac, *History and Spirit*.

109. Building from *oikonomia* as a form of "ethical accommodation" in biblical exegesis, Kathy Eden focuses on Basil of Caesarea and Augustine of Hippo to argue for the principle of *oikonomia* as still dominant in the fourth century. See Eden, *Hermeneutics and the Rhetorical Tradition*, 42; Aurelii Augustini, *De Doctrina Christiana*; and Augustine of Hippo, *On Christian Doctrine*, translated by D. W. Robertson.

110. Young, *Biblical Exegesis and the Formation of Christian Culture*, 186.

111. de Lubac, *Medieval Exegesis*, 134–135; Caplan, *Of Eloquence*, 98–99. Caplan maintains the following translation of the mnemonic device from Nicolas of Lyra: "*The literal gives the deeds, / Allegory tells what to believe, / The moral tells how to act, / Anagogical, the direction one tends.*" See also Brun, *Hermeneutics Ancient and Modern*, 139–158.

112. *Conf.* 14.15.

113. Guyette, "John Cassian on Faith and Action," 91.

114. Clark, *The Origenist Controversy*, 59.

115. Weaver, "Access to Scripture," 367.

116. Humphries, *Ascetic Pneumatology*, 17.

117. *Inst.* 2.14. *ita ut quid ex quo pendeat, haud facile possit a quoquam discerni, id est, utrum propter meditationem spiritalem incessabile manuum opus exerceant, an propter operis iugitatem tam praeclarum spiritus profectum scientiaeque lumen acquirant.*

118. Stroumsa, "The Scriptural Movement of Late Antiquity and Christian Monasticism," 70.

119. *Conf.* 14.14.

120. I follow how Rachel J. D. Smith's argument regarding Thomas of Cantimpré's hagiographies "considers *how* they seek to edify and offer figures for emulation; it argues that these works are theological documents that perform their theologizing in a rhetorically specific way." See Smith, *Excessive Saints*, 6.

121. *Conf.* 14.16.

122. Colish, *The Stoic Tradition from Antiquity to the Early Middle Ages*, 115.

123. Stewart, *Cassian the Monk*, 40.

124. Ibid., 7.

125. Humphries, *Ascetic Pneumatology*, 13.

126. Casiday, *Tradition and Theology in St. John Cassian*, 6–9.

127. Rousseau, *Ascetics, Authority, and the Church*; Harmless, *Desert Christians*; and Goodrich, *Contextualizing Cassian* are particularly notable. For research on reading practices and discourse analysis, see Leyser, *Authority and Asceticism*, and Driver, *John Cassian and the Reading of Egyptian Monastic Culture*.

128. Shaw, *The Burden of the Flesh*.

129. Kardong, "John Cassian's Evaluation of Monastic Practice," 103.

130. *Conf.* 1.15.

Chapter 3   CASSIAN ON HUMAN EFFORT

1. *Conf.* 13.1. The previous conference is *Conference* 12, "On Chastity" (*De castitate*).

2. *Conf.* 13.1. *meritum humanae cassasset industriae . . . summum desiderium incognitae nobis castitatis.*

3. *Conf.* 1.17.1. *Alioquin nec liberum in homine maneret arbitrium nec in nobis staret nostrae correctionis industria.*

4. *Conf.* 13.3.1. *nihilque laborantibus illam iugem sudoris instantiam contulisse, quia non fuit domini opitulatione directa.*

5. Ibid. *nisi eau et pluuiarum oportunitas et hiemis tranquilla serenitas subsequatur.*

6. *Conf.* 13.3.3. *exercendum omne opus ruris.*

7. *Conf.* 13.3.4.

8. *Conf.* 13.3.1.

9. Rebecca Weaver stresses Cassian's "highly variegated" understanding of divine grace as present in Origen's works as well: "The notion of grace as variegated was important to Cassian's position, for it served to protect the self-initiating character of the human will. . . . Origen had insisted on the preponderance of grace and, at the same time, maintained human self-initiative. The result was a doctrine of grace as self-initiated divine action, portrayed in both healing and teaching images, interacting with self-initiated human action, consisting of thinking and willing as well as doing." See Weaver, *Divine Grace and Human Agency*, 72.

10. Elizabeth Castelli importantly challenges assumptions of dualisms in early Christianity: "On closer examination, however, this dualism which operates as an uninterrogated given in the conceptual framework of many studies of early Christianity comes to appear less thoroughgoing, more mediated or open to competing interpretation, and ultimately less helpful a heuristic concept in trying to understand what was at stake for early Christians in their sometimes extreme pieties of the body." See Castelli, "Mortifying the Body, Curing the Soul," 137.

11. *Conf.* 13.9.4.

12. *Conf.* 13.11.4. *Haec ergo duo, id est uel gratia dei uel liberum arbitrium sibi quidem inuicem uidentur aduersa, sed utraque concordant et utraque nos pariter debere suscipere pietatis ratione colligimus, ne unum horum homini subtrahentes ecclesiasticae fidei regulam excessisse uideamur.*

13. *Conf.* 13.12.1. *Nec enim talem deus hominem fecisse credendus est, qui nec uelit umquam nec possit bonum. alioquin nec liberum ei permisit arbitrium, si ei tantummodo malum ut uelit et possit, bonum uero a semet ipso nec uelle nec posse concessit.*

14. *Conf.* 13.9.5. *quod beneficio creatoris indultum est.*

15. *Conf.* 13.12.5. *ut nihil nisi id quod malum atque peruersum est humanae ascribamus naturae.*

16. Cassian asks, in this respect: "What is the point of having longed for the grace of good health if God, who has bestowed the use of life itself,

does not also impart vigorous well-being?" *Quid autem prodest sanitatis gratiam concupisse, nisi deus, qui uitae ipsius usum tribuit, etiam uigorem incolumitatis inpertiat?* See *Conf.* 13.9.5.

I take *sanitatis* in the sense of soundness of body, mind, and health: "sāni-tas, ātis, f. sanus, I. *Soundness of body, health*; II. Trop. A. *Soundness of mind* (opp. to passionate excitement), *right reason, good sense, discretion, sanity*, etc.; B. Of style, *soundness* or *correctness of style, propriety, regularity, purity*, etc." See Lewis and Short, eds., *A Latin Dictionary*.

17. *Conf.* 13.12.8.

18. *Conf.* 13.12.7. In one of a handful of extrabiblical citations in the *Conferences*, Cassian cites *The Shepherd of Hermas*, 6, no. 2 (ed. Bart D. Ehrman), as teaching that "freedom of will is at a human being's disposal to a certain degree. In it two angels—that is, a good one and a bad one—are said to be attached to each one of us, but it is up to the human to choose which to follow."

19. Weaver, *Divine Grace and Human Agency*, 235.

20. *Conf.* 13.12.3.

21. *Conf.* 4.12.1.

22. *Conf.* 13.10.2; see also *Conf.* 13.10.1, "freedom of our will" (*liber-tatem . . . nostri . . . arbitrii*) and "power of free will" (*uirtutem liberi arbitrii*).

23. *Conf.* 13.18.5.

24. *Conf.* 13.8.4. *Et non solum sancta desideria benignus inspirat, sed etiam occasiones praestruit uitae et oportunitatem boni effectus ac salutaris uiae directionem demonstrat errantibus.*

25. *Conf.* 13.3.2, 5.

26. *Inst.* 12.18.

27. *Conf.* 13.14.9.

28. In these cases, Cassian seems to protect divine power by making room for divine grace to act in unconstrained and mysterious ways. *Conf.* 13.16.1; *Conf.* 13.17.1.

29. For the influence of Augustine on Cassian (which should not be confused with approval), see Goodrich, *Contextualizing Cassian*, 65–116, and, "John Cassian," *The Oxford Guide to the Historical Reception of Augustine*, 1221–1224, and Ramsey, "John Cassian: Student of Augus-tine," and "John Cassian and Augustine," 117–118. Cassian probably knew Augustine's writings that were circulating in Gaul at the time: "This reading included at least the *De mendacio*, the *Contra mendacium*, the *Confessions*, one or two sermons on the Gospel of John, and Letters 130 and 137." See Ramsey, "John Cassian: Student of Augustine," 14.

30. Brown, *The Body and Society*, 420.

31. Weaver, *Divine Grace and Human Agency*, 71.

32. Augustine of Hippo, *On the Free Choice of the Will*, xviii–xix.

33. Brown, *The Body and Society*, 422.

34. Augustine of Hippo, *City of God*, 22.30.

35. Brown, *The Body and Society*, 422.

36. *Inst.* 6. For Cassian's work on the struggle in the monastic life and the need for spiritual encouragement, see Millican, "Spiritual Encouragement in the *Conferences* of John Cassian (Part II)."

37. Ramsey, *Conferences*, 461.

38. Weaver, *Divine Grace and Human Agency*, 106.

39. A.M.C. Casiday notes how little is known about Prosper, mainly gleaned through his works and Gennadius; he reiterates the unverifiable claim that "Prosper belonged to Cassian's monastery." See Casiday, *Tradition and Theology in St. John Cassian*, 20.

40. Abba Chaeremon's third conference is *Conference* 13, which Ramsey calls the "most controversial of all twenty-four" and "almost certainly . . . responsible for the fact that Cassian hardly enjoys the title of saint in the West, despite his vast influence." See Ramsey, *Conferences*, 459.

41. *Conf.* 13.8.4. *Qui cum in nobis ortum quendam bonae uoluntatis inspexerit, inluminat eam confestim atque confortat et incitat ad salutem, incrementum tribuens ei quam uel ipse plantauit uel nostro conatu uiderit emersisse.*

42. *Conf.* 13.9.5. *Ut autem euidentius clareat etiam per naturae bonum, quod beneficio creatoris indultum est, nonnumquam bonarum uoluntatum prodire principia, quae tamen nisi a domino dirigantur ad consummationem uirtutum peruenire non possunt, apostolus testis est dicens: uelle enim adiacet mihi, perficere autem bonum non inuenio.*

43. Hwang, "Manifold Grace in John Cassian and Prosper of Aquitaine," 99.

44. Hwang, "Prosper, Cassian, and Vincent."

45. Matthew Pereira articulates Cassian's distance from Pelagius and Augustine alike: "On the one hand, Cassian's evaluation of the mutual reciprocation between divine grace and human agency distanced himself from Pelagius's overemphasis on free will, whereas on the other hand, his belief in the possibility that the faithful could take the initial step toward God placed him in direct opposition against Augustine." See Pereira, "Augustine, Pelagius, and the Southern Gallic Tradition," 185.

46. Harmless, *Desert Christians*, 400.

47. Ibid. For the support given by the Council of Orange (529 CE) to Augustine's view as an implicit rejection of Cassian, see Goodrich, "John Cassian," 1221–1224.

48. Ramsey, *Conferences*, 459; Harmless, *Desert Christians*, 400.

49. Casiday, "Rehabilitating John Cassian," 284. In *Tradition and Theology in St. John Cassian*, Casiday also argues that Cassian was fighting not Augustine but Pelagians.

We should question, however, whether we are to understand Cassian as "pre-Augustinian," as Michael Hanby suggests (and therefore not yet informed by Augustine's critique of the pagan virtues), since to frame the issue in those terms is to assume that a damning critique of pagan virtue is necessary. See Hanby, "Augustine and Descartes."

50. *Conf.* 13.11.1. *Et ita sunt haec quodammodo indiscrete permixta atque confusa, ut quid ex quo pendeat inter multos magna quaestione uoluatur, id est utrum quia initium bonae uoluntatis praebuerimus misereatur nostri deus, an quia deus misereatur consequamur bonae uoluntatis initium. multi enim singula haec credentes ac iusto amplius adserentes uariis sibique contrariis sunt erroribus inuoluti.*

51. Ibid.

52. Weaver, *Divine Grace and Human Agency*, 129–130.

53. Ibid., 236. For more on Cassian and Origenism, see Keech, "John Cassian and the Christology of Romans 8:3." For more on Christology in relation to anthropology, see Grillmeier, "Jesus Christ, the Kyriakos Anthropos," 292.

54. Brown, *The Body and Society*, 422.

55. *Conf.* 13.13.5.

56. *Inst.* 12.13. *quam affectu atque uirtute et experimentis propriis.*

57. Consider, for instance, Peter Munz, who defends Cassian's view of divine grace and the human will by noting that Cassian's volition focuses on a negative conception of freedom (Munz, "John Cassian"). Similarly, Michael Hanby states: "The emphasis tends to fall on the negative capacity for rejection." See Hanby, "Augustine and Descartes," 467. See also Macqueen, "John Cassian on Grace and Free Will with Particular Reference to *Institutio* XII and *Collatio* XIII."

Philip Rousseau challenges Munz's reading of Cassian as rejecting the world by asserting Cassian's affirmation of the cenobitic life. See Rousseau, "Cassian, Contemplation, and the Coenobitic Life," 118. Rousseau argues convincingly that Cassian affirms divine grace when referring to its anteriority (*Conf.* 7.8.1; 13.3.5) and insists that "the beginning of a good will is bestowed upon us at the Lord's inspiration" (*Conf.* 3.8.1).

58. Babcock, "Grace, Freedom and Justice," 13.

59. Weaver, *Divine Grace and Human Agency*, 130.

60. Colish, *The Stoic Tradition from Antiquity to the Early Middle Ages*, 116. For an account foregrounding a synergist anthropology, see Sergey Horujy's *Practices of the Self and Spiritual Practices*, in which he situates the possibilities for the hermeneutics of the subject in relation to a synergistic anthropology that "has as its phenomenal base a particular kind of constitutive anthropological experience: *extreme human experience*, which it describes in terms of 'extreme anthropological manifestations.'" See Horujy, *Practices of the Self and Spiritual Practices*, 123.

61. Ibid.

62. *Conf.* 13.7.

63. *Conf.* 13.8.4. *Et idcirco hoc ab omnibus catholicis patribus definitur, qui perfectionem cordis non inani disputatione uerborum, sed re atque opere didicerunt, diuini esse muneris primum ut accendatur unusquisque ad desiderandum omne quod bonum est, sed ita ut in alterutram partem plenum sit liberae uoluntatis arbitrium: item que etiam secundum diuinae esse gratiae ut effici ualeant exercitia praedicta uirtutum, sed ita ut possibilitas non extinguatur arbitrii: tertium quoque ad dei munera pertinere ut adquisitae uirtutis perseuerantia teneatur, sed ita ut captiuitatem libertas addicta non sentiat.*

64. Ibid. *in alterutram partem plenum sit liberae uoluntatis arbitrium.*

65. Ibid. *possibilitas non extinguatur arbitrii.*

66. Ibid.

67. *Conf.* 13.9.4. *Nisi quod in his omnibus et gratia dei et libertas nostri declaratur arbitrii, quia etiam suis interdum motibus homo ad uirtutum adpetitus possit extendi, semper uero a domino indigeat adiuuari?*

68. For a succinct treatment of the correlation among dangerous thoughts, spirits, demons, and emotions, see Sorabji, *Emotion and Peace of Mind*, 357.

69. *Inst.* 5.1; Inst. 5.2.1 "harmful passions" (*noxias passiones*); *Conf.* 5.26.1, 2 "passion of gourmandizing" (*gulae passione*).

70. *Conf.* 5.27.2; *Inst.* 5.23.1.

71. Brakke, *Demons and the Making of the Monk*, 5.

72. *Inst.* 10.25. *tolerantia potius et conflictu didiceris triumphare.* Brakke also links the production of demonology in relation to "new modes of withdrawal." See David Brakke, "The Making of Monastic Demonology,"

48. With Cassian's translation of desert asceticism to Gallic monasticism, identity formation occurs less through the struggles of withdrawal and more through the struggles of community formation. My reading of Cassian through social and embodied lenses as well as with attention to his psychological acumen seeks to articulate the intersection of the "seemingly subjective" and the "more cultural" (ibid., 19–20).

73. *Inst.* 12.5.

74. Ibid.

75. *Inst.* 4.37. *Uersutus enim serpens calcanea nostra semper obseruat, id est insidiatur exitui nostro et usque ad finem uitae nostrae nos subplantare conatur.*

76. *Conf.* 7.24.

77. Shaw, *The Burden of the Flesh*, 149.

78. *Inst.* 5; *Inst.* 10.1.

79. Charles Stewart, "Erotic Dreams and Nightmares from Antiquity to the Present," 304, citing Evagrius, *Praktikos*, 36.

80. *Conf.* 14.16.9. *Qua coniugatione uirtutum euidentissime nos uoluit erudire de uigiliis atque ieiuniis ad castitatem, de castitate ad scientiam, de scientia ad longanimitatem, de longanimitate ad suauitatem, de suauitate ad spiritum sanctum, de spiritu sancto ad caritatis non fictae praemia peruenire.*

81. Note *Conference* 4, where the three sources of thoughts are discussed. Similarly, dreams could come from God, the devil, or the person (see Tertullian, *On the soul*, 47). According to Stewart, "This tripartite scheme was apparently adapted from pre-Christian philosophical traditions" ("Erotic Dreams," 289).

82. *Conf.* 24.15.1–3.

83. *Inst.* 12.19. *Qui simplicem piscatorum fidem corde simplici retinentes non eam syllogismis dialecticis et Tulliana facundia spiritu concepere mundano, sed experimento uitae sinceris actuque purissimo, correctione quoque uitiorum, et ut uerius dixerim in ipsa perfectionis inesse naturam oculatis indiciis deprehenderunt, sine qua nec pietas in deum nec uitiorum purgatio nec emendatio morum nec uirtutum consummatio poterit adprehendi.*

84. *Conf.* 13.9.5.

85. *Conf.* 13.6.4. *Nam neque remotionis silentium nec districtionem ieiuniorum nec lectionis instantiam etiam illo quo possumus tempore pro nostro arbitrio retentamus, sed quibusdam occurrentibus causis etiam inuitissimi frequenter retrahimur a salutaribus institutis, ita ut uel loci uel temporis copiam, in quo haec exercere possimus, necesse sit nos a domino deprecari.*

86. Hiu, "Defining and Reconstitution of Man," 200.

87. *Inst.* 6.13.2. *Dum enim fortis, spiritus scilicet noster, domum suam custodit armatus, recessus cordis sui dei timore communiens, in pace erit omnis substantia eius, id est emolumenta laborum ac uirtutes longo tempore conquisitae. si autem fortior superueniens uicerit eum, id est diabolus cogita-tionum consensu, arma eius diripiet, in quibus confidebat, id est memoriam scripturarum uel timorem dei, et spolia eius diuidet, uirtutum scilicet merita per contraria uitia quaeque dispergens.*

88. Any reading of *oikonomia* in Cassian still suffers from not rec-ognizing the stakes of a "sexually differentiated theological anthropology" that Benjamin Dunning has argued in relation to other early Christian texts that might construct "an eschatological vision of the human that could still admit of fragmentation, partialness, and undomesticated difference—that is, an eschatology not about closing gaps, but about inhabiting (and being inhabited by) them." See Dunning, *Specters of Paul*, 155.

89. *Conf.* 1.21.2.

90. *Conf.* 1.22.1.

91. For thoughts as living creatures, see *Conf.* 24.3.2, 24.5.1.

92. *Inst.* 2.18, 6.2.1; *Conf.* 2.5.2.

93. For demonic thoughts attempting to intrude, see *Conf.* 2.13.7, 2.13.11, 7.5.5, 12.6.3, 12.11.3.

94. *Conf.* 1.17.

95. *Conf.* 1.10. Cassian also says that one should "cultivate the earth of our heart with the gospel plough—that is, with the continual remembering of the Lord's cross—and we shall be able to root out from ourselves the nests of harmful animals and the hiding places of venomous serpents" (*Conf.* 1.22.2).

96. Humphries, *Ascetic Pneumatology*, 31.

97. *Conf.* 24.15.3; 24.16.

98. *Conf.* 9.6.5, 11.4, 11.6.3, 11.7.3, 11.9.2.

99. Demacopoulos, *Five Models of Spiritual Direction*, 109.

100. Humphries argues that such radical transformation involves both "external actions of the monk" and "internal motivations of the monk, his thoughts and desires." See Humphries, *Ascetic Pneumatology*, 22.

101. Harmless, *Desert Christians*, 390.

102. For example, see *Inst.* 6.3: "But this disease [fornication] requires solitude and distance, along with affliction of body and contrition of heart, so that, once the dangerous fever of seething emotions has passed, a state of integral health may be acquired."

103. Shaw, *The Burden of the Flesh*, 43. Shaw describes how Galen, the second-century CE physician from Pergamon, "demonstrates as well as any

figure in antiquity that the modern disciplinary boundaries between science and religion or philosophy and medicine are artificial" (ibid., 46).

104. Stewart vitally contextualizes the work of Pseudo-Macarian homilies in relation to Syriac Christian influence. See Columba Stewart, "'Working the Earth of the Heart.'"

105. Stewart, *Cassian the Monk*, 115.

106. Dysinger, *Psalmody and Prayer in the Writings of Evagrius Ponticus*, 28.

107. *Inst.* 5.6.1, 5.7.1, 5.8.1, 5.10.1.

108. *Inst.* 6.2.

109. As I will argue in chapter 4, fasting is important, according to Cassian, because "if the flesh be filled with an excess of food, it be found at odds with the salutary precepts of the soul and insolently reject the governance of its own spirit" (*Inst.* 6.2).

110. *Inst.* 6.4.1.

111. *Inst.* 3.8.3.

112. *Conf.* 14.19. *quia efficacius semper corde concipitur, quidquid sensim et absque nimio labore corporis intimatur.*

113. *Inst.* 8.17.

114. *Inst.* 5.10.1, 5.41.1.

115. *Conf.* 6.10, 12.5.5, 16.22.2.

Chapter 4 BODILY PRACTICES

1. *Inst.* 10.1, 10.2.3.

2. *Inst.* 10.1. *ut quaedam febris ingruens tempore praestituto ardentissimos aestus accessionum suarum solitis ac statutis horis animae inferens aegrotanti.*

3. Evagrius Ponticus, *The Praktikos and Chapters on Prayer*, 19. On Evagrius's teachings on prayer, see Dysinger, *Psalmody and Prayer in the Writings of Evagrius Ponticus*; Linge, "Leading the Life of Angels"; and Stewart, "Imageless Prayer and the Theological Vision of Evagrius Ponticus."

4. *Inst.* 10.2.1. *ad omne quoque opus quod intra septa sui cubilis est, facit desidem et inertem. Non eum in cellula residere, non operam sinit inpendere lectioni.*

5. *Inst.* 10.2.3.

6. *Inst.* 10.2.1.

7. *Inst.* 10.2.3, 10.6.

8. "So filled is he with a kind of irrational confusion of mind, like a foul mist, and so disengaged and blank has he become with respect to any spiritual activity that he thinks that no other remedy for such an attack can be found than the visit of a brother or the solace of sleep alone." *Et ita quadam inrationabili mentis confusione uelut taetra subpletur caligine omnique actu spiritali redditur otiosus ac uacuus, ut nulla re alia tantae obpugnationis remedium quam uisitatione fratris cuiuspiam seu somni solius solacio posse aestimet inueniri. Inst.* 10.2.3.

9. In a modern corollary, consider Gustave Flaubert's *ennui*, that silent spider weaving its way into the corners of Emma Bovary's heart: "Et l'ennui, araignée silencieuse, filait sa toile dans l'ombre à tous les coins de son coeur." See Flaubert, *Madame Bovary,* 47.

10. *Inst.* 10.2.3. On *acedia* in Cassian's monastic context, see Folsom, "Anger, Dejection, and Acedia in the Writings of John Cassian," 219–248. *Acedia* has been treated as the precursor to melancholy from a number of perspectives. See Bynum, "Discarded Diagnoses"; Cvetkovich, *Depression,* esp. 84–114; and Solomon, *The Noonday Demon,* esp. 285–334. Cvetkovich challenges Solomon's "routine dismissal of acedia as an aberration from the 'dark ages'" (*Depression,* 87), but does not critique Solomon's assumption that Cassian represents acedia "as a state that resembles contemporary depression as a sin" (ibid., 88). This reflects broader problems with periodization in the history of depression that Solomon reinforces. See Stewart, "Erotic Dreams and Nightmares from Antiquity to the Present," 304. The force of the "noonday demon" for understanding ecological collapse through a Surrealist lens has been taken up powerfully by artists Jennifer Allora and Guillermo Calzadilla in their commissioned exhibition at the Menil Collection, *Specters of Noon,* May 15–October 11, 2020. See Michelle White, "Allora & Calzadilla's Land of Marvels."

11. *Inst.* 10.3.

12. *Inst.* 3.2. *Ita namque ab eis incessanter operatio manuum priuatim per cellulas exercetur, ut psalmorum quoque uel ceterarum scripturarum meditatio numquam penitus omittatur, cui preces et orationes per singula momenta miscentes in his officiis, quae nos statuto tempore celebramus, totum diei tempus absumunt.*

13. Ibid. *incessanter operatio manuum . . . adiectione spontanee celebrantur.*

14. For an excellent survey of readings including psychoanalytic, poststructuralist, postmetaphysical, theological, and epistemological-ethical approaches, see Anderson and Clack, eds., *Feminist Philosophy of Religion.*

15. Bell, *Ritual Theory, Ritual Practice*, 194.

16. Furey, "Body, Society, and Subjectivity in Religious Studies," 9.

17. Mauss, "Body Techniques," 104, 122.

18. Bourdieu, *The Logic of Practice*, 73.

19. Asad, *Genealogies of Religion*, 75. Asad also cites Mauss, "Body Techniques," 122. See also Asad, "Remarks on the Anthropology of the Body," 49.

20. Coakley, "Introduction," 3.

21. Ibid.

22. Mary Douglas illustrates this view of "the body" as overlaid with cultural symbolism in the Lele: "Just as the focus of all pollution symbolism is the body, the final problem to which the perspective of pollution leads is bodily disintegration." See Douglas, *Purity and Danger*, 174.

23. Butler, *Gender Trouble*, 10; *The Psychic Life of Power*, esp. 1–30, 167–200; and *Excitable Speech*, 1–42.

24. Mahmood's approach to subject formation through embodied practices informs my own approach: "*Politics of Piety* is not a hermeneutical exercise in another important sense: its primary preoccupation has less to do with the meaning of practices than with the work they perform in the making of subjects, in creating life worlds, attachments, and embodied capacities." See Mahmood, *Politics of Piety*, xi.

Discourses of embodiment in critical race theory are also vital to expanding understandings of subjectivity, as exemplified by Anthony B. Pinn in "Black Bodies in Pain and Ecstasy"; see also Pinn, *Terror and Triumph*.

25. Harvey, *Scenting Salvation*, 1–10.

26. Miller, "Desert Asceticism and 'The Body from Nowhere,'" 137. Miller continues to correlate "the angelic life" with forms of human subjectivity in the *Historia monachorum* in "Strategies of Representation in Collective Biography," 231.

27. I read Cassian's account of the body in asceticism as closer to Dale Martin's account of "the Strong" persons at Corinth, who "value sexual asceticism not out of some fear of pollution from the body . . . but because of a concern for the continued strength, and therefore health, of the body when it is properly controlled and its hierarchy maintained." See Martin, *The Corinthian Body*, 208.

28. In these ways, Cassian characterizes himself and Germanus as "striving with great effort to endure the barrenness and the vastness of the desert and to imitate their rigorous way of life" (*perlustratis egestatem ac*

uastitatem heremi tolerare et imitari rigorem conuersationis illorum tanto opere niteremur). See *Conf.* 3.2.1.

29. *Inst.* 1.3. Cassian's list of the clothing discussed includes 1. Belt (*Inst.* 1.1.4); 2. Garment (*Inst.* 1.2); 3. Hoods (*Inst.* 1.3); 4. *colobia* (a linen cloak with shortened sleeves) (*Inst.* 1.4); 5. *analaboi* (cords) (*Inst.* 1.5); 6. *mafortes* (short cape) (*Inst.* 1.6); 7. *melotis* (goatskin or *pera*) (*Inst.* 1.7); 8. Staffs (*Inst.* 1.7); 9. Footwear (*Inst.* 1.9).

30. Cassian's own preface indicates that he did not intend for the books to circulate independently. See Chadwick, *John Cassian*, 195.

31. *Conf.* 3.2.1. *ieiunia, uigiliae, meditatio scripturarum, nuditas ac priuatio omnium facultatum non perfectio, sed perfectionis instrumenta sunt; Conf.* 1.7 *pro hac ieiunia, uigilias, labores, corporis nuditatem, lectionem ceterasque uirtutes; Inst.* 4.12. "It is this that they prefer not only to manual labor or to reading or to the peace and quiet of their cells but even to all other virtues . . ." *Quam non solum operi manuum seu lectioni uel silentio et quieti cellae, uerum etiam cunctis uirtutibus ita praeferunt.*

32. On fasting, see *Inst.* 2.18; 5.5; 5.20; 5.24; 6.23; *Conf.* 2.5.2; 2.16; 2.21.1–2; 2.22.1; 2.23.1; 12.11.2; 21.11; 21.29.2; 22.3.2; 22.6.4.

33. *Conf.* 2.19; see Rousselle, *Porneia*, 160–178; Shaw, *The Burden of the Flesh*, 117–118. For the list of Greek words Cassian employs in relation to food, see Stewart, "From Logos to Verbum," 12–13.

34. *Conf.* 8.1.1–2.

35. *Conf.* 8.1. Cassian refers to *labsanion* (salted greens) mixed with water as a particular "delicacy" for the abstemious (*Inst.* 4.11). He also says that "dry and uncooked food, and the leaves of leeks that are cut every month, charlock, granulated salt, olives, and tiny salted fish, which they call maenomenia, are their highest pleasure" (*Inst.* 4.22.). See also Dembińska, "Diet," esp. 441.

36. *Inst.* 4.11; 4.22. *Conf.* 2.26; 8.1; 12.15; 21.23.

37. Stewart, *Cassian the Monk*, 73.

38. Brown, *The Body and Society*, 218–224.

39. *Inst.* 4.21–22. See also Palladius, *Historia Lausiaca*, 11, on Ammonius's diet of uncooked foods, and Rousselle, *Porneia*, 220–221.

40. *Conf.* 12.11; 22.6; *Inst.* 5.23; 6.17.

41. *Conf.* 22.3.2.

42. Stewart, *Cassian the Monk*, 72–73.

43. Rouselle, *Porneia*, 175–178; Brown, *The Body and Society*, 218–24.

44. Shaw, *The Burden of the Flesh*, 52.

45. Pigeaud, *La Maladie de l'âme*, 27; cited in Shaw, *The Burden of the Flesh*, 52fn91.

46. Shaw, *The Burden of the Flesh*, 52.

47. Brown, *The Body and Society*, 421.

48. Musurillo, "The Problem of Ascetical Fasting in the Greek Patristic Writers."

49. *Conf.* 22.3.2.

50. *Inst.* 5.11.1. *interioris hominis castitas uirtutis huius consummatione discernitur.*

51. *Inst.* 10.22.

52. Ibid.

53. Caner, *Wandering, Begging Monks*, 42. Maria Doerfler analyzes Augustine's treatise *De opera monachorum* (*On the Work of Monks*), emphasizing how manual labor could not be construed merely spiritually (addressing monks who shirked labor and wore long hair in order to show their renunciant status). See Doerfler, "'Hair!'"

54. Caner, *Wandering, Begging Monks*, 44.

55. Ibid. Forms of female labor (including textile work) can be gleaned from other sources. Consider, for example, Macrina, who, as Gregory of Nyssa narrates in the *Life of Saint Macrina*, "exercised her hand mainly in working wool" (5.30) but branched out by baking bread, which was considered scandalous because it was "work strictly reserved for slaves." See Elm, *Virgins of God*, 46.

56. Doerfler, "'Hair!,'" 91.

57. *Inst.* 10.22. *actum cordis ac profectum patientiae et humilitatis sedulitate operis metientes.*

58. *Inst.* 10.24. *Ut cum hoc fieri nequaquam necessitas uictus exigeret, pro sola purgatione cordis et cogitationum soliditate, ac perseuerantia cellae, uel acediae ipsius uictoria et expugnatione perficeret.* Cassian continues: "Without manual labor a monk can neither stay in one spot nor ever mount to the summit of perfection." *Sine opere manuum nec in loco posse monachum perdurare, nec ad perfectionis culmen aliquando conscendere.*

59. *Inst.* 10.22; 10.24.

60. *Inst.* 10.23. *Operantem monachum daemone uno pulsari, otiosum uero innumeris spiritibus deuastari.*

61. Stewart, *Cassian the Monk*, 107; see also *Conf.* 10.14.2; 4.12.4; *Inst.* 2.1.4, 7, 10.

62. "For Cassian, the monk is a contemplative and is most truly himself when he prays." See Harmless, *Desert Christians*, 392.

63. Columba Stewart, "Prayer," 753.

64. *Inst.* 2.7.2.

65. *Conf.* 9.3.3. *Quamobrem quales orantes uolumus inueniri, tales nos ante orationis tempus praeparare debemus.*

66. See Bitton-Ashkelony, "Demons and Prayers," esp. 203–206.

67. *Inst.* 2.14. *Ita ut, quid ex quo pendeat, haud facile possit a quoquam discerni, id est, utrum propter meditationem spiritalem incessabile manuum opus exerceant, an propter operis iugitatem tam praeclarum spiritus profectum scientiaeque lumen acquirant.*

68. Stewart, *Cassian the Monk*, 132, and "Prayer," 754.

69. Kardong, "John Cassian's Teaching on Perfect Chastity," 249–263. See Cassian, *Cassian on Chastity*, translated and with an introduction by Terrence G. Kardong.

70. Cassian, *Conferences*, trans. Edgar C. S. Gibson.

71. Chadwick, *John Cassian*, 42–43, 94–95, 102–103.

72. See Bibliothèque nationale de France, NAF 28730, Dossier No. XXII, "Pères de l'Église" and Dossier No XXIV, "Seminaire 'Dire vrai sur soi-même.'" Foucault's early notes on Cassian are from French editions by le Sieur de Saligny from the seventeenth century. See "Les Institutions de Cassien" (1667) and "Les Conférences de Cassien" (1687). Philip Rousseau's "Cassian, Contemplation, and the Coenobitic Life" opens the very worn folder on "Cassien," an article Foucault received from Peter Brown after their 1980 meeting.

73. Mayra Rivera's reading of Foucault's use of "'flesh for an artifact of power a discursive apparatus, and 'body' for what that apparatus seeks to control" and her own use of "'flesh' to point to a vital materiality" that is "shaped by cultures, languages, and representations, but is not determined by them" parallels my embrace of embodiment here as that which is shaped but not determined. See Rivera, *Poetics of the Flesh*, 94.

74. *Inst.* 6.22; see also *Inst.* 3.5.1. *Huc usque igitur festinandum est nobis et eo usque aduersus animae motus uel carnis incentiua pugnandum, donec ista carnis condicio necessitatem naturae expleat, non suscitet uoluptatem, concretam exuberantiam sine ullo pruritu noxaque propellens, non pugnam suscitans castitati.*

75. See also Casiday, "Apatheia and Sexuality in the Thought of Augustine and Cassian," and Wei, "The Absence of Sin in Sexual Dreams in the Writings of Augustine and Cassian."

76. *Inst.* 6.10.

77. *Inst.* 7.3.1; *Conf.* 22.3.5.

78. *Inst.* 6.4. *ad similem puritatis statum per laborem longum et industriam integritate mentis et corporis peruenerunt et aculeos carnis non tam inpugnatione concupiscentiae turpis, quam naturae tantummodo motu sentiunt.*

79. *Conf.* 22.3.4. *omnem perfectionis et castimoniae summam in sola credat exterioris hominis castigatione consistere.*

80. Ibid. *disciplinis interioris hominis instituta.*

81. Brakke, "The Problematization of Nocturnal Emissions in Early Christian Syria, Egypt, and Gaul," esp. 448.

82. *Inst.* 2.13.1, 2; 6.10.

83. Stewart, *Cassian the Monk*, 125.

84. *Conf.* 20.8.11. Barbara Rosenwein notes the "wordless signs of emotional outpouring" in Cassian's *conpunctio* (Rosenwein, *Emotional Communities in the Early Middle Ages*, 49).

85. *Conf.* 20.7.

86. *Conf.* 9.27.

87. Hausherr, *Penthos*, 6.

88. *Conf.* 9.27.

89. Ibid.

90. *Conf.* 9.30.1. See also Stewart, *Cassian the Monk*, 128.

91. Kallistos Ware, "An Obscure Matter," 244–245. Ware describes Cassian's emphasis on the spontaneity of tears and how they cannot be induced through willful effort but are instead a gift of God, while also noting that tears for sin can have utility even for beginners.

92. Stewart, *Cassian the Monk*, 124.

93. Merton, *Cassian and the Fathers*, 210.

94. *Inst.* 2.14. *Nam pariter exercentes corporis animaeque uirtutes exterioris hominis stipendia cum emolumentis interioris exaequant, lubricis motibus cordis et fluctuationi cogitationum instabili operum pondera uelut quandam tenacem atque inmobilem anchoram praefigentes, cui uolubilitas ac peruagatio cordis innexa intra claustra cellae uelut in portu fidissimo ualeat contineri.*

95. In this respect Stewart stresses that "Cassian does not, however, oppose the 'practical' and 'contemplative' aspects of the monastic life. Monastic life is *always* both 'practical' and 'contemplative'; contemplation includes and situates action without eliminating its necessity." See *Cassian the Monk*, 54.

96. *Conf.* 1.8.

97. Dysinger, *Psalmody and Prayer in the Writings of Evagrius Ponticus*, 34.

98. *Conf.* 1.3; 1.4.

99. Stewart, *Cassian the Monk*, 131.

100. Ibid.

101. Humphries, *Ascetic Pneumatology*, 28.

102. *Conf.* 9.25.1. I particularly like Elizabeth Clark's translation of Gabriel Bunge on Cassian's "pure prayer" as "glowing prayer," for some of the modern assumptions concerning purity, evacuation, and representation do not apply. See Clark, *The Origenist Controversy*, 66.

103. *Conf.* 9.25.1. *conglobatis sensibus uelut de fonte quodam copiosissimo effundit ubertim atque ineffabiliter eructat ad deum.*

104. *Conf.* 9.25.1. *quanta nec eloqui facile nec percurrere mens in semet ipsam reuersa praeualeat.*

105. *Inst.* 3.2. *per totum diei spatium iugiter cum operis adiectione spontanee celebrantur.*

106. *Inst.* 5.9; 6.23; *Conf.* 21.23.

107. This is closer to Foucault's admiration for how a Greek or Roman philosopher "submits to a *forma* (a form)" rather than "obey a *regula* (a rule)." See Foucault, *The Hermeneutics of the Subject*, 424.

108. *Inst.* 3.2.1; see also *Inst.* 6.2. *gratius uoluntarium munus quam functiones quae canonica conpulsione redduntur.*

109. *Inst.* 3.2.1. *plus enim est id quod incessanter offertur quam quod per temporis interualla persoluitur.*

Chapter 5 AFFECTIVE PRACTICES

1. *Conf.* 2.13.4.

2. Ibid. *Ille amarissimis eum increpans uerbis miserabilemque et indignum nec monachi nomine censendum esse pronuntians, qui potuerit huiusmodi uitio et concupiscentia titillari.*

3. Ibid. *summa desperatione deiectum ac letali tristitia consternatum.*

4. *Conf.* 2.13.8.

5. *Conf.* 2.13.9. *Ad cellam tandemque te intellege uel ignoratum hactenus a diabolo uel despectum nec in eorum numero reputatum, quibus ille cotidie confligere et conluctari profectibus eorum ac studiis instigatur.*

6. For more on reading methods as "potentially a spiritual act" in medieval and modern times, see Duncan Robertson, "*Lectio divina* and Literary Criticism."

7. Ioannis Papadogiannakis argues that using the emotions as a distinct category of historical analysis can illuminate religious change and

requires more substantive engagement in late ancient Christian texts. See Papadogiannakis, "Introduction." Such inquiry amplifies the possibilities for studying "emotion" as πάθη in late ancient Christianity. Knuuttila, in *Emotion and Peace of Mind*, and Konstan, in *The Emotions of the Ancient Greeks*, engage in classical antiquity. Knuuttila notes that more on the emotions in ancient sources has been done than in medieval ones. See Knuuttila, *Emotions in Ancient and Medieval Philosophy*, 145.

8. For Schleiermacher, "Religion's essence is neither thinking nor acting, but intuition and feeling." See Schleiermacher, *On Religion*, 22. For Hegel, by contrast, this "natural feeling" is "cut off from freedom, right, the rule of law; and a people [is] unhappy and miserable where it is only such feeling that is exclusively cultivated, that alone possesses beauty." See Hegel, *Lectures on the Philosophy of Religion, Vol. 2*, 122.

9. Kant, *Metaphysics of Morals*, 166.

10. James, "The Physical Basis of Emotion," 307.

11. Jameson, *Postmodernism*, 10, 15, 16.

12. Pellegrini and Puar, "Affect," 36.

13. Deleuze and Guattari, "Percept, Affect, Concept," 465.

14. Citing from Deleuze's lectures, Charles Stivale, *Gilles Deleuze*, 183. For an approximate definition of "affections, affects," see Deleuze, *Spinoza*, 48–51.

15. Deleuze and Guattari, *A Thousand Plateaus*, xvi. Massumi develops this idea: "From the point of view of a given context, affect is the quasi-causal openness of a characteristic interaction under way in that context to a sensing of 'something new,' the arrival or irruption of which is expressed in a global qualitative change in the dynamic of the intersection, to sometimes striking effect." See Massumi, *Parables of the Virtual*, 227.

16. Berlant, *Cruel Optimism*, 8–9.

17. See Sedgwick, *Touching Feeling*, 60. See also Sedgwick's adaptation of scientific literature on the emotions by Silvan Tomkins in Sedgwick and Frank, eds., *Shame and Its Sisters*.

18. Brennan, *The Transmission of Affect*, 1–2. Brennan continues to make the distinction between feelings and affects: "Feelings can be sifted from affects, and better known to consciousness, through the deployment of living attention or love." Ibid., 139.

19. Berlant, *Cruel Optimism*, 8. See Ahmed, *Queer Phenomenology*, 158, and Ahmed, *Willful Subjects*, 4, 9. According to Ahmed, "This analysis of how we 'feel our way' approaches emotion as a form of cultural politics or world making. . . . Attention to emotions allows us to address the question

of how subjects become invested in particular structures such that their demise is felt as a kind of living death." See Ahmed, *The Cultural Politics of Emotion*, 12. Eugenie Brinkema signals its undifferentiated perils: "One of the symptoms of appeals to affect in the negative theoretical sense—as signaling principally a rejection: not semiosis, not meaning, not structure, not apparatus, but the felt visceral, immediate, sensed, embodied, excessive—is that 'affect' in the turn to affect has been deployed almost exclusively in the singular, as the capacity for movement or disturbance in general." See Brinkema, *The Forms of the Affects*, xii–xiii, 261, xi.

20. Vasquez, *More than Belief*, 5, and Schaefer, *Religious Affects*, 8.

21. Gray, "Enfleshing the Subject."

22. Since the early 1980s, the emotions have become increasingly recognized as central to philosophical reflection on human action and cognition (for example, in Amelie Rorty's 1980 *Explaining Emotions*, Ronald deSousa's 1987 *The Rationality of Emotion*, Jesse Prinz's 2004 *Gut Reactions*, and Robert Solomon's 2004 *Thinking about Feeling*). Research in experimental psychology on the emotions' vital role in moral judgment by researchers including Joshua Greene, Fiery Cushman, and Walter Sinnott-Armstrong rejects the computational model of human cognition and displaces the centrality of rationality. I do not engage these disciplines here because of the complicated (and perhaps epistemologically intractable) intersection between scientific and humanistic discourses. See Niki Kasumi Clements, *Mental Religion*.

23. Leys, "The Turn to Affect," 443.

24. Nussbaum, *Upheavals of Thought*; Sorabji, *Emotion and Peace of Mind*; and Rosenwein, *Emotional Communities in the Early Middle Ages*.

25. Davis, *The Weight of Love*, 23. For medieval affects, see also Smith, *Excessive Saints*.

26. Davis, *The Weight of Love*, 7. Michelle Voss Roberts relatedly notes that "Bernard and his medieval contemporaries affirm divine love as the perfection rather than the antithesis of human affect (*affectus*)." See Voss Roberts, *Tastes of the Divine*, 87.

27. Douglas Burton-Christie, "Early Monasticism," 51.

28. Thomas Bestul notes of *meditatio*: "Meditation is almost always seen as training or preparation for the higher activity of prayer or contemplation, an intermediate stage rather than an end in itself. In considering meditation, it is useful to distinguish between meditation as a practice or spiritual exercise and meditation as a written form." See Bestul, "*Meditatio*/Meditation," 157.

29. While there is debate on whether reading involved recitation or was silent (William A. Johnson, "Toward a Sociology of Reading in Classical

Antiquity"), Bestul notes that *meditari* "usually means the private recitation of a text, with a view toward memorizing it." See Bestul, *Meditatio/Meditation*,"157.

30. Burton-Christie, *The Word in the Desert*, 123.

31. Duncan Roberston notes: "Pronunciation remained necessary at all subsequent stages of the reading process, particularly in the work of memorization, which formed the basis of the monastic meditatio." See Robertson, *Lectio Divina*, xiv.

32. *Conf.* 14.10.4. *Diligenter memoriae conmendanda est et incessabiliter recensenda sacrarum series scripturarum.*

33. Christopher Kelly, *Cassian's Conferences*, 3.

34. Cassian clearly draws from the tradition expressed in Athanasius's *Epistula ad Marcellinum* 1. See also Athanasius, *The Life of Antony and the Letter to Marcellinus*, trans. Robert C. Gregg.

35. Reference to the Psalms is missing only from *Conf.* 15. Direct citations of the Psalms in the *Conferences* are found in *Conf.* 3.4.6; 3.9.1; 6.9.1, 4, 6; 7.4.3; 7.32.4; 9.17.1; 9.29.4; 9.34.11; 11.3.1; 11.13.3; 12.6.2; 12.11.1; 13.10.2; 13.11.4; 14.9.2; 16.26.2 (×2); 17.27; 18.6 (×3); 19.8.3, 4; 21.26.3 (×3). Main references to the practice of prayer and psalmic recitation include those in *Conf.* 1.3.1, 17.3, 23.6.2, 23.7.2 (on the practice of prayer); *Conf.* 10.10.8 (on singing psalms at synaxis); *Conf.* 23.5.9 (on singing a psalm to God); *Conf.* 8.16 (on demonic intrusions and singing psalms for synaxis); *Conf.* 23.16.1 (on the mind's leading one to do bad things); *Conf.* 7.23.1 (on the vigil at night with psalmic protection); and *Conf.* 20.1.3 (on reciting psalms for entrance to a monastery). Consider also Cassian's treatment in *Inst.* 4.19.2.

36. On a few occasions, Cassian refers to poor singing of psalms, including *Conf.* 10.13.1–2 (on the mind's whirling around distractedly from psalm to psalm), *Conf.* 14.12 (on images of poetry cropping up even when singing psalms), and *Conf.* 16.15 (on an ascetic's angrily singing psalms out of annoyance at other ascetics).

37. *Conf.* 11.15. References to the exemplary or salubrious effects of singing the Psalms are developed throughout the *Conferences*, especially in *Conf.* 1.17.2 and 6.10.3 (on singing the Psalms as a mark of a good person); *Conf.* 9.26.1 (on reciting a verse of the Psalms as precipitating fiery prayer); *Conf.* 10.11.4 (on experiencing a psalm as one's own); *Conf.* 10.11.6 (on the presence in the Psalms of all the dispositions of a person); *Conf.* 10.11.5 (on the goodness of all recitation); *Conf.* 11.15 (on reciting the Psalms as a way of life); *Conf.* 14.9.3 (on the belief that one who sings the Psalms with a pure heart will

understand what one reads); *Conf.* 18.2.3 (on the markers of identity including the manner of fasting, singing psalms, and dressing); and *Conf.* 18.11.2 (on the Psalms as guides for prayer). Consider also Cassian's treatment in *Inst.* 2.7.3.

38. Hadot, *Philosophy as a Way of Life*, 104; Krueger, *Writing and Holiness*, 89; Paul R. Kolbet, "Athanasius, the Psalms, and the Reformation of the Self," 100.

39. Kolbet, "Athanasius, the Psalms, and the Reformation of the Self," 101.

40. *Conf.* 18.2.3.

41. *Conf.* 9.1. In the *Institutes*, Books 2 ("The Canonical Method of the Nighttime Prayers and Psalms") and 3 ("The Canonical Method of the Daytime Prayers and Psalms") have many references to practices of psalmody and prayer. See also Harmless, *Desert Christians*, 380.

42. *Conf.* 10.11.5. *Eundem namque recipientes cordis affectum, quo quisque decantatus uel conscriptus est psalmus, uelut auctores eius facti praecedemus magis intellectum ipsius quam sequemur, id est ut prius dictorum uirtutem quam notitiam colligentes, quid in nobis gestum sit uel cotidianis geratur incursibus superueniente eorum meditatione quodammodo recordemur.*

43. *Conf.* 14.13.3.

44. Kolbet, "Athanasius, the Psalms, and the Reformation of the Self," 101.

45. Hollywood, "Song, Experience, and the Book in Benedictine Monasticism," 68.

46. Robertson, *Lectio Divina*, 101.

47. Ibid., 132.

48. Psalm 70:1, cited in *Conf.* 10.10.2 and throughout *Conf.* 10.10.

49. *Conf.* 10.12. *unius uersiculi uolutatione a cunctis uisibilium terminis emigrare.*

50. Ibid.; *Conf.* 10.10.3. *recipit enim omnes adfectus quicumque inferri humanae possunt naturae et ad omnem statum atque uniuersos incursus proprie satis et conpetenter aptatur.*

51. *Conf.* 10.10.

52. *Conf.* 10.10.14. *Hunc in opere quolibet seu ministerio uel itinere constitutus decantare non desinas. Hunc et dormiens et reficiens et in ultimis naturae necessitatibus meditare.*

53. As Christopher Kelly notes, "For Cassian, the monk's very life becomes the hermeneutical medium for understanding divine revelation, an understanding experienced in the light of theories." See Kelly, *Cassian's Conferences*, 97.

54. Though in a different context, I read in Cassian's texts a connection between the affective and reflective that Robert Davis draws between *affectus* and *intellectus* in Bonaventure: "Affective experience was anything but unreflective in medieval mystical texts." See Davis, *The Weight of Love*, 14.

55. *Conf.* 10.11.5.

56. Ibid. As Columba Stewart unfolds in Cassian, "the constant repetition of the biblical 'formula' or the name of Jesus is not only a protection against demonic assault or other kinds of distraction but also a means of unceasing prayer and a way to some kind of 'higher prayer.'" See Stewart, *Cassian the Monk*, 111. See also: *Conf.* 9.26.1.

57. *Inst.* 4.23.

58. Krawiec, "Monastic Literacy in John Cassian."

59. *Conf.* 14.13.3; *Conf.* 14.15.

60. *Conf.* 7.1.

61. *Conf.* 7.2.1–2.

62. *Conf.* 21.1.1.

63. *Conf.* 21.8.1.

64. *Conf.* 20.1. This same story is told in *Inst.* 4.30. Ramsey notes that the story could be modeled on a similar one told of Macarius of Alexandria in Palladius's *Historia Lausiaca* 18.12–16. See Ramsey, *Conferences*, 687.

65. *Inst.* 4.30–32.

66. *Inst.* 4.41.3. Ramsey, *Conferences*, 5.

67. *Conf.* 8.18–19.

68. *Conf.* 8.19.2.

69. *Conf.* 2.2.

70. *Conf.* 2.5.

71. *Conf.* 2.6.1–3. This is important for chastening Foucault's stress on obedience in Cassian.

72. *Conf.* 10.3.5.

73. According to Douglas Burton-Christie, Cassian's *Conferences* are considered parallel to the *Apophthegmata Patrum*, Evagrius's *Praktikos*, Palladius's *Historia Lausiaca*, Athanasius's *Vita Antonii*, and Socrates's *Historia Ecclesiastica*. See Burton-Christie, *The Word in the Desert*, 93.

74. *Conf.* 14.4.1, 18.6.2; 21.4.2.

75. *Conf.* 24.26.18.

76. *Inst.* 4.23. See Niki Kasumi Clements, "Emotions and Ascetic Formation in John Cassian's *Collationes*."

77. *Conf.* 1.1. *Ab eodem abbate aedificationis sermonem fusis lacrimis posceremus.*

78. *Apophthegmata Patrum*, Abba Cassian, 5: "They asked him to leave them a concise and salutary saying as their inheritance, which would enable them to become perfect in Christ."

79. *Conf.* 1.1.

80. Ibid.

81. Thomas L. Humphries Jr. stresses that desire in itself is not negative in Cassian and argues that Cassian believes that "the Holy Spirit is the reformer of desire and emotion." See Humphries, *Ascetic Pneumatology*, 35.

82. *Conf.* 1.4.3; *Conf.* 1.9.

83. *Conf.* 1.23.1–2.

84. *Conf.* 1.23.5.

85. *Conf.* 2.1.1; *Conf.* 2.26.4.

86. *Conf.* 2.1.1.

87. They state: "The words of the conference so inflamed us that, leaving the old man's cell with greater spiritual ardor than when we arrived, we thirsted for the accomplishment of his teaching" (*Conf.* 8.25.5). *Nos conlationis huius sermo flammauit, ut maiore mentis ardore abeuntes a cella senis quam ante uenientes doctrinae eius plenitudinem sitiremus.*

88. *Conf.* 9.36.3. *His sancti Isaac sermonibus stupefacti potius quam repleti uespertina synaxi celebrata sopore paululum membra.*

89. *Conf.* 16.28. *ad custodiendam sodalitatis perpetuam caritatem ardentius incitauit.*

90. *Conf.* 18.16.15.

91. *Conf.* 1.23.4.

92. *Conf.* 12.16.4.

93. *Conf.* 13.1.

94. *Conf.* 14.12.1. *Ad haec ego occulta primum conpunctione permotus.*

95. *Conf.* 17.2.3. *Cumque sic aestuantes quid super statu salutis nostrae definiendum esset nequaquam inuenire possemus.*

96. *Conf.* 17.2.1.

97. *Conf.* 17.10.

98. *Conf.* 20.2.3. *Igitur desperatione deiecti et ipso etiam uultu intimam cogitationum amaritudinem non celantes ad beatum senem satis anxia mente recucurrimus.*

99. *Conf.* 20.6.2.

100. *Conf.* 3.22.4. For compunction as an emotion in monastic literature, see Hausherr, *Penthos.*

101. *Conf.* 6.1.2; *Conf.* 6.17.3.

102. This recalls Psalm 126:6: "Those who go out weeping, carrying seed to sow, will return with songs of joy, carrying their sheaves."

103. *Conf.* 10.3.5; *Conf.* 10.4.1–2.

104. *Conf.* 10.4.1–2. *Non enim parua desperatione deicimur considerantes eum labores tantos.*

105. *Conf.* 21.36.1. *Studium quidem uestrum, quo perfectionis uiam non transitorie, sed plene atque perfecte desideratis adtingere.*

106. *Conf.* 22.1.1, 3. This conference on nocturnal emissions also features Germanus experiencing embarrassment while questioning the *abba* on this enduring problem (*Conf.* 22.4).

107. *Conf.* 24.1.2.

108. Ibid. *Igitur ad hunc Abraham inpugnationem cogitationum nostrarum anxia confessione detulimus.*

109. *Conf.* 7.34.2. *Reuersi post synaxin ea, quae Dominus ad instructionem communem pro desiderio uestro largitus fuerit, duplicato gaudio conferemus.*

110. *Conf.* 8.25.5. *Nos conlationis huius sermo flammauit, ut maiore mentis ardore abeuntes a cella senis quam ante uenientes doctrinae eius plenitudinem sitiremus.*

111. *Conf.* 9.36.3.

112. *Conf.* 10.3.5; 10.4.1–2.

113. *Conf.* 10.8.1.

114. *Conf.* 10.14.3.

115. Of the many excellent questions posed by Ioannis Papadogiannakis, I address this one vis-à-vis Cassian: "How did Christian authors employ emotions to remake social relationships, ideals and values along the lines of their new religious vision?" See Papadogiannakis, "Introduction," 8.

116. Ramsey, *Conferences*, 13–14.

117. Ibid.

118. Hollywood, "Song, Experience, and the Book in Benedictine Monasticism," 67.

119. *Conf.* 11.6.1.

120. *Conf.* 1.10.5.

121. Even as he urges that the separation be nuanced, Marcus Plested notes: "The contrast between Evagrian and Macarian conceptions of the spiritual life could, at first sight, hardly be more striking. Evagrius is a staunch Origenist and a sophisticated philosopher in his own right; Macarius less cultivated and to a degree the product of the vivid and emotive world of Syrian asceticism." See Plested, *The Macarian Legacy*, 64.

122. *Conf.* 10.11.

123. *Conf.* 10.11.6.

124. *Conf.* 14.10.2–3.

125. Aaron Stalnaker has discussed a similar sense of virtue acquisition as skill building in early Confucian texts. See Stalnaker, "Virtue as Mastery in Early Confucianism," 420–426.

126. *Conf.* 14.10.4.

127. *Conf.* 10.8.5–6.

128. *Conf.* 14.10.4.

129. Krueger, *Writing and Holiness*, 95.

130. *Conf.* 14.11.1; *Conf.* 14.9.3. *ille enim psallens intelleget quae canuntur, qui in uia inmaculata gressu puri cordis innititur.* We can see modern corollaries to scriptural recitation in the work of Anna Gade, whose analysis of recitation practices as constitutive of subjectivities of Muslim practitioners in Indonesia foregrounds "a site of creative agency or problem solving" involving "moral, cognitive and especially affective modes." See Gade, *Perfection Makes Practice*, 72–74.

131. Burton-Christie, *The Word in the Desert*, viii.

132. *Conf.* 14.9.3. *Inpossibile namque est animam, quae mundanis uel tenuiter distentionibus occupatur, donum scientiae promereri uel generatricem spiritalium sensuum aut tenacem sacrarum fieri lectionum.*

Chapter 6   COMMUNAL PRACTICES

1. *Inst.* 12.1.

2. Ibid.

3. *Inst.* 12.1; 12.4.2.

4. Ibid.

5. *Inst.* 12.5. *in protoplastum serpens infirmitates omnium uitiorum et materias germinauit.*

6. *Inst.* 12.3.2.

7. *Inst.* 12.27.2. *per quae iam non monasterii iugum sustinere contentus est, non senioris ullius institui disciplina.*

8. *Conf.* 2.5.

9. *Inst.* 12.2. This story is similar in form to that of Abba Patermutus from *Conference* 1, yet contrasts the virtue of obedience and the vice of pride.

10. *Inst.* 12.2.

11. *Inst.* 12.27.2. *ne ipsam quidem auribus suis doctrinam perfectionis admittit.*

12. *Inst.* 12.27.3–4. *Pro suspiriis enim salutaribus sputa de sicco gutture contrahuntur, excreationes etiam sine ulla interpellatione flegmatis prouocantur, digiti ludunt et in modum quiddam scribentis uolitant atque depingunt, et ita huc atque illuc uniuersa membra corporis commouentur, ut, dum, spiritalis agitatur conlatio, totum se uel scatentibus uermibus uel acutissimis sudibus credat insidere, et quidquid simplex conlatio ad aedificationem protulerit audientium, ob suam suggillationem aestimet esse prolatum. totoque tempore, quo uitae spiritalis examinatio uentilatur, suis suspicionibus occupatus non quid exinde ad profectum suum capere debeat aucupatur, sed causas, cur unumquodque sit dictum, sollicita mente perquirit, uel quid eis possit obicere tacita intra se cordis uolutatione coniectat.*

13. *Inst.* 12.29.3. *Et ita fit ut etiam incapax consilii salutaris effecta in omnibus suo potius credit quam seniorum iudicio.*

14. *Inst.* 12.27.5. *deinde post haec excelsa uox, sermo rigidus, amara turbulentaque responsio, incessus erectus ac mobilis.* Cassian's account of *acedia* is famous for its psychological acumen, but his account of pride is similarly astute for its reflection on the academic (or sometimes the political) temperament.

15. Asad, *Genealogies of Religion*, 125–170.

16. Furey, "Body, Society, and Subjectivity in Religious Studies," 7.

17. Ibid.

18. Moore, "Friendship and the Cultivation of Religious Sensibilities," 439.

19. Carruthers, *The Craft of Thought*, 21.

20. Krueger, *Liturgical Subjects*, 12.

21. Harvey, *Scenting Salvation*, 3.

22. Judith Butler's account is helpful for analyzing Cassian's own construction of social constitution from a place of vulnerability. See Butler, "Afterword," 467.

23. *Conf.* 1. *cum quo mihi ab ipso tirocinio ac rudimentis militiae spiritalis ita indiuiduum deinceps contubernium tam in coenobio quam in heremo fuit, ut cuncti ad significandam sodalitatis ac propositi nostri parilitatem pronuntiarent unam mentem atque animam duobus inesse corporibus.*

24. Ibid.

25. *Inst.* 2.12.3. *quam aut solus aut cum alio tantum inhabitare permittitur, quem scilicet societas operationis uel discipulatus et disciplinae*

inbutio copulauit uel certe quem similitudo uirtutum conparem fecit. See Derek Krueger, "Between Monks."

26. In a narrative move resonant with Cassian's, John Panteleimon Manoussakis analyzes the particular ways in which Gregory Nazianzus and Basil of Caesarea do not theorize friendship as such but attend autobiographically to their particular relationships. See Manoussakis, "Friendship in Late Antiquity," 174.

Brian Patrick McGuire reflects on the ascetic anxiety over the bonds of friendship as reconciled through a "monastic *apatheia*, the removal of the passions in the pursuit of perfect peace." See McGuire, *Friendship and Community*, 15.

27. *Conf.* 16.1.

28. Carolinne White, *Christian Friendship in the Fourth Century*, 175–176.

29. *Conf.* 16.1. *non carnali, sed spiritali essemus fraternitate deuincti.*

30. Rapp, "Ritual Brotherhood in Byzantium."

31. *Conf.* 16.2.1. *Amicitiarum ac sodalitatis multa sunt genera, quae diuersis modis humanum genus dilectionis societate conectunt.*

32. Konstan, *Friendship in the Classical World*, 152, 235.

33. *Conf.* 16.2.1. *Quosdam enim praecedens conmendatio primum notitiae, post etiam amicitiae fecit inire conmercia. In quibusdam uero contractus quidam seu dati acceptiue depectio caritatis foedera copulauit.*

34. *Conf.* 16.2.2. *quod instinctu naturae ipsius et consanguinitatis lege conectitur.*

35. Ibid. *uerum etiam omnibus alitibus atque animantibus.*

36. Ibid. *basilisci uel monocerotes uel grypes . . . intolerabilis feritas ac letale uirus.*

37. *Conf.* 16.3.1.

38. *Conf.* 16.2.3. *diuersis uel lucri uel libidinis uel consanguinitatis ac necessitudinum uariarum societatibus . . . gemina amicorum perfectione ac uirtute concrescit.*

39. White, *Christian Friendship*, 177.

40. *Conf.* 16.14.5. "Although it loves everyone in a general way, nonetheless it makes an exception for itself of those whom it should embrace with a particular affection." *quaeque, cum generaliter diligat cunctos, excipit tamen sibi ex his quos debeat peculiari affectione conplecti.*

41. *Inst.* 4.9.

42. Basil of Caesarea, *The Rule of St. Basil*, 115, 163.

43. *Inst.* 12.32.1.

44. Other pedagogical practices occur in these relations, such as the interpretation of Scripture by the elder to help guide the novice. See Philip Rousseau, *Ascetics, Authority, and the Church in the Age of Jerome and Cassian*, 189–198.

45. *Inst.* 4.1; Rousseau, *Ascetics, Authority, and the Church*, 197.

46. Ramsey, *Conferences*, 78. Aristotle's influence, mediated to Cassian either through the cultural milieu or the works of Cicero, is relevant to thinking about *phronesis* as practical knowledge and its association with Cassian's understanding of *discretio*. See Aristotle, *Nicomachean Ethics*, 6.5.

47. The polyvalence of discernment as a skill, as a critical faculty, as a practical discipline, and as not bound to the legalistic is meticulously presented by Anthony D. Rich in *Discernment in the Desert Fathers*.

48. *Inst.* 2.2.

49. *Conf.* 2.2.4. *Nec enim alia lapsus eorum causa deprehenditur, nisi quod minus a senioribus instituti nequaquam potuerunt rationem discretionis adipisci, quae praetermittens utramque nimietatem uia regia monachum docet semper incedere et nec dextra uirtutum permittit extolli, id est feruoris excessu iustae continentiae modum inepta praesumptione transcendere, nec oblectatum remissione deflectere ad uitia sinistra concedit, hoc est sub praetextu gubernandi corporis contrario spiritus tepore lentescere.*

50. *Conf.* 2.1.4. *Non terrenum nec paruum esse discretionis munus, sed diuinae gratiae maximum praemium.* Kallistos Ware writes on discernment (διάκρισις) as one of "the three gifts of the spiritual father." See Ware, "The Spiritual Father in Orthodox Christianity."

51. Ibid. *Quam nisi monachus omni intentione fuerit adsecutus et ascendentium in sese spirituum discretionem certa ratione possederit, necesse est eum uelut in nocte caeca taetrisque tenebris oberrantem non solum perniciosis foueis ac praeruptis incidere, sed etiam in planis ac directis frequenter offendere.*

52. Lawrence J. Johnson, *Worship in the Early Church*, 159–175.

53. *Inst.* 2. Books 2 and 3 of the *Institutes* treat "the canonical method of prayer and psalmody that must be observed in the daytime gatherings in all monasteries."

54. *Inst.* 2.3.1. "We see that the correct number of prayers is maintained in the evening gatherings and at the night vigils." *Legitimum orationum modum in uespertinis conuentibus seu nocturnis uigiliis uidimus retentari.* Chadwick also notes that offices that start with Psalm 70:1 show Cassian's direct influence. See Chadwick, *John Cassian*, 70, 76.

55. *Inst.* 2.3.1. *per successiones ac traditiones maiorum usque in hodiernum diem uel permanent uel mansura fundantur.*

56. *Inst.* 3.5.2.

57. *Inst.* 2.5.3.

58. *Inst.* 2.5.5. *Cumque sedentibus cunctis, ut est moris nunc usque in Aegypti partibus, et in psallentis uerba omni cordis intentione defixis undecim psalmos orationum interiectione distinctos contiguis uersibus parili pronuntiatione cantasset, duodecimum sub alleluiae responsione consummans ab uniuersorum oculis repente subtractus quaestioni pariter et caerimoniis finem inposuit.*

59. Crouan, *The History and the Future of the Roman Liturgy*, 52.

60. Harvey, "Liturgy and Ethics in Ancient Syriac Christianity," 310.

61. *Inst.* 2.6.

62. Ibid.

63. Ibid. Additional changes for observance of the Sabbath include not kneeling and not keeping to the rule of fasting from Saturday evening through dawn on Sunday morning until the following evening, as well as for the entirety of Pentecost. *Inst.* 2.18.

64. This contrasts with many genres of documentation that treat the liturgical institutions of the fourth and fifth centuries, noted by Marcel Metzger as "church order, homilies, catecheses, letters, stories" that typically "allow us to reconstruct almost entirely the rituals in use for several churches." (Marcel Metzger, *History of the Liturgy: The Major Stages*, 67.)

65. *Inst.* 2.11.1. *eos pro numero uersuum duabus uel tribus intercisionibus cum orationum interiectione diuisos distinctim particulatimque consummant.*

66. *Inst.* 2.11.3. *si duo fuerint fratres, senos psallant, si tres, quaternos, si quattuor, ternos. . . . numquam amplius psallunt in synaxi quam quattuor fratres.*

67. *Inst.* 2.11.2.

68. *Inst.* 2.10.1; *Inst.* 3.10.2.

69. *Inst.* 2.15. *absoluta nullus eorum uel ad modicum subsistere aut sermocinari audet cum altero.*

70. *Inst.* 3.2.

71. *Inst.* 2.12.1–2. *ut has easdem congregationum sollemnitates ex more celebrantes absque eo, qui dicturus in medium psalmos surrexerit, cuncti sedilibus humillimis insidentes a uoce psallentis omni cordis intentione dependeant. ita namque ieiuniis et operatione totius diei noctisque lassescunt, ut,*

nisi huiuscemodi refectione adiuuentur, ne hunc quidem numerum stantes explere praeualeant.

72. Ibid.

73. Chadwick, *John Cassian*, 76.

74. *Inst.* 2.7.1–2. Compare this to *The Rule of St. Benedict (RB)* 20.4–5: "Prayer should therefore be short and pure, unless perhaps it is prolonged under the inspiration of divine grace. In community, however, prayer should always be brief; and when the superior gives the signal, all should rise together."

75. *Inst.* 2.6. Cassian mentions the singing of Psalms 50, 62, and 89 during this service as an innovation.

76. See Psalms 148:1, 149:1, and 150:1, 6 (*New Revised Standard Version*): "Praise the Lord from the heavens; praise him in the heights!" "Sing to the Lord a new song, his praise in the assembly of his faithful people." "Praise God in his sanctuary; praise him in his mighty firmament!"

77. Harvey, "Liturgy and Ethics in Ancient Syriac Christianity," 309.

78. *Inst.* 3.5.2. *ut eos superueniens lux matutina in hoc feruore spiritus repperiat constitutos ac per totum diei tempus feruentiores sollicitioresque custodiat, praeparatos eos suscipiens ad conflictum et contra diurnam conluctationem diaboli nocturnarum exercitio uigiliarum ac spiritali meditatione firmatos.*

79. *Inst.* 3.1.

80. As discussed earlier, Cassian differentiates the cenobites who observe "the offices that we are obliged to render to the Lord at different hours and at intervals of time, at the call of the summoner" from the Egyptian ascetics, whose prayer is "celebrated continuously and spontaneously throughout the course of the whole day." *Inst.* 3.2.

81. *Inst.* 3.3.1. "In the monasteries of Palestine and Mesopotamia and the entire Orient the services at the aforesaid hours are done every day with three psalms." *in Palaestinae uel Mesopotamiae monasteriis ac totius Orientis supra dictarum horarum sollemnitates trinis psalmis cotidie finiuntur. Inst.* 3.1.

82. *Inst.* 3.3.1. *in his siquidem promissionum perfectio et summa nostrae salutis est adinpleta.*

83. *Inst.* 3.3.2.

84. *Inst.* 3.3.3.

85. *Inst.* 3.3.6.

86. *Inst.* 3.3.4.

87. Chadwick, *John Cassian*, xiii.

88. *Conf.* 16.15.

89. *Conf.* 16.22.1. *Sicut paulo ante dictum est, non solum res ipsa quae geritur, sed etiam qualitas mentis et propositum facientis est intuendum.*

Conf. 16.18.1. "As if it were words alone and not the will in particular that is declared guilty in the sight of God, and just the sinful deed and not only the wish and the intention that should be considered wrong, and only what each person has done and not also what he wanted to do that should be submitted to judgment." *Quasi uero apud deum uerba tantummodo et non praecipue uoluntas uocetur in culpam, et opus solum peccati et non etiam uotum ac propositum habeatur in crimine, aut hoc tantum quid unusquisque fecerit et non quid etiam facere disposuerit in iudicio sit quaerendum.*

90. *Conf.* 16.6.5. *non tam proprio iudicio quam fratris credere decreuit examini, pro eius scilicet arbitrio.*

91. *Conf.* 16.3.4. "Therefore love can abide unbroken only in those in whom there is one chosen orientation and one desire, one willing and one not willing. If you also wish to preserve this inviolable, you must first strive, after having expelled your vices, to put to death your own will and, with common earnestness and a common chosen orientation, to fulfill diligently what the prophet takes such great delight in." *Et idcirco in his tantum indisrupta potest dilectio permanere, in quibus unum propositum ac uoluntas, unum uelle ac nolle consistit. Quam si uos quoque cupitis inuiolabilem retentare, festinandum est uobis, ut expulsis primitus uitiis mortificetis proprias uoluntates et ut unito studio atque proposito illud quo propheta admodum delectatur gnauiter impleatis.*

92. Ramsey, *Conferences*, 79.

93. *Conf.* 16.3.4.

94. *Conf.* 16.24.

95. Rousseau, *Ascetics, Authority, and the Church in the Age of Jerome and Cassian*, 187.

96. *Inst.* 2.3.1. *Non enim quisquam conuenticulo fratrum, sed ne sibi quidem ipsi praeesse conceditur, priusquam non solum uniuersis facultatibus suis reddatur externus, sed ne sui quidem ipsius esse se dominum uel potestatem habere cognoscat.*

97. *Inst.* 2.3.4.

98. *Conf.* 2.26.4.

99. *Conf.* 17.30.2.

100. *Conf.* 6.27.3.

101. Germanus expresses sustained embarrassment in *Conf.* 22.8 and 22.15.1–3.

102. Cassian describes himself as a "foreigner" like Hiram, commissioned to advise Solomon on the building of the Temple in 3 Kings 7:13–14, yet when read in relation to Benjamin Dunning's theorization of "the alien" topos that "lays claim to a rhetoric of marginality in order to formulate *the self as other*," Cassian's designation can be seen to authorize and even "*valorize* that alien status." See Dunning, *Aliens and Sojourners*, 6, 92.

103. *Inst.* 4.40. *exempla tibi sunt imitationis ac uitae perfectae in congregatione commoranti a paucis . . . quod ad perfectionem propositi huius, id est coenobialis uitae, diligentius quis unius inbuitur ac formatur exemplo.*

104. *Inst.* 2.13.1–3.

105. Cassian describes the friends going to bed in "solemn stillness, at once burning with joy as a result of the conference that had been given and excited by the prospect of the discussion that had been promised." *Conf.* 1.23.4.

106. Abba Moses remarks: "Seeing you inflamed with such a burning desire, I have the impression that the very short time of rest which I wanted to take away from our spiritual conference and devote to the refreshment of the flesh did not help your bodily repose." *Conf.* 2.1.1.

107. *Conf.* 3.1.1. Cassian says: "Instructed by these words and not so much cheerful as moved with compunction in our hearts, we were dismissed by Abba Paphnutius from his cell before midnight." *Conf.* 3.22.4.

108. *Conf.* 7.34.1.

109. *Conf.* 8.25.5.

110. *Conf.* 9.36.3.

111. *Conf.* 11.15.

112. *Conf.* 12.1.1.

113. *Conf.* 12.16.4.

114. *Conf.* 13.1.

115. *Conf.* 15.1.1.

116. *Conf.* 17.1–3.

117. *Conf.* 18.16.15.

118. *Conf.* 22.1.1.

119. *Conf.* 24.15.

120. Weaver, *Divine Grace and Human Agency*, 236.

121. Brown, *The Body and Society*, 432.

122. Brakke, "The Problematization of Nocturnal Emissions," 448.

123. Harvey, "Liturgy and Ethics in Ancient Syriac Christianity," 316.

124. White, *Christian Friendship*, 184.

125. Alford, "The Scriptural Self," 20.

126. Foucault, "Technologies of the Self," 18.

127. Paul Dilley writes an excellent study on the formation of such mechanisms during Cassian's time, when "cenobitic monasteries expanded and systematized training in the cognitive disciplines in Scripture, fear of God, and prayer, which it shared with anchoritic groups, while maintaining the role of the individual monastic leader in instruction." See Dilley, *Monasteries and the Care of Souls in Late Antique Christianity*, 22.

128. Nathan D. Mitchell, *Liturgy and the Social Sciences*, 65.

129. Demacopoulos, *Five Models of Spiritual Direction in the Early Church*, 126.

130. Ibid., 125.

131. Colish, *The Stoic Tradition from Antiquity to the Early Middle Ages*, 116; Weaver, *Divine Grace and Human Agency*, 236.

132. Carruthers, *The Craft of Thought*, 21.

133. *Inst.* 5.32.2.

134. Adele Fiske develops Cassian's influence on "the friendship ideals that took deep root in the monastic life of the Middle Ages and produced rich fruit from the time of St. Benedict to that of St. Aelred of Rievaulx." See Fiske, "Cassian and Monastic Friendship," 190.

CONCLUSION

1. *Conf.* 1.1. *monachorum probatissimi patres et omnis commorabatur perfectio.*

2. Ibid.

3. *Conf.* 2.26.4. *abrenuntiandi rationem et destinationem finemque propositi.*

4. Ibid.

5. *Conf.* 3.5.2. *quicquam defuit ad perfectae beatitudinis meritum.*

6. Although Boniface Ramsey claims that Cassian's Abba Moses is not the reformed criminal "Moses the Ethiopian" (catalogued in Palladius's *Historia Lausiaca* 19 and Sozomen's *Ecclesiastical History* 6.29), I agree with Columba Stewart's reading that affirms this identity: "There can be little doubt that Cassian is still referring to the Moses of *Conferences* 1–2" when describing Moses as a "repentant murderer" in *Conference* 3 (Stewart, *Cassian the Monk*, 139). See Ramsey, *Conferences*, 35.

7. *Conf.* 3.5.2.

8. Ibid.

9. Cameron, *Christianity and the Rhetoric of Empire*, 69.

10. Asad, *Genealogies of Religion*, 15; "agent" correlates with "the principle of effectivity" and "subject" with "consciousness."

11. Keller, cited in Hollywood, *Acute Melancholia*, 125.

12. Ibid.

13. I find Cassian's contribution to the study of religion perhaps a historical antecedent to that argued of Bataille, who is noted as "perhaps *the* thinker for instigating the overcoming of the 'autonomous subject of modernity.'" See Biles and Britnall, eds., *Negative Ecstasies*, 9.

14. Hollywood, "Afterword," 244.

15. Athanasius of Alexandria, *Vita Antonii*, 14; see Athanasius, *The Life of Antony and the Letter to Marcellinus*, 43.

16. For a philosophical account of achievements as valuable due to their difficulty as to the effort humans expend, see Gwendolyn Bradford, *Achievement*.

17. *Conf.* 1.17.1.

18. *Conf.* 1.1.

19. Surely there are intimations of modernity in the development of Christianity, but these disjunctive drives—as I read in Sarah Coakley's comparative analysis of fourteenth-century texts, where, "while spiritual texts in the West were dividing the person . . . the East, in its public acceptance of Palamas's viewpoint, was restructuring and resynthesizing it"—do not come for quite a while in western Christianity even if they intimate aspects of Cartesian "individualism." See Coakley, *Powers and Submissions*, 73.

20. I aim, following Tyler Roberts, to approach questions of ethics and subjectivity "in a constructive and affirmative way, as opposed to simply an explanatory or historicist way." See Roberts, *Encountering Religion*, 19.

21. Perhaps Foucault's attention to *parresia*, developed over his last two years as a political and ethical practice in ancient Greek and Roman contexts, would have found exemplary correlates in the arts of living and the possibility of "an other world" (*un mode autre*) in early Christianity, as Foucault suggests in his final lecture at the Collège de France. See Foucault, *The Courage of Truth*, 325–342.

Agamben, Giorgio. *The Highest Poverty: Monastic Rules and Form-of-Life*. Palo Alto, CA: Stanford University Press, 2013.

——. *The Use of Bodies*. Palo Alto, CA: Stanford University Press, 2015.

Ahmed, Sara. *The Cultural Politics of Emotion*. New York: Routledge, 2014.

——. *Queer Phenomenology: Orientations, Objects, Others*. Durham, NC: Duke University Press, 2006.

——. *Willful Subjects*. Durham, NC: Duke University Press, 2014.

Alford, John A. "The Scriptural Self." In *The Bible in the Middle Ages: Its Influence on Literature and Art*, 1–22. Edited by Bernard S. Levy. Binghamton, NY: State University of New York, 1992.

Anderson, Pamela Sue, and Beverley Clack, eds. *Feminist Philosophy of Religion: Critical Readings*. New York: Routledge, 2004.

Apophthegmata patrum (Sayings of the Desert Fathers). Edited by Jacques Paul Migne. *Patrologiae graeca*, Vol. 65. Paris: J. P. Migne, 1864.

Aristotle. *Nicomachean Ethics*. Translated by Harris Rackham. Cambridge, MA: Harvard University Press, 1934.

Asad, Talal. *Genealogies of Religion*. Baltimore, MD: Johns Hopkins University Press, 1993.

——. "Remarks on the Anthropology of the Body." In *Religion and the Body*. Edited by Sarah Coakley. Cambridge: Cambridge University Press, 1997.

Athanasius of Alexandria. *Epistula ad Marcellinum*. Edited by Jacques Paul Migne. *Patrologia graeca*, Vol. 27. Paris: J. P. Migne, 1886.

——. *The Life of Antony and the Letter to Marcellinus*. Translated by Robert C. Gregg. Mahwah, NJ: Paulist Press, 1980.

——. *Vita Beati Antonii Abbatis*. Edited by Jacques Paul Migne. *Patrologia graeca*, Vol. 26. Paris: J. P. Migne, 1887.

Atkins, Kim. *Self and Subjectivity*. Malden, MA: Blackwell, 2005.

Augustine of Hippo. *City of God*. Translated by Marcus Dods. New York: Modern Library, 2000.

———. *On Christian Doctrine*. Translated by D. W. Robertson. New York: Liberal Arts Press, Pearson, 1958.

———. *On the Free Choice of the Will, On Grace and Free Choice, and Other Writings*. Translated by Peter King. New York: Cambridge University Press, 2010.

———. *Treatises on Various Subjects*. Edited by Roy Deferrari. Washington, DC: Catholic University of America Press, 1952.

Aurelii Augustini. *De civitate Dei*. Edited by Emanuel Hoffmann. In *Corpus Scriptorum Ecclesiasticorum Latinorum*. Vienna: Tempsky, 1899.

———. *De Doctrina Christiana*. Edited by William M. Green. *Corpus Scriptorum Ecclesiasticorum Latinorum* 89. Vienna: Tempsky, 1963.

Babcock, William S. "Grace, Freedom and Justice: Augustine and the Christian Tradition." *Perkins Journal* (Summer 1972): 1–15.

Basil of Caesarea. *The Rule of St. Basil*. Translated by Anna M. Silvas. Collegeville, MN: Liturgical Press, 2013.

Behr, John. *Asceticism and Anthropology in Irenaeus and Clement*. Oxford: Oxford University Press, 2000.

Bell, Catherine. *Ritual Theory, Ritual Practice*. Oxford: Oxford University Press, 1992.

Benedict of Nursia. *RB 1980: The Rule of St. Benedict in Latin and English with Notes*. Edited and translated by Timothy Fry, O.S.B. Collegeville, MN: Liturgical Press, 1981.

Berlant, Lauren. *Cruel Optimism*. Durham, NC: Duke University Press, 2011.

Berzon, Todd S. *Classifying Christians: Ethnography, Heresiology, and the Limits of Knowledge in Late Antiquity*. Oakland: University of California Press, 2016.

Bestul, Thomas H. "Meditatio/*Meditation*." In *Cambridge Companion to Christian Mysticism*. Edited by Amy Hollywood and Patricia Z. Beckman. New York: Cambridge University Press, 2012.

Biblia sacra iuxta vulgatam versionem. Edited by B. Fischer, J. Gribomont, H.F.D. Sparks, W. Thiele, and R. Weber. Turnhout, Belgium: Brepols, 1975.

Biles, Jeremy, and Kent L. Britnall, eds. *Negative Ecstasies: Georges Bataille and the Study of Religion*. New York: Fordham University Press, 2015.

Bitton-Ashkelony, Brouria. "Demons and Prayers: Spiritual Exercises in the Monastic Community of Gaza in the Fifth and Sixth Centuries." *Vigiliae Christianae* 57, no. 2 (2003): 200–221.

——. *Encountering the Sacred: The Debate on Christian Pilgrimage in Late Antiquity.* Berkeley, CA: University of California Press, 2005.

Blowers, Paul M. "Doctrine of Creation." In *The Oxford Handbook of Early Christian Studies.* Edited by Susan Ashbrook Harvey and David G. Hunter. Oxford: Oxford University Press, 2008.

——. "Pity, Empathy, and the Tragic Spectacle of Human Suffering: Exploring the Emotional Culture of Compassion in Late Ancient Christianity." *Journal of Early Christian Studies* 18, no. 1 (Spring 2010): 1–27.

Bourdieu, Pierre. *The Field of Cultural Production.* Edited by Randal Johnson. Cambridge, MA: Polity Press, 1993.

——. *The Logic of Practice.* Stanford, CA: Stanford University Press, 1990.

——. *Outline of a Theory of Practice.* Cambridge: Cambridge University Press, 1977.

Boyarin, Daniel, and Elizabeth A. Castelli. "Introduction: Foucault's *The History of Sexuality*: The Fourth Volume; or, A Field Left Fallow for Others to Till." *Journal of the History of Sexuality* 10, nos. 3 and 4 (July–October 2001): 357–374.

Bradford, Gwendolyn. *Achievement.* Oxford: Oxford University Press, 2015.

Brakke, David. *Demons and the Making of the Monk: Spiritual Combat in Early Christianity.* Cambridge, MA: Harvard University Press, 2006.

——. "The Early Church in North America: Late Antiquity, Theory, and the History of Christianity." *Church History* 71, no. 3 (September 2002): 473–491.

——. "The Lady Appears: Materializations of 'Woman' in Early Monastic Literature." *Journal of Medieval and Early Modern Studies* 33, no. 3 (2003): 387–402.

——. "The Making of Monastic Demonology: Three Ascetic Teachers on Withdrawal and Resistance." *Church History* 70, no. 1 (March 2001): 19–48.

——. "Making Public the Monastic Life: Reading the Self in Evagrius Ponticus's Talking Back." In *Religion and the Self in Antiquity.* Edited by David Brakke, Michael Satlow, and Steven Weitzman. Bloomington, IN: Indiana University Press, 2005.

——. "The Problematization of Nocturnal Emissions in Early Christian Syria, Egypt, and Gaul." *Journal of Early Christian Studies* 3, no. 4 (Winter 1995): 419–460.

Brakke, David, Michael Satlow, and Steven Weitzman, eds. *Religion and the Self in Late Antiquity.* Bloomington, IN: Indiana University Press, 2005.

Brennan, Teresa. *The Transmission of Affect*. Ithaca, NY: Cornell University Press, 2004.

Brinkema, Eugenie. *The Forms of the Affects*. Durham, NC: Duke University Press, 2014.

Brown, Peter. *The Body and Society: Men, Women and Sexual Renunciation in Early Christianity*. New York: Columbia University Press, 1988.

———. "The Rise and Function of the Holy Man in Late Antiquity." *Journal of Roman Studies* 61 (1971): 80–101.

———. *The World of Late Antiquity: AD 150–750*. New York: Norton, 1989.

Brun, Gerald. *Hermeneutics Ancient and Modern*. New Haven, CT: Yale University Press, 1995.

Bucar, Elizabeth M. "The Ambiguity of Moral Excellence." *Journal of Religious Ethics* 38, no. 3 (2010): 429–435.

———. *Creative Conformity: The Feminist Politics of U.S. Catholic and Iranian Shi'i Women*. Washington, DC: Georgetown University Press, 2011.

———. "Dianomy: Understanding Religious Women's Moral Agency as Creative Conformity." *Journal of the American Academy of Religion* 78, no. 3 (2010): 662–686.

———. "Methodological Invention as a Constructive Project: Exploring the Production of Ethical Knowledge through the Interaction of Discursive Logics." *Journal of Religious Ethics* 36, no. 3 (2008): 355–373.

Bucar, Elizabeth M., with Grace Kao and Irene Oh. "Sexing Comparative Religious Ethics." *Journal of Religious Ethics* 38, no. 4 (2010): 654–659.

Bucar, Elizabeth M., and Aaron Stalnaker, eds. *Religious Ethics in a Time of Globalism*. New York: Palgrave Macmillan, 2012.

Burrus, Virginia. *"Begotten, Not Made": Conceiving Manhood in Late Antiquity*. Stanford, CA: Stanford University Press, 2000.

———. *Saving Shame: Martyrs, Saints, and Other Abject Subjects*. Philadelphia: University of Pennsylvania Press, 2007.

———. *The Sex Lives of Saints: An Erotics of Ancient Hagiography*. Philadelphia: University of Pennsylvania Press, 2010.

Burton-Christie, Douglas. "Early Monasticism." In *Cambridge Companion to Christian Mysticism*. Edited by Amy Hollywood and Patricia Z. Beckman. New York: Cambridge University Press, 2012.

———. *The Word in the Desert: Scripture and the Quest for Holiness in Early Christian Monasticism*. New York: Oxford University Press, 1993.

Bush, Stephen. *Visions of Religion: Experience, Meaning, and Power*. New York: Oxford University Press, 2014.

Butler, Judith. "Afterword." In *Loss: The Politics of Mourning*. Edited by David L. Eng and David Kazanjian. Berkeley: University of California Press, 2002.

———. *Bodies That Matter: On the Discursive Limits of "Sex."* New York: Routledge, 1993.

———. *Excitable Speech: A Politics of the Performative*. New York: Routledge, 1997.

———. *Gender Trouble: Feminism and the Subversion of Identity*. New York: Routledge, 2007.

———. *Giving an Account of Oneself*. New York: Fordham University Press, 2005.

———. *Precarious Life: The Powers of Mourning and Violence*. New York: Verso, 2006.

———. *The Psychic Life of Power: Theories of Subjection*. Stanford, CA: Stanford University Press, 1997.

———. "Rethinking Vulnerability and Resistance." In *Vulnerability in Resistance*. Edited by Judith Butler, Zeynep Gambetti, and Leticia Sabsay. Durham, NC: Duke University Press, 2016.

———. *Senses of the Subject*. New York: Fordham University Press, 2015.

———. *Undoing Gender*. New York: Routledge, 2004.

———. "What Is Critique?" In *The Judith Butler Reader*. Edited by Sara Salih. Oxford: Wiley-Blackwell, 2004.

Bynum, Bill. "Discarded Diagnoses: Acedia." *Lancet* 357 (June 16, 2001): 1985.

Cabrol, Fernand. "Cassien." In *Dictionnaire d'archéologie chrétienne et de liturgie*, 2348–2357. Paris: Letouzey et Ané, 1953.

Caeserius of Arles. *The Rule for Nuns of St. Caesarius of Arles: A Translation with a Critical Introduction*. Translated by Maria Caritas McCarthy. Washington, DC: Catholic University of America Press, 1960.

Cameron, Alan. "The Transmission of Cassian." *Revue d'histoire des textes* VI (2011): 361–365.

Cameron, Averil. *Christianity and the Rhetoric of Empire: The Development of Christian Discourse*. Berkeley: University of California Press, 1994.

———. *The Mediterranean World in Late Antiquity: AD 395–600*. New York: Routledge, 1993.

———. "Redrawing the Map: Early Christian Territory after Foucault." *Journal of Roman Studies* 76 (1986): 266–71.

Caner, Daniel. *Wandering, Begging Monks: Spiritual Authority and the Promotion of Monasticism in Late Antiquity*. Berkeley: University of California Press, 2002.

Caplan, Harry. *Of Eloquence: Studies in Ancient and Medieval Rhetoric.* Edited by Anne King and Helen North. Ithaca, NY: Cornell University Press, 1970.

Cappuyns, Maïeul. "Cassien." In *Dictionnaire d'histoire et de géographie ecclésiastique*, XI, 1319–1348. Edited by Alfred Henri Marie Baudrillart. Paris: Letouzey et Ané, 1949.

Carrette, Jeremy R. *Foucault and Religion: Spiritual Corporality and Political Spirituality.* New York: Routledge, 2000.

———. *Religion and Culture: Michel Foucault.* New York: Routledge, 1999.

Carrithers, Michael, Steven Collins, and Steven Lukes, eds. *The Category of the Person: Anthropology, Philosophy, History.* Cambridge: Cambridge University Press, 1985.

Carruthers, Mary. *The Craft of Thought: Meditation, Rhetoric, and the Making of Images, 400–1200.* Cambridge: Cambridge University Press, 1998.

Casey, Michael. *Sacred Reading: The Ancient Art of Lectio Divina.* Liguori, MO: Liguori, 1997.

Casiday, A.M.C. "Apatheia and Sexuality in the Thought of Augustine and Cassian." *St. Vladimir's Quarterly* 45, no. 4 (2001): 339–394.

———. "Grace and the Humanity of Christ according to St. Vincent of Lerins." *Vigiliae Christianae* 59 (2005): 298–314.

———. "Rehabilitating John Cassian: An Evaluation of Prosper of Aquitaine's Polemic against the 'Semipelagians.'" *Scottish Journal of Theology* 58, no. 3 (August 2005): 270–284.

———. *Tradition and Theology in St. John Cassian.* Oxford: Oxford University Press, 2007.

———. "Tradition as a Governing Theme in the Writings of John Cassian." *Early Medieval Europe* 16, no. 2 (2008): 191–214.

Cassian, John. *Cassian on Chastity: Institute 6, Conference 12, Conference 22.* Translated and with an introduction by Terrence G. Kardong. Richardton, ND: Assumption Abbey Press, 1993.

———. *Conferences (Conf.).* Edited and translated by Boniface Ramsey. Mahwah, NJ: Newman Press, 1997.

———. *Conferences.* Introduced by Owen Chadwick. Translated by Colm Luibheid. Mahwah, NJ: Paulist Press, 1985.

———. *Conferences.* Translated by Edgar C. S. Gibson. A Select Library of Nicene and Post-Nicene Fathers of the Christian Church. 2nd series, Vol. 11. New York, 1894.

———. *Institutes (Inst.)*. Edited and translated by Boniface Ramsey. Mahwah, NJ: Newman Press, 2000.

Cassianus, Iohannes. *Conlationes XXIIII (Conf.)*. Edited by Michael Petschenig. *Corpus Scriptorum Ecclesiasticorum Latinorum* 13. Vienna: Geroldus, 1886.

———. *De incarnatione domini contra Nestorium libri VII*. Edited by Michael Petschenig. *Corpus Scriptorum Ecclesiasticorum Latinorum* 17. Vienna: Tempsky, 1888.

———. *De institutis coenobiorum et de octo principalium vitiorum remediis libri XII (Inst.)*. Edited by Michael Petschenig. *Corpus Scriptorum Ecclesiasticorum Latinorum* 17. Vienna: Tempsky, 1888.

Cassien, Jean. *Conférences*. Introduction, translation, and notes by Dom E. Pichery. In *Sources chrétiennes*, Nos. 42, 54, et 64. Paris: Les Éditions du Cerf, 1955, 1958, and 1959.

———. *Les Conférences de Cassien*. Tomes I et II. Translated by le Sieur de Saligny. Lyon: Chez Jean-Mathieu Martin & V. Carteron, 1687.

———. *Institutions Cénobitiques*. Introduction, translation, and notes by Jean-Claude Guy, S.J. In *Sources chrétiennes*, no. 109. Paris: Les Éditions du Cerf, 1965.

———. *Les Institutions de Cassien*. Translated by le Sieur de Saligny. Lyon: Chez Jean-Mathieu Martin & V. Carteron, 1667.

———. *Traité de l'Incarnation: Contre Nestorius*. Translated by Marie-Anne Vannier. *Sagesses chrétiennes*. Paris: Cerf, 1999.

Castelli, Elizabeth A. "Heteroglossia, Hermeneutics, and History: A Review Essay of Recent Feminist Studies of Early Christianity." *Journal of Feminist Studies in Religion* 10, no. 2 (Fall 1994): 73–98.

———. *Martyrdom and Memory: Early Christian Culture Making*. New York: Columbia University Press, 2004.

———. "Mortifying the Body, Curing the Soul: Beyond Ascetic Dualism in the Life of Saint Syncletica." *differences* 4, no. 2 (1992): 134–153.

Cates, Diana Fritz. *Aquinas on the Emotions: A Religious-Ethical Inquiry*. Washington, DC: Georgetown University Press, 2009.

Chadwick, Owen. *John Cassian*. 2nd ed. Cambridge: Cambridge University Press, 1968.

———, ed. *Western Asceticism*. Philadelphia, PA: Westminster John Knox Press, 1958.

Chevallier, Philippe. *Foucault et le christianisme*. Lyon: École normale supérieure Éditions, 2011.

Chidester, David. *Word and Light: Seeing, Hearing and Religious Discourse.* Chicago: University of Illinois Press, 1992.

Chitty, Derwas J. *The Desert a City: An Introduction to the Study of Egyptian and Palestinian Monasticism under the Christian Empire.* Oxford: Blackwell, 1966.

Clark, Elizabeth A. "Foucault, the Fathers, and Sex." *Journal of the American Academy of Religion* 56 (1988): 619–641.

———. "From Patristics to Early Christian Studies." In *The Oxford Handbook of Early Christian Studies*, 7–41. Edited by Susan Ashbrook Harvey and David G. Hunter. Oxford: Oxford University Press, 2008.

———. *History, Theory, Text: Historians and the Linguistic Turn.* Cambridge, MA: Harvard University Press, 2004.

———. *The Origenist Controversy: The Cultural Construction of an Early Christian Debate.* Princeton, NJ: Princeton University Press, 1992.

———. *Reading Renunciation: Asceticism and Scripture in Early Christianity.* Princeton, NJ: Princeton University Press, 1999.

Clements, Niki Kasumi. "Asceticism and Self-Cultivation." In *The Blackwell Companion to Religious Ethics*, Vol. 1. 2nd ed. Edited by William Schweiker, David Clairmont, Elizabeth Bucar, and Maria Antonaccio. Oxford: Wiley-Blackwell, 2020.

———. "The Asceticism of Interpretation: John Cassian, Hermeneutical Askēsis, and Religious Ethics." In *Scripture, Tradition, and Reason in Christian Ethics: Normative Dimensions.* Edited by Bharat Ranganathan and Derek Woodard-Lehman. New York: Palgrave Macmillan, 2019.

———. "Emotions and Ascetic Formation in John Cassian's Collationes." *Studia Patristica.* Edited by Markus Vinzent and Ioannis Papadogiannakis. Special Vol. 83, no. 9 (2017): 241–270.

Coakley, Sarah. "Introduction: Religion and the Body." In *Religion and the Body.* Edited by Sarah Coakley. Cambridge: Cambridge University Press, 1997.

———. *The New Asceticism: Sexuality, Gender and the Quest for God.* London: Bloomsbury Continuum, 2015.

———. *Powers and Submissions: Spirituality, Philosophy, and Gender.* Malden, MA: Blackwell, 2002.

Colish, Marcia. *Medieval Foundations of the Western Intellectual Tradition.* New Haven, CT: Yale University Press, 1999.

———. *The Stoic Tradition from Antiquity to the Early Middle Ages.* Leiden, The Netherlands: Brill, 1985.

Coman, Jean. "Les 'Scythes' Jean Cassien et Denys le Petit et leurs relations avec le monde Méditerranéen." *Kleronomia: Periodikon demosieuma tou Patriarchikou Hidrymatos Paterikon Meleton* 7 (1975): 27–46.

Cooper, John. *Pursuits of Wisdom: Six Ways of Life in Ancient Philosophy from Socrates to Plotinus.* Princeton, NJ: Princeton University Press, 2013.

Cristiani, Leon. *Jean Cassien.* 2 vols. Abbaye de Saint-Wandrille: Éditions de Fontenelle, 1946.

Crouan, Denis. *The History and the Future of the Roman Liturgy.* Translated by Michael Miller. San Francisco: Ignatius, 2005.

Csordas, Thomas J. "Embodiment as a Paradigm for Anthropology." *Ethos* 18, no. 1 (1990): 5–47.

Cvetkovich, Ann. *Depression: A Public Feeling.* Durham, NC: Duke University Press, 2012.

Damian, Theodor. "Some Critical Considerations and New Arguments Reviewing the Problem of St. John Cassian's Birthplace." *Orientalia Christiana Periodica* 57 (1991): 257–280.

Davis, Robert. *The Weight of Love: Affect, Ecstasy, and Union in the Theology of Bonaventure.* New York: Fordham University Press, 2016.

DeConick, April D., Gregory Shaw, and John D. Turner, eds. *Practicing Gnosis: Ritual, Magic, Theurgy and Liturgy in Nag Hammadi, Manichean, and Other Ancient Literature; Essays in Honor of Birger A. Pearson.* Leiden, The Netherlands: Koninklijke Brill, 2013.

Deleuze, Gilles. *Spinoza: Practical Philosophy.* Translated by Robert Hurley. San Francisco: City Lights, 2001.

Deleuze, Gilles, and Felix Guattari. "Percept, Affect, Concept." In *The Continental Aesthetics Reader.* Florence, KY: Psychology Press, 2000.

———. *A Thousand Plateaus: Capitalism and Schizophrenia.* Translation and foreword by Brian Massumi. Minneapolis: University of Minnesota Press, 1987.

de Lubac, Henri. *History and Spirit: The Understanding of Scripture According to Origen.* San Francisco: Ignatius Press, 2007.

———. *Medieval Exegesis: The Four Senses of Scripture.* Grand Rapids, MI: Eerdmans, 1998.

Demacopoulos, George E. *Five Models of Spiritual Direction in the Early Church.* Notre Dame, IN: University of Notre Dame Press, 2006.

Dembińska, Maria. "Diet: A Comparison of Food Consumption between Some Eastern and Western Monasteries in the Fourth–Twelfth Centuries." *Byzantion* (1985): 433–462.

de Vogüé, Aldabert. *Histoire littéraire du mouvement monastique dans l'antiquité*. Paris: Éditions du Cerf, 1991–1998.

——. "Les mentions des oeuvres de Cassien chez Benoît et ses contemporains." *Studia Monastica* 20 (1978): 275–85.

——. "The Spiritual Father in Orthodox Christianity." *Cross Currents: The Journal of the Association for Religion and Intellectual Life* 24, nos. 2–3 (Summer/Fall 1974): 296–313.

——. *To Love Fasting: The Monastic Experience*. Petersham, MA: Saint Bede's Publications, 1993.

Devos, Paul. "Saint Jean Cassien et Saine Moïse l'Ethiopien." *Analecta Bollandiana* 103 (1985): 61–72.

Dietz, Maribel. *Wandering Monks, Virgins, And Pilgrims: Ascetic Travel in the Mediterranean World, A.D. 300–800*. University Park, PA: Pennsylvania State University Press, 2005.

Dilley, Paul. *Monasteries and the Care of Souls in Late Antique Christianity*. New York: Cambridge University Press, 2017.

Dillon, John M. "Rejecting the Body, Refining the Body: Some Remarks on the Development of Platonist Asceticism." In *Asceticism*. Edited by Vincent L. Wimbush and Richard Valantasis. New York: Oxford University Press, 1995.

Doerfler, Maria E. "'Hair!': Remnants of Ascetic Exegesis in Augustine of Hippo's *De Opere Monachorum*." *Journal of Early Christian Studies* 22, no. 1 (2014): 77–111.

Douglas, Mary. *Purity and Danger: An Analysis of Concepts of Pollution and Taboo*. New York: Routledge, 1966.

Driver, Steven D. "From Palestinian Ignorance to Egyptian Wisdom: Cassian's Challenge to Jerome's Monastic Teaching." *American Benedictine Review* 48 (1997): 293–315.

——. *John Cassian and the Reading of Egyptian Monastic Culture*. New York: Routledge, 2002.

Dunn, Geoffrey. "Cassian in Syria?: The Evidence of Innocent I." *Vigiliae Christianae* 69 (2015): 3–17.

Dunn, Marilyn. "Asceticism and Monasticism, Vol. 2: Western." In *The Cambridge History of Christianity, Vol. 2: Constantine to c. 600*. Edited by Augustine Casiday and Frederick W. Norris. Cambridge: Cambridge University Press, 2007.

——. *The Emergence of Monasticism: From the Desert Fathers to the Early Middle Ages*. London: Blackwell, 2000.

Dunning, Benjamin. *Aliens and Sojourners: Self as Other in Early Christianity*. Philadelphia: University of Pennsylvania Press, 2009.

———. *Specters of Paul: Sexual Difference in Early Christian Thought*. Philadelphia: University of Pennsylvania Press, 2011.

Dysinger, Luke. "Evagrius Ponticus, Exegete of the Soul." In *Evagrius and His Legacy*. Edited by Joel Kalvesmaki and Robin Darling Young. Notre Dame, IN: University of Notre Dame Press, 2016.

———. *Psalmody and Prayer in the Writings of Evagrius Ponticus*. Oxford: Oxford University Press, 2005.

Eden, Kathy. *Hermeneutics and the Rhetorical Tradition: Chapters in the Ancient Legacy and Its Humanist Reception*. New Haven, CT: Yale University Press, 1997.

Ehrman, Bart D., ed. *The Apostolic Fathers*, Vol. 2: *Epistle of Barnabas, Papias and Quadratus, Epistle to Diognetus, The Shepherd of Hermas*. Translated by Bart D. Ehrman. Cambridge, MA: Harvard University Press, 2003.

Elm, Susanna. *Virgins of God: The Making of Asceticism in Late Antiquity*. Oxford: Clarendon, 1994.

Evagrius Ponticus. *Evagrius of Pontus: The Greek Ascetic Corpus*. Translated by Robert E. Sinkewicz. Oxford: Oxford University Press, 2006.

———. *Evagrius's Kephalaia Gnostika: A New Translation of the Unreformed Text from the Syriac*. Translated with an introduction and commentary by Ilaria L. E. Ramelli. Atlanta, GA: Society of Biblical Literature Press, 2015.

———. *The Praktikos and Chapters on Prayer*. Translated by John Eudes Bamberger. Spencer, MA: Cistercian Publications, 1972.

Fairbairn, Donald. *Grace and Christology in the Early Church*. Oxford: Oxford University Press, 2003.

Falcasantos, Rebecca Stephens. *Constantinople: Ritual, Violence, and Memory in the Making of a Christian Imperial Capital*. Oakland: University of California Press, 2020.

Fiore, Benjamin. "Parenesis and Protreptic." In *The Anchor Bible Dictionary*, Vol. 5. Edited by David Noel Freedman. New York: Doubleday, 1992.

Fiske, Adele. "Cassian and Monastic Friendship." *American Benedictine Review* 12 (1961): 190–205.

Flaubert, Gustave. *Madame Bovary*. Collection Folio classique [n° 3512]. Paris: Éditions Gallimard, 1972.

Flood, Gavin. *Beyond Phenomenology: Rethinking the Study of Religion*. New York: Continuum, 1999.

Folsom, Cassian. "Anger, Dejection, and Acedia in the Writings of John Cassian." *American Benedictine Review* 35, no. 3 (September 1984): 219–248.

Foucault, Michel. "About the Beginning of the Hermeneutics of the Self: Two Lectures at Dartmouth." *Political Theory* 21, no. 2 (May 1993): 198–227.

———. "An Aesthetics of Existence." In *Politics, Philosophy, Culture*. Edited by Lawrence D. Kritzman. New York: Routledge, 1988.

———. *Les Aveux de la chair*. Vol. 4 of *Histoire de la sexualité*. Edited by Frédéric Gros. Paris: Gallimard, 2018. There is no English translation yet. All translations are my own.

———. "The Battle for Chastity." In *Essential Works of Foucault, 1954–1984*, Vol. 1: *Ethics: Subjectivity and Truth*. Edited by Paul Rabinow. Translated by Robert Hurley. New York: New Press, 2000.

———. "Berkeley et New York University, 1980." Dossier no. XL. Fonds Michel Foucault. NAF 28730, Bibliothèque nationale de France.

———. "Le combat de la chasteté." In *Dits et Ecrits*, Tome 2: *1976–1988*. Paris: Éditions Gallimard, 2001.

———. "The Concern for Truth." In *Michel Foucault: Politics, Philosophy, Culture; Interviews and other writings 1977–1984*. Translated by Alan Sheridan. New York: Routledge, 1990.

———. *Le Courage de la vérité, Le Gouvernement de soi et des autres II: Cours au Collège de France: 1983–1984*. Paris: Éditions de Seuil, 2009.

———. *The Courage of Truth: Lectures at the Collège de France, 1983–1984*. Translated by Graham Burchell. Hampshire, UK: Palgrave Macmillan, 2011.

———. *Discipline and Punish*. Translated by Robert Hurley. New York: Vintage Books, 1997.

———. *Essential Works of Foucault 1954–1984*, Vol. 1: *Ethics: Subjectivity and Truth*. Edited by Paul Rabinow. Translated by Robert Hurley. New York: New Press, 2000.

———. "Ethics as the Care of the Self as a Practice of Freedom." In *The Final Foucault*. Edited by James Bernauer. Cambridge: MIT Press, 1987.

———. *The Foucault Reader*. Edited by Paul Rabinow. New York: Penguin, 1986.

———. *Du Gouvernement de vivants: Cours au Collège de France: 1979–1980*. Paris: Éditions de Seuil, 2012.

———. *Le Gouvernement de soi et des autres: Cours au Collège de France: 1982–1983*. Paris: Éditions de Seuil, 2008.

———. *The Government of Self and Others: Lectures at the Collège de France, 1982–1983*. Translated by Graham Burchell. Hampshire, UK: Palgrave Macmillan, 2011.

———. *The Hermeneutics of the Subject: Lectures at the Collège de France 1981–1982*. Translated by Graham Burchell. New York: Palgrave Macmillan, 2005.

———. *Herméneutique du sujet: Cours au Collège de France: 1981–1982*. Paris: Éditions de Seuil, 2001.

———. *The History of Sexuality*, Vol. 1: *An Introduction*. Translated by Robert Hurley. New York: Vintage Books, 1990.

———. *The History of Sexuality*, Vol. 2: *The Use of Pleasure*. Translated by Robert Hurley. New York: Vintage Books, 1990.

———. *The History of Sexuality*, Vol. 3: *The Care of the Self*. Translated by Robert Hurley. New York: Vintage Books, 1990.

———. *The History of Sexuality*, Vol. 4: *Confessions of the Flesh*. Paris: Éditions Gallimard, 2018. There is no published translation yet. All translations are my own.

———. "Notes de lecture." Dossier no. XXI. Fonds Michel Foucault. NAF 28730, Bibliothèque nationale de France.

———. "Notes de la fin de sa vie pour ses derniers livres." Dossier no. XXIII. Fonds Michel Foucault. NAF 28730, Bibliothèque nationale de France.

———. "On the Genealogy of Ethics: An Overview of Work in Progress; Interview with Paul Rabinow." In *The Foucault Reader*. Edited by Paul Rabinow. New York: Penguin, 1986.

———. *On the Government of the Living: Lectures at the Collège de France, 1979–1980*. Translated by Graham Burchell. Hampshire, UK: Palgrave Macmillan, 2014.

———. "Pères de l'Église." Dossier no. XXII. Fonds Michel Foucault. NAF 28730, Bibliothèque nationale de France.

———. *Sécurité, Territoire, Population: Cours au Collège de France: 1977–1978*. Paris: Éditions de Seuil, 2004.

———. *Security, Territory, Population: Lectures at the Collège de France, 1977–1978*. Translated by Graham Burchell. New York: Palgrave Macmillan, 2009.

———. "Self-Writing." In *Essential Works of Foucault, 1954–1984*, Vol. 1: *Ethics: Subjectivity and Truth*. Edited by Paul Rabinow. Translated by Robert Hurley. New York: New Press, 2000.

———. *Le souci de soi*. Paris: Éditions Gallimard, 1994.

——. *Surveiller et punir: Naissance de la prison*. Paris: Éditions Gallimard, 1993.

——. "Technologies of the Self." In *Essential Works of Foucault, 1954–1984*, Vol. 1: *Ethics: Subjectivity and Truth*. Edited by Paul Rabinow. Translated by Robert Hurley. New York: New Press, 2000.

——. "Ultimes Papiers." Dossier no. XXVIII. Fonds Michel Foucault. NAF 28730, Bibliothèque nationale de France.

——. "Une esthétique de l'existence." *Dits et Ecrits*, Tome IV. Edited by Daniel Defert and Francois Ewald. Texte n° 357, Reprise du texte n° 352, Paris, 1994.

——. *L'Usage des plaisirs*. Paris: Éditions Gallimard, 1994.

——. *La Volonté de savoir*. Paris: Éditions Gallimard, 1994.

Foucault, Michel, and Richard Sennett. "Sexuality and Solitude." *London Review of Books* 3, no. 9 (May 21, 1981).

Frank, Georgia. "Dialogue and Deliberation: The Sensory Self in the Hymns of Romanos the Melodist." In *Religion and the Self in Antiquity*, 163–182. Edited by David Brakke, Michael L. Satlow, and Steven Weitzman. Bloomington: Indiana University Press, 2005.

——. *The Memory of the Eyes: Pilgrims to Living Saints in Christian Late Antiquity*. Berkeley: University of California Press, 2000.

Frank, Karl Suso. "John Cassian on John Cassian." *Studia Patristica* 30 (1996): 418–433.

Frankenberry, Nancy, ed. *Radical Interpretation in Religion*. Cambridge: Cambridge University Press, 2002.

Fraser, Nancy. *Unruly Practices: Power, Discourse, and Gender in Contemporary Social Theory*. Minneapolis: University of Minnesota Press, 1989.

Furey, Constance M. "Body, Society, and Subjectivity in Religious Studies." *Journal of the American Academy of Religion* 80, no. 1 (2012): 7–33.

Gaca, Kathy L. *The Making of Fornication: Eros, Ethics, and Political Reform in Greek Philosophy and Early Christianity*. Berkeley: University of California Press, 2003.

Gadamer, Hans-Georg. *Dialogue and Dialectic: Eight Hermeneutical Studies on Plato*. Translated and introduced by P. Christopher Smith. New Haven, CT: Yale University Press, 1980.

Gade, Anna. *Perfection Makes Practice: Learning, Emotion, and the Recited Qur'ān in Indonesia*. Honolulu: University of Hawaii Press, 2004.

Galliard, Michel Olphe. "Jean Cassien." In *Dictionnaire de Spiritualité*, 214–276. Paris: Beauchesne, 1953.

——. "Vie contemplative et vie active d'après Cassien." *Revue d'Ascétique et de Mystique* 16 (1935): 252–288.

Gill, Christopher. *The Structured Self in Hellenistic and Roman Thought.* Oxford: Oxford University Press, 2006.

Godet, Paul. "Jean Cassien." In *Dictionnaire de Théologie Catholique*, 1823–1834. Paris: Letouzey et Ané, 1932.

Godlove, Terry. "Saving Belief: On the New Materialism in Religious Studies." In *Radical Interpretation in Religion*, 10–24. Edited by Nancy Frankenberry. Cambridge: Cambridge University Press, 2002.

Golitzin, Alexander. "A Testimony to Christianity as Transfiguration: The Macarian Homilies and Orthodox Spirituality." In *Orthodox and Wesleyan Spirituality*, 129–156. Edited by Steven T. Kimbrough. Crestwood, NY: St. Vladimir's Seminary, 2002.

Goodrich, Richard J. *Contextualizing Cassian: Aristocrats, Asceticism, and Reformation in Fifth-Century Gaul.* Oxford: Oxford University Press, 2007.

——. "John Cassian." In *The Oxford Guide to the Historical Reception of Augustine*, 1221–1224. Oxford: Oxford University Press, 2013.

Gray, Biko Mandela. "Enfleshing the Subject: Race and Religion in the Development of Subjectivity." Ph.D. dissertation, Rice University, Houston, May 2017.

Green, Ronald. *Religious Reason: The Rational and Moral Basis of Religious Belief.* Oxford: Oxford University Press, 1978.

Gregory of Nyssa. *The Life of Saint Macrina.* Translated by Kevin Corrigan. Eugene, OR: Wipf and Stock, 2005.

Griffe, Elie. "Cassien a-t-il été prêtre d'Antioche?" *Bulletin de la Littérature Ecclésiastique* 55 (1954): 240–244.

——. "La Gaule chrétienne à l'époque romaine." *Revue d'histoire de l'Église de France* 37 (1951): 40–52.

Grillmeier, Alois. "Jesus Christ, the Kyriakos Anthropos." *Theological Studies* 38 (1977): 275–293.

Guy, Jean-Claude. "Jean Cassien, Historien du Monachisme Egyptien?" *Studia Patristica* 8 (1966).

——. *Recherches sur la Tradition Grecque des Apophthegmata Patrum. Subsidia hagiographica* 36. Bruxelles: Société des Bollandistes, 1962.

Guyette, Fred. "John Cassian on Faith and Action: Implications for Protestant-Catholic Dialogue." *Pro Ecclesia* 12, no. 1 (2003): 89–98.

Hadot, Pierre. *Exercices spirituels et philosophie antique.* Paris: Éditions Albin Michel, 2002.

——. *La philosophie comme maniere de vivre: Entretiens avec Jeannie Car-lier et Arnold I. Davidson*. Paris: Éditions Albin Michel, 2011.

——. *Philosophy as a Way of Life: Spiritual Exercises from Socrates to Fou-cault*. Translated by Michael Chase. New York: Blackwell, 1995.

Hagan, Harry. "The Master's Rearrangement of John Cassian's Signs of Humility: RM 10 and Institutes 4.39." *American Benedictine Review* 66, no. 1 (March 2015): 70–100.

Hagg, Tomas, and Philip Rousseau, eds. *Greek Biography and Panegyric in Late Antiquity*. Berkeley: University of California Press, 2000.

Hall, Donald E. *Subjectivity*. New York: Routledge, 2004.

Hanby, Michael. "Augustine and Descartes: An Overlooked Chapter in the Story of Modern Origins." *Modern Theology* 19, no. 4 (October 2003): 455–582.

Harmless, William. "Cassian." In *The Oxford Classical Dictionary*, 287. Edited by Simon Hornblower and Antony Spawforth. Oxford: Oxford University Press, 2003.

——. *Desert Christians: An Introduction to the Literature of Early Monas-ticism*. New York: Oxford University Press, 2004.

Harper, James. "John Cassian and Sulpicius Severus." *Church History* 34, no. 4 (December 1965): 371–380.

Harpham, Geoffrey. *The Ascetic Imperative in Culture and Criticism*. Chi-cago, IL: University of Chicago Press, 1992.

Harrison, Nonna Verna. *God's Many-Splendored Image: Theological Anthropology for Christian Formation*. Grand Rapids, MI: Baker Aca-demic, 2010.

——. "Gregory of Nyssa on Human Unity and Diversity." *Studia Patris-tica* 41 (2006): 333–344.

Harvey, Susan Ashbrook. "Asceticism." In *Late Antiquity: Guide to the Postclassical World*, 317–318. Edited by G. W. Bowersock, Peter Brown, and Oleg Grabar. Cambridge, MA: Harvard University Press, 1999.

——. "Liturgy and Ethics in Ancient Syriac Christianity: Two Paradigms." *Studies in Christian Ethics* 26, no. 3 (2013): 300–316.

——. "Locating the Sensing Body: Perception and Religious Identity in Late Antiquity." In *Religion and the Self in Antiquity*, 140–162. Edited by David Brakke, Michael L. Satlow, and Steven Weitzman. Blooming-ton, IN: Indiana University Press, 2005.

——. *Scenting Salvation*. Berkeley: University of California Press, 2006.

Harvey, Susan Ashbrook, and David G. Hunter, eds. *The Oxford Handbook of Early Christian Studies*. Oxford: Oxford University Press, 2008.

Hausherr, Irénée. *Penthos: The Doctrine of Compunction in the Christian East*. Kalamazoo, MI: Cistercian Publications, 1982.

Hedstrom, Darlene L. Brooks. "The Geography of the Monastic Cell in Early Egyptian Monastic Literature." *Church History* 78, no. 4 (2009): 756–791.

Hegel, G.W.F. *Lectures on the Philosophy of Religion*, Vol. 2: *Determinate Religion*. Edited by Peter C. Hodgson. Oxford: Oxford University Press, 2008.

Herdt, Jennifer. *Putting On Virtue: The Legacy of the Splendid Vices*. Chicago: University of Chicago Press, 2012.

Hiu, Ion-Valeriu. "Defining and Reconstitution of Man through Word, Text and Speech, in Relation with the Transcendent: Ontological Vocation of the Human Spirit and Vision about Self and World in the Work of Saint John Cassian." In *Language and Literature: European Landmarks of Identity*, 194–200. Piteşti, Romania: University of Piteşti Press, 2012.

Hollywood, Amy. *Acute Melancholia and Other Essays: Mysticism, History, and the Study of Religion*. New York: Columbia University Press, 2016.

———. "Afterword." In *Negative Ecstasies: Georges Bataille and the Study of Religion*, 239–244. Edited by Jeremy Biles and Kent L. Britnall. New York: Fordham University Press, 2015.

———. "Performativity, Citationality, Ritualization." *History of Religions* 42 (November 2002): 93–115.

———. "Practice, Belief, and Feminist Philosophy of Religion." In *Feminist Philosophy of Religion: Critical Readings*, 225–240. Edited by Pamela Sue Anderson and Beverly Clack. New York: Routledge, 2004.

———. *Sensible Ecstasy*. Chicago, IL: University of Chicago Press, 2002.

———. "Song, Experience, and the Book in Benedictine Monasticism." In *The Cambridge Companion to Christian Mysticism*, 59–79. Edited by Amy Hollywood and Patricia Z. Beckman. New York: Cambridge University Press, 2012.

Hollywood, Amy, and Patricia Z. Beckman, eds. *Cambridge Companion to Christian Mysticism*. New York: Columbia University Press, 2012.

Horujy, Sergey. *Practices of the Self and Spiritual Practices: Michel Foucault and the Eastern Christian Discourse*. Translated by Boris Jakim. Grand Rapids, MI: Eerdmans, 2015.

Humphries Jr., Thomas L. *Ascetic Pneumatology from John Cassian to Gregory the Great*. Oxford: Oxford University Press, 2013.

———. "Prosper's Pneumatology: The Development of an Augustinian." In *Grace for Grace: The Debates after Augustine and Pelagius*, 97–113.

Edited by Alexander Y. Hwang, Brian J. Matz, and Augustine Casiday. Washington, DC: Catholic University of America Press, 2014.

Hungerford, Amy. *Postmodern Belief: American Literature and Religion since 1960*. Princeton, NJ: Princeton University Press, 2010.

Hwang, Alexander Y. "Manifold Grace in John Cassian and Prosper of Aquitaine." *Scottish Journal of Theology* 63, no. 1 (February 2010): 93–108.

———. "Prosper, Cassian, and Vincent: The Rule of Faith in the Augustinian Controversy." In *Tradition and the Rule of Faith in the Early Church*, 68–85. Edited by Ronnie J. Rombs and Alexander Y. Hwang. Washington, DC: Catholic University of America Press, 2010.

Hwang, Alexander Y., Brian Matz, and Augustine Casiday, eds. *Grace for Grace: The Debates after Augustine and Pelagius*. Washington, DC: Catholic University of America Press, 2014.

James, William. "The Physical Basis of Emotion." In *Essays in Psychology*. Cambridge, MA: Harvard University Press, 1983.

Jameson, Fredric. *Postmodernism; or, The Cultural Logic of Late Capitalism*. Durham, NC: Duke University Press, 1991.

Johnson, Lawrence J. *Worship in the Early Church: An Anthology of Historical Sources*, Vol. 3. Collegeville, MN: Liturgical Press, 2010.

Johnson, William A. "Toward a Sociology of Reading in Classical Antiquity." *The American Journal of Philology* 121, no. 4 (Winter 2000): 593–627.

Jones, Tamsin. *A Genealogy of Marion's Philosophy of Religion: Apparent Darkness*. Bloomington, IN: Indiana University Press, 2011.

Jordan, Mark D. *Convulsing Bodies: Religion and Resistance in Foucault*. Stanford, CA: Stanford University Press, 2015.

———. *The Ethics of Sex*. Malden, MA: Blackwell, 2002.

———. *Teaching Bodies: Moral Formation in the* Summa *of Thomas Aquinas*. New York: Fordham University Press, 2017.

Jotischky, Andrew. *A Hermit's Cookbook: Monks, Food and Fasting in the Middle Ages*. London: Continuum International, 2011.

Kalvesmaki, Joel, and Robin Darling Young, eds. *Evagrius and His Legacy*. Notre Dame, IN: University of Notre Dame Press, 2016.

Kant, Immanuel. *Groundwork of the Metaphysics of Morals*. Translated by Mary Gregor and Jens Timmermann. New York: Cambridge University Press, 2012.

———. *Metaphysics of Morals*. Translated by Mary J. Gregor. New York: Cambridge University Press, 1996.

———. *Prolegomena to Any Future Metaphysics*. Cambridge: Cambridge University Press, 1997.

Kao, Grace Y. *Grounding Human Rights in a Pluralist World*. Washington, DC: Georgetown University Press, 2011.

Kardong, Terrence G. "John Cassian's Evaluation of Monastic Practices." *American Benedictine Review* 43 (1992): 82–105.

———. "John Cassian's Teaching on Perfect Chastity." *American Benedictine Review* 30 (1979): 249–263.

———. *Pillars of Community: Four Rules of Pre-Benedictine Monastic Life*. Collegeville, MN: Liturgical Press, 2010.

Keech, Dominic. "John Cassian and the Christology of Romans 8:3." *Vigiliae Christianae* 64 (2010): 280–299.

Kelly, Christopher J. *Cassian's Conferences: Scriptural Interpretation and the Monastic Ideal*. Farnham, Surrey: Ashgate, 2012.

Khawaja, Noreen. *The Religion of Existence: Asceticism in Philosophy from Kierkegaard to Sartre*. Chicago, IL: University of Chicago Press, 2016.

Klingshirn, William. *Caesarius of Arles: The Making of a Christian Community in Late Antique Gaul*. Cambridge: Cambridge University Press, 1994.

Knuuttila, Simo. *Emotion and Peace of Mind: From Stoic Agitation to Christian Temptation*. Oxford: Oxford University Press, 2000.

———. *Emotions in Ancient and Medieval Philosophy*. Oxford: Oxford University Press, 2004.

Kolbet, Paul R. "Athanasius, the Psalms, and the Reformation of the Self." *Harvard Theological Review* (1999): 85–101.

———. *Augustine and the Cure of Souls*. Notre Dame, IN: University of Notre Dame Press, 2011.

Konstan, David. *The Emotions of the Ancient Greeks: Studies in Aristotle and Classical Literature*. Toronto: University of Toronto Press, 2007.

———. *Friendship in the Classical World*. Cambridge: Cambridge University Press, 1997.

Korsgaard, Christine. *Self-Constitution: Agency, Identity, and Integrity*. New York: Oxford University Press, 2009.

———. *The Sources of Normativity*. Cambridge: Cambridge University Press, 1996.

Kraemer, Ross, ed. *Women's Religions in the Greco-Roman World: A Sourcebook*. New York: Oxford University Press, 2004.

Krawiec, Rebecca. "Literacy and Memory in Evagrius' Monasticism." *Journal of Early Christian Studies* 21, no. 3 (Fall 2013): 363–390.

———. "Monastic Literacy in John Cassian: Toward a New Sublimity." *Church History* 81, no. 4 (December 2012): 765–795.

——. *Shenoute and the Women of the White Monastery: Egyptian Monasticism in Late Antiquity*. New York: Oxford University Press, 2002.

Krueger, Derek. "Between Monks: Tales of Monastic Companionship in Early Byzantium." *Journal of the History of Sexuality* 20, no. 1 (January 2011): 28–61.

——. *Liturgical Subjects: Christian Ritual, Biblical Narrative, and the Formation of the Self in Byzantium*. Philadelphia: University of Pennsylvania Press, 2014.

——. *Writing and Holiness: The Practice of Authorship in the Early Christian East*. Philadelphia, PA: University of Pennsylvania Press, 2004.

Lake, Stephen. "Knowledge of the Writings of John Cassian in Early Anglo-Saxon England." *Anglo-Saxon England* 32 (2004): 27–41.

——. "Usage of the Writings of John Cassian in Some Early British and Irish Writings." *Journal of the Australian Early Medieval Association* 7 (2011): 95–121.

Lamberigts, Mathijs. "Pelagius and Pelagians." In *The Oxford Handbook of Early Christian Studies*, 258–279. Edited by Susan Ashbrook Harvey and David G. Hunter. Oxford: Oxford University Press, 2008.

LeClerq, Jean, O.S.B. *The Love of Learning and the Desire for God: A Study of Monastic Culture*. New York: Fordham University Press, 1992.

Lewis, Charlton T., and Charles Short, eds. *A Latin Dictionary*. Oxford: Clarendon, 1879.

Lewis, Thomas A. "Ethical Formation and Ordinary Life in the Modern West: The Case of Work." In *Religious Ethics in a Time of Globalism*, 27–48. Edited by Elizabeth M. Bucar and Aaron Stalnaker. New York: Palgrave Macmillan, 2012.

——. "Ethnography, Anthropology, and Comparative Religious Ethics." *Journal of Religious Ethics* 38, no. 3 (2010): 395–403.

——. "Frames of Comparison: Anthropology and Inheriting Traditional Practices." *Journal of Religious Ethics* 33, no. 2 (2005): 225–253.

——. *Freedom and Tradition in Hegel: Reconsidering Anthropology, Ethics, and Religion*. Notre Dame, IN: University of Notre Dame Press, 2005.

——. *Why Philosophy Matters to the Study of Religion, and Vice Versa*. New York: Oxford University Press, 2015.

Lewis, Thomas A., Jonathan Wyn Schofer, Aaron Stalnaker, and Mark Berkson. "Anthropos and Ethics: Categories of Inquiry and Procedures of Comparison." *Journal of Religious Ethics* 33, no. 2 (2005): 177–185.

Leys, Ruth. "The Turn to Affect: A Critique." *Critical Inquiry* 37, no. 3 (2011): 434–472.

Leyser, Conrad. *Authority and Asceticism from Augustine to Gregory the Great*. Oxford: Oxford University Press, 2000.

———. "Masculinity in Flux: Nocturnal Emissions and the Limits of Celibacy in the Early Middle Ages." In *Masculinity in Medieval Europe*. Edited by Dawn Hadley. London: Longman, 1999.

———. "'This Sainted Isle': Panegyric, Nostalgia, and the Invention of Lerinian Monasticism." In *The Limits of Ancient Christianity: Essays on Late Antique Thought and Culture in Honor of R. A. Markus*. Edited by William E. Klingshirn and Mark Vessey. Ann Arbor, MI: University of Michigan Press, 1999.

———. "The Uses of the Desert in the Sixth-Century West." In *The Encroaching Desert: Egyptian Hagiography and the Medieval West*. Edited by Jitse Dijkstra and Mathilde van Dijk. Leiden, The Netherlands: Brill, 2006.

Liddell, Henry George, and Robert Scott, eds. *A Greek-English Lexicon*. Oxford: Clarendon, 1940.

Linge, David E. "Leading the Life of Angels: Ascetic Practice and Reflection in the Writings of Evagrius of Pontus." *Journal of the American Academy of Religion* 68, no. 3 (September 2000): 537–568.

Little, David, and Sumner Twiss. *Comparative Religious Ethics: A New Method*. San Francisco: Harper & Row, 1978.

Logan, Dana. "The Lean Closet: Asceticism in Postindustrial Consumer Culture." *Journal of the American Academy of Religion* 85, no. 3 (2017): 600–628.

Lorenzini, Daniele, Ariane Revel, and Arianna Sforzini, eds. *Michel Foucault: Éthique et vérité, 1980–1984*. Paris: Vrin, 2013.

Loseby, Simon T. "Marseille: A Late Antique Success Story?" *The Journal of Roman Studies* 82 (1992): 165–185.

MacIntyre, Alasdair. *After Virtue*. Notre Dame, IN: University of Notre Dame Press, 1984.

———. *Dependent Rational Animals: Why Human Beings Need the Virtues*. Peru, IL: Carus Publishing, 1999.

———. *Three Rival Versions of Moral Inquiry*. Notre Dame, IN: University of Notre Dame Press, 1991.

Macqueen, D. J. "John Cassian on Grace and Free Will with Particular Reference to *Institutio* XII and *Collatio* XIII." *Recherches de théologie ancienne et médiévale* 44 (1977): 5–28.

Mahmood, Saba. *Politics of Piety*. Princeton, NJ: Princeton University Press, 2005.

Malina, Bruce J. "Pain, Power, and Personhood: Ascetic Behavior in the Ancient Mediterranean." In *Asceticism*. Edited by Vincent Wimbush and Richard Valantasis. New York: Oxford University Press, 1995.

Manoussakis, John Panteleimon. "Friendship in Late Antiquity: The Case of Gregory Nazianzen and Basil the Great." In *Ancient and Medieval Concepts of Friendship*. Edited by Suzanne Stern-Gillet and Gary M. Gurtler. New York: State University of New York Press, 2014.

Markus, Robert A. *The End of Ancient Christianity*. Cambridge: Cambridge University Press, 1991.

Marrou, Henri Irénée. "Jean Cassien à Marseille." *Revue du Moyen Age Latin* (1945): 1–17.

———. "La patrie de Jean Cassien." *Orientalia Christiana Periodica* 13 (1947): 588–596.

Marsili, Salvatore. *Giovanni Cassiano ed Evagrio Pontico: Dottrina sulla carità e contemplazione*. Rome: S.A.L.E.R. Herder, 1936.

Martin, Dale B. *The Corinthian Body*. New Haven, CT: Yale University Press, 1999.

Martin, Dale, and Patricia Cox Miller, eds. *The Cultural Turn in Late Ancient Studies: Gender, Asceticism, and Historiography*. Durham, NC: Duke University Press, 2005.

Martin, Luther H., Huck Gutman, and Patrick H. Hutton, eds. *Technologies of the Self: A Seminar with Michel Foucault*. Amherst, MA: University of Massachusetts Press, 1988.

Massumi, Brian. *Parables for the Virtual: Movement, Affect, Sensation*. Durham, NC: Duke University Press, 2002.

Masuzawa, Tomoko. *The Invention of World Religions; or, How European Universalism Was Preserved in the Language of Pluralism*. Chicago: University of Chicago Press, 2005.

Mauss, Marcel. "Body Techniques." In *Sociology and Psychology: Essays*. Translated by Ben Brewster. London: Routledge, 1979.

———. "Les techniques du corps." *Journal de Psychologie* 32, nos. 3–4 (1936).

McGinn, Bernard. *The Foundations of Mysticism*. New York: Crossroad Publishing, 1991.

———. *The Growth of Mysticism*. New York: Crossroad Publishing, 1994.

McGuire, Brian Patrick. *Friendship and Community: The Monastic Experience, 350–1250*. Ithaca, NY: Cornell University Press, 2010.

McGuckin, John. "The Strategic Adaptation of Deification in the Cappadocians." In *Partakers of the Divine Nature: The History and Development of Deification*. Edited by Michael Christensen and Jeffrey Wittung. Grand Rapids, MI: Baker, 2008.

McMahon, Lori Mitchell. "'O God, Come to My Assistance': A Journey with Cassian's Prayer." *Journal of Spiritual Formation & Soul Care* 5, no. 1 (2012): 135–143.

McNamara, Jo Ann, and John E. Halborg with E. Gordon Whatley, ed. and trans. *Sainted Women of the Dark Ages*. Durham, NC: Duke University Press, 1992.

Merton, Thomas. *Cassian and the Fathers: Initiation into the Monastic Tradition*. Kalamazoo, MI: Cistercian Publications, 2005.

Metzger, Marcel. *History of the Liturgy: The Major Stages*. Translated by Madeleine Beaumont. Collegeville, MN: Liturgical Press, 1997.

Miller, Patricia Cox. *Biography in Late Antiquity: A Quest for the Holy Man*. Berkeley: University of California Press, 1983.

———. *The Corporeal Imagination: Signifying the Holy in Late Ancient Christianity*. Philadelphia: University of Pennsylvania Press, 2009.

———. "Desert Asceticism and 'The Body from Nowhere.'" *Journal of Early Christian Studies* 2 (1994): 137–153.

———. "Shifting Selves in Late Antiquity." In *Religion and the Self in Antiquity*, 15–39. Edited by David Brakke, Michael L. Satlow, and Steven Weitzman. Bloomington: Indiana University Press, 2005.

———. "Strategies of Representation in Collective Biography." In *Greek Biography and Panegyric in Late Antiquity*. Edited by Tomas Hagg and Philip Rousseau. Berkeley: University of California Press, 2000.

Millican, Sofia. "Spiritual Encouragement in the *Conferences* of John Cassian (Part II)." *Cistercian Studies Quarterly* 49, no. 3 (2014): 279–297.

Mitchell, Nathan D. *Liturgy and the Social Sciences*. Collegeville, MN: Liturgical Press, 1999.

———. "The Poetics of Space." *Worship* 67, no. 4 (July 1993): 363–367.

Moore, Brenna. "Friendship and the Cultivation of Religious Sensibilities." *Journal of the American Academy of Religion* 83, no. 2 (June 2015): 437–463.

Moxnes, Halvor. "Asceticism and Christian Identity in Antiquity: A Dialogue with Foucault and Paul." *Journal for the Study of the New Testament* 26, no. 1 (2003): 3–29.

Munz, Peter. "John Cassian." *Journal of Ecclesiastical History* 11, no. 1 (1960): 6–12.

Murray, Jacqueline. "Men's Bodies, Men's Minds: Seminal Emissions and Sexual Anxiety in the Middle Ages." *Annual Review of Sex Research* 8 (1997): 1–26.

Musurillo, Herbert. "The Problem of Ascetical Fasting in the Greek Patristic Writers." *Traditio* 12 (1956): 1–64.

New Revised Standard Version Bible. New York: HarperCollins, 1993.

Nietzsche, Friedrich. *The Genealogy of Morals.* Translated by Walter Kaufmann. New York: Vintage, 1989.

Nussbaum, Martha. *The Fragility of Goodness: Luck and Ethics in Greek Tragedy and Philosophy.* Cambridge: Cambridge University Press, 2001.

———. *Therapy of Desire.* Princeton, NJ: Princeton University Press, 2009.

———. *Upheavals of Thought: The Intelligence of Emotions.* Cambridge: Cambridge University Press, 2003.

O'Leary, Timothy. *Foucault and the Art of Ethics.* New York: Continuum, 2006.

Olphe-Galliard, Michel. "Jean Cassien." In *Dictionnaire de Spiritualité.* Paris: Beauchesne, 1937.

———. "Vie contemplative et vie active d'après Cassien." *Revue d'Ascétique et de Mystique* 16 (1935): 252–288.

Palladius. *Historia Lausiaca.* Translated by Robert T. Meyer. Mahwah, NJ: Paulist Press, 1991.

Papadogiannakis, Ioannis. "'Encyclopedism' in the Byzantine Question-and-Answer Literature: The Case of Pseudo-Kaisarios." In *Encyclopedic Trends in Byzantium?* Edited by Peter van Deun and Caroline Macé. Leuven, Belgium: Peeters, 2011.

———. "Instruction by Question and Answer: The Case of Late Antique and Byzantine Erotapokriseis." In *Greek Literature in Late Antiquity: Dynamism, Didacticism, Classicism.* Edited by Scott Fitzgerald Johnson. Burlington, VT: Ashgate, 2006.

———. "Introduction: The Study of Emotions in Patristic Literature: *Status Quaestionis* and Future Prospects." Edited by Markus Vincent and Ioannis Papadogiannakis. *Studia Patristica* 83, no. 9 (2017): 1–18.

Pellegrini, Ann, and Jasbir Puar. "Affect." *Social Text* 27, no. 3 (2009): 35–38.

Pereira, Matthew J. "Augustine, Pelagius, and the Southern Gallic Tradition: Faustus of Riez's De gratia Dei." In *Grace for Grace: The Debates after Augustine and Pelagius.* Edited by Alexander Y. Hwang, Brian J. Matz, and Augustine Casiday. Washington, DC: Catholic University of America Press, 2014.

Perkins, Judith. *The Suffering Self: Pain and Narrative Representation in the Early Christian Era.* New York: Routledge, 1995.

Pfau, Thomas. *Minding the Modern: Human Agency, Intellectual Traditions, and Responsible Knowledge.* Notre Dame, IN: University of Notre Dame Press, 2013.

Phelan Jr., John E. "The Long Shadow of Augustine." *Ex Auditu* 30 (2014): 1–21.

Pigeaud, Jackie. *La Maladie de l'âme: Étude sur la relation de l'âme et du corps dans la tradition médico-philosophique antique.* Paris: Société d'édition "Les Belles Lettres," 1981.

Pinn, Anthony B. "Black Bodies in Pain and Ecstasy: Terror, Subjectivity, and the Nature of Black Religion." *Nova Religio: The Journal of Alternative and Emergent Religions* 7, no. 1 (2003): 76–89.

———. *Terror and Triumph: The Nature of Black Religion.* Minneapolis, MN: Augsburg Fortress Publishers, 2003.

Plested, Marcus. *The Macarian Legacy: The Place of Macarius-Symeon in the Eastern Christian Tradition.* Oxford: Oxford University Press, 2004.

Prosperi Aquitani. *De Gratia Dei et Libero Arbitrio contra Collatorem. Patrologiae latinae* 51. 1861.

Ramsey, Boniface. "John Cassian and Augustine." In *Grace for Grace: The Debates after Augustine and Pelagius.* Edited by Alexander Y. Hwang, Brian J. Matz, and Augustine Casiday. Washington, DC: Catholic University of America Press, 2014.

———. "John Cassian: Student of Augustine." *Cistercian Studies Quarterly* 28 (1993): 5–15.

Rapp, Claudia. "Desert, City, and Countryside." In *The Encroaching Desert: Egyptian Hagiography and the Medieval West.* Edited by Jitse Dijkstra and Mathilde Van Dijk. Leiden, The Netherlands: Koninklijke Brill, 2006.

———. "Ritual Brotherhood in Byzantium: Origins and Context." *Traditio* 52 (1997): 285–326.

Reeder, John P. Jr. "What Is a Religious Ethic?" *Journal of Religious Ethics* 25, no. 3 (1998): 157–181.

Rich, Anthony D. *Discernment in the Desert Fathers: Διάκρισις in the Life and Thought of Early Egyptian Monasticism.* London: Paternoster, 2007.

Rivera, Mayra. *Poetics of the Flesh.* Durham, NC: Duke University Press, 2015.

Roberts, Tyler. *Encountering Religion: Responsibility and Criticism after Secularism.* New York: Columbia University Press, 2013.

Robertson, Duncan. *Lectio Divina: The Medieval Experience of Reading.* Collegeville, MN: Liturgical Press, 2011.

——. *"Lectio Divina* and Literary Criticism: From John Cassian to Stanley Fish." *Cistercian Studies Quarterly* 46, no. 1 (2011): 83–93.

Rosenwein, Barbara. *Emotional Communities in the Early Middle Ages.* Ithaca, NY: Cornell University Press, 2007.

Rousseau, Philip. *Ascetics, Authority, and the Church in the Age of Jerome and Cassian.* New York: Oxford University Press, 1978.

——. *Basil of Caesarea.* Berkeley: University of California Press, 1998.

——. "Cassian, Contemplation, and the Coenobitic Life." *Journal of Ecclesiastical History* 26, no. 2 (1975): 113–126.

——. *Pachomius: The Making of a Community in Fourth-Century Egypt.* Berkeley: University of California Press, 1999.

Rousselle, Aline. *Porneia: On Desire and the Body in Antiquity.* Translated by Felicia Pheasant. Lyndhurst, NJ: Barnes and Noble, 1996.

Rubenson, Samuel. *The Letters of St. Antony: Origenist Theology, Monastic Tradition and the Making of a Saint.* Lund, Sweden: Lund University Press, 1990.

——. "Wisdom, Paraenesis, and the Roots of Monasticism." In *Early Christian Paraenesis in Context.* Edited by James Starr and Troels Engberg-Pedersen. Boston: Walter de Gruyter, 2005.

Russell, Norman. *The Doctrine of Deification in the Greek Patristic Tradition.* Oxford: Oxford University Press, 2006.

Ryle, Gilbert. "Knowing How and Knowing That." In *The Concept of Mind.* Chicago, IL: University of Chicago Press, 2000.

Saak, Eric L. "Ex Vita Patrum Formatur Vita Fratrum: The Appropriation of the Desert Fathers in the Augustinian Monasticism of the Later Middle Ages." *Church History and Religious Culture* 86 (2006): 191–228.

Satlow, Michael L. "'And on the Earth You Shall Sleep': 'Talmud Torah' and Rabbinic Asceticism." *Journal of Religion* 83, no. 2 (April 2003): 204–225.

——. "Disappearing Categories: Using Categories in the Study of Religion." *Method & Theory in the Study of Religion* 17, no. 4 (2005): 287–298.

Schaefer, Donovan. *Religious Affects: Animality, Evolution, and Power.* Durham, NC: Duke University Press, 2015.

Schatzki, Theodore R. *The Site of the Social: A Philosophical Account of the Constitution of Social Life and Change.* University Park, PA: Pennsylvania State University Press, 2002.

———. *The Timespace of Human Activity: On Performance, Society, and History as Indeterminate Teleological Events*. Lanham, MD: Lexington Books, 2010.

Schilbrack, Kevin. *Philosophy and the Study of Religions: A Manifesto*. Malden, MA: Wiley-Blackwell, 2014.

———. *Thinking Through Rituals: Philosophical Perspectives*. New York: Routledge, 2004.

Schleiermacher, Friedrich. *On Religion: Speeches to Its Cultured Despisers*. Translated by Richard Crouter. Cambridge: Cambridge University Press, 1996.

Schneewind, Jerome B. *The Invention of Autonomy: A History of Modern Moral Philosophy*. New York: Cambridge University Press, 1998.

Schofer, Jonathan Wyn. "The Beastly Body in Rabbinic Self-Formation." In *Religion and the Self in Antiquity*. Edited by David Brakke, Michael Satlow, and Steven Weitzman. Bloomington: Indiana University Press, 2005.

———. *Confronting Vulnerability*. Chicago, IL: University of Chicago Press, 2010.

———. "Embodiment and Virtue in a Comparative Perspective." *Journal of Religious Ethics* 35, no. 4 (2007): 715–728.

———. "Self, Subject, and Chosen Subjection: Rabbinic Ethics and Comparative Possibilities." *Journal of Religious Ethics* 33, no. 2 (2005): 255–91.

Schroeder, Caroline T. *Monastic Bodies: Discipline and Salvation in Shenoute of Atripe*. Philadelphia: University of Pennsylvania Press, 2007.

Schweiker, William. "Religious Ethics." In *The Blackwell Companion to Religious Ethics*. Edited by William Schweiker. Oxford: Blackwell, 2005.

Sedgwick, Eve Kosofsky. *Touching Feeling: Affect, Pedagogy, Performativity*. Durham, NC: Duke University Press, 2003.

Sedgwick, Eve Kosofsky, and Adam Frank, eds. *Shame and Its Sisters: A Silvan Tomkins Reader*. Durham, NC: Duke University Press, 1995.

Seiler, Tracy Keefer. "Gennadius of Marseille's *De Viris Inlustribus* and John Cassian." *Journal of the Australian Early Medieval Association* 3 (2007): 307–326.

Shaw, Teresa M. *The Burden of the Flesh: Fasting and Sexuality in Early Christianity*. Minneapolis, MN: Fortress, 1998.

Shepherd Jr., Massey H. "John Cassian by Owen Chadwick." *Church History* 19, no. 3 (September 1950): 200–202.

Smith, Jonathan Z. *Drudgery Divine: On the Comparison of Early Christianities and the Religions of Late Antiquity*. Chicago, IL: University of Chicago Press, 1990.

Smith, Rachel J. D. *Excessive Saints: Gender, Narrative, and Theological Invention in Thomas of Cantimpré's Mystical Hagiographies*. New York: Columbia University Press, 2018.

Smith, William George, Henry Wace, and John Murray, eds. *A Dictionary of Christian Biography, Literature, Sects and Doctrines*. Whitefish, MT: Kessinger, 2004.

Solomon, Andrew. *The Noonday Demon: An Atlas of Depression*. New York: Simon & Schuster, 2001.

Sorabji, Richard. *Emotion and Peace of Mind: From Stoic Agitation to Christian Temptation*. New York: Oxford University Press, 2003.

Stalnaker, Aaron. "Comparative Religious Ethics and the Problem of 'Human Nature.'" *Journal of Religious Ethics* 33, no. 2 (2005): 187–224.

——. *Overcoming Our Evil: Human Nature and Spiritual Exercises in Xunzi and Augustine*. Washington, DC: Georgetown University Press, 2006.

——. "Virtue as Mastery in Early Confucianism." *Journal of Religious Ethics* 38, no. 3 (2010): 404–428.

Stewart, Charles. "Erotic Dreams and Nightmares from Antiquity to the Present." *Journal of Royal Anthropological Institute* 8 (2002): 279–309.

Stewart, Columba. "Another Cassian?" *Journal of Ecclesiastical History* 66, no. 2 (April 2015): 372–376.

——. *Cassian the Monk*. New York: Oxford University Press, 1998.

——. "Evagrius Beyond Byzantium: The Latin and Syriac Receptions." In *Evagrius and His Legacy*, 206–235. Edited by Joel Kalvesmaki and Robin Darling Young. Notre Dame, IN: University of Notre Dame Press, 2016.

——. "From *logos* to *verbum*: John Cassian's Use of Greek in the Development of a Latin Monastic Vocabulary." In *The Joy of Learning and the Love of God: Studies in Honor of Jean Leclerq*. Kalamazoo, MI: Cistercian Publications, 1994.

——. "Imageless Prayer and the Theological Vision of Evagrius Ponticus." *Journal of Early Christian Studies* 9, no. 2 (Summer 2001): 173–204.

——. "Prayer." In *The Oxford Handbook of Early Christian Studies*. Edited by Susan Ashbrook Harvey and David G. Hunter. Oxford: Oxford University Press, 2008.

——. "We"? Reflections on Affinity and Dissonance in Reading Early Monastic Literature." *Spiritus* 1, no. 1 (Spring 2001): 93–102.

———. *"Working the Earth of the Heart": The Messalian Controversy in History, Texts, and Language to A.D. 431.* Oxford: Clarendon, 1991.

———. "Writing about John Cassian in the 1990s." *American Benedictine Review* 48, no. 4 (1997): 341–346.

Stivale, Charles. *Gilles Deleuze: Key Concepts.* Quebec: McGill-Queen's University Press, 2005.

Stock, Brian. *Augustine's Inner Dialogue: The Philosophical Soliloquy in Late Antiquity.* Cambridge: Cambridge University Press, 2010.

———. *Ethics through Literature: Ascetic and Aesthetic Reading in Western Culture.* Waltham, MA: Brandeis University Press, 2008.

———. "Reading and Self-Knowledge." In *After Augustine: The Meditative Reader and the Text.* Philadelphia: University of Pennsylvania Press, 2001.

Stowers, Stanley. *Letter Writing in Greco-Roman Antiquity.* Philadelphia: Westminster John Knox Press, 1986.

Stroumsa, Gedaliahu G. "'Caro salutis cardo': Shaping the Person in Early Christian Thought." *History of Religions* 30, no. 1 (1990): 25–50.

———. "The Scriptural Movement of Late Antiquity and Christian Monasticism." *Journal of Early Christian Studies* 16, no. 1 (2008): 61–77.

Sulpicius Severus. "Dialogues." In *A Select Library of the Nicene and Post-Nicene Fathers of the Christian Church, Second Series.* Edited by Philip Schaff. Buffalo, NY: Christian Literature Co., 1886.

———. *Life of Martin of Tours (Vita Sancti Martini).* In *Early Christian Lives.* Translated by Carolinne White. New York: Penguin Classics, 1998.

Taylor, Charles. *Ethics of Authenticity.* Cambridge, MA: Harvard University Press, 1991.

———. *Sources of the Self: The Making of the Modern Identity.* Cambridge: Cambridge University Press, 1989.

Taylor, Mark C., ed. *Critical Terms for Religious Studies.* Chicago, IL: University of Chicago Press, 1998.

Tertullian. *Apologetical Works and Minicius Felix Octavius.* Translated by Rudolph Arbesmann, Emily Joseph Daly, and Edwin Quain. Washington, DC: Catholic University of America Press, 2008.

Teselle, Eugene. "The Background: Augustine and the Pelagian Controversy." In *Grace for Grace: The Debates after Augustine and Pelagius.* Edited by Alexander Y. Hwang, Brian J. Matz, and Augustine Casiday. Washington, DC: Catholic University of America Press, 2014.

Teuber, Bernhard. "Chair, ascèse et allégorie sur la généalogie chrétienne du sujet désirant selon Michel Foucault." *Vigiliae Christianae* 48, no. 4 (1994): 367–384.

Torjesen, Karen Jo. *Hermeneutical Procedure and Theological Structure in Origen's Exegesis.* New York: De Gruyter, 1986.

Turcescu, Lucian. *Gregory of Nyssa and the Concept of Divine Persons.* Oxford: Oxford University Press, 2005.

Twiss, Sumner B. "Comparison in Religious Ethics." In *The Blackwell Companion to Religious Ethics.* Edited by William Schweiker. Oxford: Blackwell, 2005.

Tzamalikos, Panayiotis. *A Newly Discovered Greek Father: Cassian the Sabaite Eclipsed by John Cassian of Marseilles.* Leiden, The Netherlands: Brill, 2012.

———. *The Real Cassian Revisited: Monastic Life, Greek Paideia, and Origenism in the Sixth Century.* Leiden, The Netherlands: Brill, 2012.

Valantasis, Richard. "Constructions of Power in Asceticism." *Journal of the American Academy of Religion* 63 (1995): 775–821.

———, ed. *Religions of Late Antiquity in Practice.* Princeton, NJ: Princeton University Press, 2000.

Valantasis, Richard, and Vincent Wimbush, eds. *Asceticism.* Oxford: Oxford University Press, 1995.

Vasquez, Manuel A. *More than Belief: A Materialist Theory of Religion.* New York: Oxford University Press, 2011.

Volgers, Annelie, and Claudio Zamagni, eds. *Erotapokriseis: Early Christian Question-and-Answer Literature in Context.* Leuven, Belgium: Peeters, 2004.

Voss Roberts, Michelle. *Tastes of the Divine: Hindu and Christian Theologies of Emotion.* New York: Fordham University Press, 2014.

Ward, Benedicta, trans. *The Sayings of the Desert Fathers: The Alphabetical Collection.* Collegeville, MN: Liturgical Press, 1984.

Ware, Kallistos. "An Obscure Matter: The Mystery of Tears in Orthodox Spirituality." In *Holy Tears: Weeping in the Religious Imagination.* Edited by Kimberley Patton and John Hawley. Princeton, NJ: Princeton University Press, 2005.

———. "The Spiritual Father in Orthodox Christianity." *Cross Currents: The Journal of the Association for Religion and Intellectual Life.* 24, nos. 2–3 (Summer/Fall 1974): 296–313.

Weaver, Rebecca Harden. "Access to Scripture: Experiencing the Text." *Interpretation* 52 (1997): 367–379.

———. *Divine Grace and Human Agency: A Study of the Semi-Pelagian Controversy.* Macon, GA: Mercer University Press, 1996.

———. "Introduction." In *Grace for Grace: The Debates after Augustine and Pelagius.* Edited by Alexander Y. Hwang, Brian J. Matz, and Augustine Casiday. Washington, DC: Catholic University of America Press, 2014.

Weber, Max. *The Protestant Ethic and the Spirit of Capitalism.* Translated by Talcott Parsons. New York: Dover, 2003.

Wei, Simon Lienyueh. "The Absence of Sin in Sexual Dreams in the Writings of Augustine and Cassian." *Vigiliae Christianae* 66 (2012): 362–378.

Wendt, Heidi. *At the Temple Gates: The Religion of Freelance Experts in the Roman Empire.* New York: Oxford University Press, 2016.

Wessel, Susan. *Leo the Great and the Spiritual Rebuilding of a Universal Rome.* Leiden, Belgium: Brill, 2008.

White, Carolinne. *Christian Friendship in the Fourth Century.* Cambridge: Cambridge University Press, 1992.

White, Michelle. "Allora & Calzadilla's Land of Marvels." In *Allora & Calzadilla: Specters of Noon.* Houston: The Menil Collection/Yale University Press, 2020.

Williams, Bernard. *Ethics and the Limits of Philosophy.* Cambridge, MA: Harvard University Press, 1985.

———. *Shame and Necessity.* Berkeley: University of California Press, 1993.

Willis, G. G. *A History of Early Roman Liturgy: To the Death of Pope Gregory the Great.* London: Boydell, 1994.

Wills, Lawrence M. "Ascetic Theology before Asceticism? Jewish Narratives and the Decentering of the Self." *Journal of the American Academy of Religion* 74, no. 4 (2006): 902–925.

Wittgenstein, Ludwig. *On Certainty.* Translated by Denis Paul and G.E.M. Anscombe. New York: Harper Torchbooks, 1969.

Wyschogrod, Edith. *Saints and Postmodernism: Revisioning Moral Philosophy.* Chicago, IL: University of Chicago Press, 1990.

Yearley, Lee. *Mencius and Aquinas: Theories of Virtue and Conceptions of Courage.* Albany, NY: State University of New York Press, 1990.

Young, Frances M. *Biblical Exegesis and the Formation of Christian Culture.* Cambridge: Cambridge University Press, 1997.

Young, Iris Marion. *On Female Body Experience: "Throwing Like a Girl" and Other Essays.* New York: Oxford University Press, 2005.

NIKI KASUMI CLEMENTS is the Watt J. and Lilly G. Jackson Assistant Professor of Religion and Allison Sarofim Assistant Professor of Distinguished Teaching in the Humanities.

9 780268 107857